Trotsky

PROFILES IN POWER

General Editor: Keith Robbins

Trotsky

Geoffrey Swain

Harlow, England • London • New York • Boston • San Francisco • Toronto
Sydney • Singapore • Hong Kong • Tokyo • Seoul • Taipei • New Delhi
Cape Town • Madrid • Mexico City • Amsterdam • Munich • Paris • Milan

PEARSON EDUCATION LIMITED

Edinburgh Gate
Harlow CM20 2JE
United Kingdom
Tel: +44 (0)1279 623623
Fax: +44 (0)1279 431059
Website: www.pearsoned.co.uk

First edition published in Great Britain in 2006

ISBN-13: 978-0-582-77190-1
ISBN-10: 0-582-77190-0

British Library Cataloguing in Publication Data
A CIP catalogue record for this book can be obtained from the British Library

Library of Congress Cataloging-in-Publication Data
Swain, Geoff.
    Trotsky / Geoffrey Swain.
        p. cm. — (Profiles in power)
    Includes bibliographical references (p. [483]–489) and index.
    ISBN-13: 978-0-582-77190-1 (pbk.)
    ISBN-10: 0-582-77190-0 (pbk.)
    1. Trotsky, Leon, 1879–1940. 2. Statesmen—Soviet Union—Biography. 3.
Revolutionaries—Soviet Union—Biography. 4. Soviet Union—Politics and
government—1917–1936. I. Title. II. Profiles in power (London, England)

DK254.T6S93 2006
947.084′092—dc22
[B]   2006040813

10   9   8   7   6   5   4   3   2   1
10   09   08   07   06

Set by 35 in 9.5/12pt Celeste
Printed in Malaysia

The Publisher's policy is to use paper manufactured from sustainable forests.

Contents

Introduction

When his American sympathiser Max Eastman wrote to Trotsky asking if he could write a biography, Trotsky replied that he could because "many people find their way to the general through the personal and in that sense biographies have their own right".[1] Readers of this biography will not find their way to Trotskyism. They may, however, gain a greater understanding of the role Trotsky played in twentieth century Russian history. This book appears in a series entitled *Profiles in Power* and I tried to live up to that ambition by concentrating as much as possible on the years that Trotsky was either in or on the fringes of power. For that reason I have taken a rather different approach to that of Isaac Deutscher in his classic trilogy *The Prophet Armed, The Prophet Unarmed, The Prophet Outcast*.[2] Deutscher devotes a whole volume to the years of exile and most of another volume to the years after Lenin's death. My approach is to give far greater prominence to the years 1917–23 when Trotsky was in power, and my consideration of the years 1924–7 is rather different to Deutscher's; rather than years of determined struggle against Stalin, Trotsky spent much of that time trying to re-establish himself in power, at times with the support of Stalin.

Deutscher went along with, and indeed helped to foster the Trotsky myth, the idea that he was "the best Bolshevik": together Lenin and Trotsky carried out the October Revolution and, with Lenin's support, Trotsky consistently challenged Stalin from the end of 1922 onwards to save the revolution from its bureaucratic degeneration; in this version of events Trotsky was Lenin's heir. This view has been challenged repeatedly in the 50 years since Deutscher's trilogy appeared and I have drawn heavily on the work of other scholars. Ian Thatcher has rediscovered the pre-1917 Trotsky as well as showing clearly how unreliable Trotsky's own writings can be.[3] James White has completely reassessed the Lenin and Trotsky relationship in 1917, showing that the two men's visions of insurrection were entirely different.[4] Eric van Ree demolished the notion that Trotsky was Lenin's heir.[5] Richard Day, writing more than 30 years ago, argued convincingly that Trotsky, far from being an internationalist, firmly believed in the possibility of building socialism in one country.[6]

1

More controversially, Nikolai Valentinov suggested nearly 50 years ago that in 1925, far from opposing Stalin, Trotsky was in alliance with him; although Valentinov's suggestion of a pact sealed at a secret meeting has not stood the test of time, other evidence confirms a period of testy collaboration.[7]

The decision to concentrate on the years in power enabled me to do justice for the first time to Trotsky and Russia's Civil War. All Trotsky's biographers have found this subject difficult: Deutscher covered it only superficially and Thatcher confessed that "the exact course of the battles of the Civil War, with the various twists in fate and fortune, are too complicated to go into in any detail".[8] However, getting to grips with the Civil War years enables the historian to see much more clearly the continuities in Trotsky's thought. These are twofold, the theory of Party organisation and the question of the peasantry; unfortunately for Trotsky both these issues would bring him into conflict with other Bolsheviks. At first glance the pre-revolutionary Trotsky seems very different from the post-revolutionary Trotsky. Before the revolution he favoured the self-organisation of workers and after the revolution his talk was always of labour discipline. The Civil War years help connect the two. Trotsky believed the Party could not presume to be all-knowing, but had to involve people on the ground. During his lifetime those changed from the St Petersburg Soviet, to leaders of the legal labour movement, to the Petrograd Soviet, to former Tsarist generals, to economic managers and planners; but Trotsky believed consistently that the Party had to involve these people in its affairs and not dictate to them. A study of the Civil War also brings out the centrality of what might be termed Trotsky's peasant obsession. In 1906 he predicted the danger of a peasant insurgency against proletarian power in his pamphlet *Results and Prospects*, in the 1920s he anticipated Thermidor, a peasant-sponsored counter-revolution; but during the Civil War, particularly its first months, Trotsky successfully defeated a peasant-inspired rebellion. He knew the potential of peasant power under arms.

It is clear, then, that by focusing on the years in power, a rather different picture of Trotsky emerges to that traditionally drawn, more of the man and less of the myth. There is little of world revolution. Trotsky believed in world revolution, but no more and no less than every other Bolshevik, and like all other Bolsheviks this belief was largely rhetorical. While he was in power, he had no qualms about talking about building socialism in the absence of a world revolution, and when he was on the fringes of power he objected to Stalin's theory of socialism in one country not because such a task was impossible but because his approach implied too many concessions to the peasantry and therefore threatened the restoration of capitalism. It was only in exile in 1933 that internationalism actually became central to Trotsky's purpose. His critique of the failed German Revolution in 1923 was simply camouflage for an attack on his then domestic opponents Zinoviev and Kamenev. It was the same with his writings on the British General Strike, although here his opponents were Bukharin and Stalin. As to his enthusiasm for China in 1927, that too was essentially domestic in focus, for Chiang Kai-shek's destruction of the Chinese Communist Party was simply a metaphor for Thermidor, for what would happen in Russia if the kulaks ever found a general willing to act on their behalf. It was only in emigration, in 1933, when he had buried the concept of Thermidor, that Trotsky explored the idea of how the revival of the working class movement in Europe might have a beneficial impact on the Soviet Union and halt the degeneration of the workers' state. Then internationalism became central to his ideas.

Trotsky scholars might be surprised to find in this biography that there are no references to Baruch Knei-Paz's great study *The Social and Political Thought of Leon Trotsky*.[9] Knei-Paz collects together Trotsky's writing under certain themes, bringing together early and later essays into a coherent exposition; this approach makes Trotsky a far greater thinker than he was in reality. Trotsky wrote an enormous amount and, as a journalist, he was always happy to write on subjects about which he knew very little. Trotsky could write beautifully, but he was no philosopher. Knei-Paz does a better job than Trotsky himself in synthesising his ideas. Trotsky was a jobbing journalist and revolutionary activist and his writings cannot be divorced from their immediate context. Trotsky's first revolutionary comrade, Grigorii Ziv, doubted that Trotsky had the patience to fully engage with Marxism as an analytical tool. A similar verdict came from Anatolii Lunacharskii, a close comrade in 1917. He concluded that Trotsky was a very orthodox Marxist: "he takes revolutionary Marxism and draws from it the conclusions applicable to a given situation; he is bold as can be in opposing liberalism and semi-socialism, but he is no innovator."[10]

Ian Thatcher aptly commented that with Trotsky "all too often the political passions of the biographer determine the nature of the biography".[11] I have tried to avoid political passion. For good or ill, the Bolsheviks would not have come to power without Trotsky, and they would have lost power in less than a year if he had not been put in charge of the Red Army. It is equally certain that if Trotsky had remained in the leadership in the 1920s, the Soviet Union would have been a more technocratic and less terrorised society. However, Trotsky was the instigator of his own downfall. Partly from personality failings, but largely because of an unresolved disagreement about how the Party should operate and an ideological obsession with the kulak danger, he turned on his colleagues as much as they turned on him.

Notes

1 M. Eastman, *Leon Trotsky: the Portrait of Youth* (London, 1926), p. v.

2 I. Deutscher, *The Prophet Armed, Trotsky: 1879–1921* (Oxford, 1970); I. Deutscher, *The Prophet Unarmed, Trotsky: 1921–1929* (Oxford, 1978); I. Deutscher, *The Prophet Outcast, Trotsky: 1929–1940* (Oxford, 1970).

3 I. Thatcher, *Leon Trotsky and World War One* (Basingstoke, 2000); I. Thatcher, *Trotsky* (London, 2003).

4 J. White, "Lenin, Trotsky and the Arts of Insurrection: the Congress of Soviets of the Northern Region 11–13 October 1917", *Slavonic and East European Review*, No. 1, 1999.

5 E. van Ree, "'Lenin's Last Struggle' Revisited", *Revolutionary Russia*, No. 2, 2001.

6 R. B. Day, *Leon Trotsky and the Politics of Economic Isolation* (Cambridge, 1973).

7 N. Valentinov, "Dopolnenie k 'Dnevniku' L. Trotskogo", *Sotsialisticheskii vestnik*, No. 2–3, 1959.

8 Thatcher, *Trotsky*, p. 100.

9 B. Knei-Paz, *The Social and Political Thought of Leon Trotsky* (Oxford, 1978).

10 G. Ziv, *Trotskii: kharakteristika po lichnym vospominaniem* (New York, 1921); A. Lunacharskii, *Revolutionary Silhouettes* (London, 1967), pp. 66–7.

11 Thatcher, *Trotsky*, p. 1.

Chapter 1

The Precocious Apprentice

Lev Davidovich Bronstein, or Trotsky as he became, was the son of a rich peasant, what the Russians term a kulak. Born on 26 October 1879, his father, David Bronstein, was an unusual kulak in that he was a Jew. Early in the 19th century Tsar Alexander I had offered Jews the chance to buy land in what was then termed "New Russia", the southern steppe land bordering on the Black Sea, land that had been captured from the Turks a quarter of a century earlier by Catherine the Great. This land needed to be settled, thus the unusual decision for a Russian tsar to encourage even Jews to establish homesteads there. Trotsky's grandparents had taken up the challenge, and by the time of Trotsky's birth his father was well established. This was somewhat against the odds, for subsequent tsars had first dropped the Jewish settlement scheme and then started to deprive Jews of their land, but Trotsky's father had stuck with farming and moved to buy up the small estate of Yanovka.

Growing Up

Yanovka was an isolated spot. The nearest post office was 15 miles away, the nearest railway station 25. When the Bronsteins moved in in spring 1879, the farm was dilapidated. The house was of leaky thatch and traditional mud walls and floors; only two rooms had wooden floors, and only one of these was painted. Yet, as Trotsky recalled, "my childhood was not one of hunger and cold; my family had already achieved a competence at the time of my birth, but it was the stern competence of a people still rising from poverty and having no desire to stop half-way." Thus on the Bronstein farm moneymaking came first. The house might need repair, but that was because it was last on the list of the many improvements Trotsky's father was determined to make. The original farm was 250 acres, but the family leased 400 acres more. There were three barns and two open sheds, as well as a machine shop, stables and a cow shed. Most important of all for a kulak, there was an engine-powered mill; Trotsky's father could not only store his grain until the market price was right, but hire out his mill to his neighbours. Wheat made David Bronstein rich and the young Trotsky wanted for little. He was, he recalled, "the son of a prosperous landowner [and] belonged to the privileged class rather than to the oppressed".[1]

There were plenty of happy moments in Trotsky's childhood. Around the house it was his job to fetch in the eggs laid by the hens, exploring under the raised floors of the barns. Where he was truly happy, however, was in the machine shed. There he idolised the machine hand Ivan Greben, and spent many happy hours in the company of this man who could rebuild an engine and repair a boiler. Greben clearly reciprocated to a degree and made the young Trotsky a bicycle and taught him to ride it. He also devised ways of making croquet balls; the future scourge of the bourgeoisie was a passionate croquet player for much of his life. Trotsky remembered twirling Greben's moustache and studying "those unmistakable hands of the artisan". He was delighted when he was allowed to cut the threads of nuts or screws. Greben also restored the family spinet, which eventually sat proudly in the parlour; the machine shop was occupied by the spinet for several winter weeks as Greben cleaned it, glued it, polished it and found new strings and keys.[2] But there were also the unhappy moments of childhood. He suffered the traditional torture inflicted by doting parents on a precocious child. When his parents discovered he had been writing poems, he was forced to read them out to their friends: "it was painfully embarrassing; I would refuse, they would urge me, gently, then with irritation, finally with threats; sometimes I would run away, but my elders knew how to get what they wanted; with a pounding heart, with tears in my eyes, I would read my verses, ashamed of my borrowed lines and limping rhymes."[3]

Like most families on the way up the social ladder, Trotsky's father was obsessed with the education of his children. David Bronstein could not read and his wife, despite developing a love of reading, only read with difficulty. At the age of seven Trotsky started school at the village of Gromoklei. The experiment was not a success. Although the village was only two and a half miles away, Trotsky had to stay during the week with his aunt and uncle; worse, all the other children in the village spoke Yiddish, a language the Bronsteins, with their social aspirations, had long since abandoned in favour of Russian. And yet the Bronsteins had a child who at the age of eight had persuaded one of his many elder cousins that they should produce a handwritten magazine. After two years Trotsky's father decided he should move to a school in Odessa. What brought this about was the visit to Yanovka of another of Trotsky's cousins, the 28-year-old Moishe Shpentser, a freelance journalist from Odessa who had been persuaded to spend the summer of 1887 at the Bronstein farm to help fight off what was believed to be incipient tuberculosis. Moishe held radical views, views which he believed had prevented him gaining a university education. Moishe and his wife were happy to bring Trotsky into their cramped house in order that he might attend the St Paul's *Realschule* in Odessa. Unfortunately, the local Gromoklei school had educated him so poorly that Trotsky failed the entrance exam and had to spend a year in the preparatory class.

Thus, at the age of nine, Trotsky started seven years of education in Odessa. He was a model student for most of that time. At the end of the preparatory year he scored maximum marks in every subject and that was to be the pattern for the rest of his time at the *Realschule*. The Shpentsers supported him, but from the start he was both self-contained and self-confident, although occasionally he missed his mother and cried himself to sleep. Trotsky later described his time in Odessa as "becoming an urbanite".

Every day there was revealed to me some aspect of a cultural environment greater than that in which I passed the first nine years of my life. Even the machine shop at home began to dim and to lose its magic as compared with the spell of classical literature and the charm of the theatre.

Part of this process of urbanisation was to shed all aspects of his Jewishness and assimilate completely into the world of Russian culture. At key moments in his later life he would remember his roots: in 1917 he told Lenin his Jewishness prevented him from serving as Commissar for Internal Affairs; in 1926 he was horrified by the way the Party's campaign against Zinoviev took on an anti-Semitic hue; but Trotsky consciously rejected all aspects of Jewish separateness.

While Trotsky was living in the Shpentser's home, Moishe moved on from journalism to establishing a publishing concern, which was eventually to become very successful. Trotsky was keen to help, and was soon familiar with the different typefaces, printing layouts and bindings. He developed a particular passion for proof-reading. "My love of the freshly printed page", he recalled, "has its origins in those far-away years as a school boy." At school his own literary work was regularly read aloud in class by the teacher as a model, and a journalist friend of Shpentser was soon encouraging him to write more and more.[4] But Trotsky was not always the model student. In his second year he was involved in a typical schoolboy prank. As a certain teacher left the room, the whole class made a humming noise, but without moving their lips so that there were no obvious culprits. The teacher responded by disciplining some likely suspects quite arbitrarily, while Trotsky, the star pupil, was left untouched. However, some of those punished reported Trotsky as the ringleader and he was summoned to the head teacher. Athough expulsion was considered, the pleadings of the Shpentser family were listened to and Trotsky escaped with a suspension. Rather to Trotsky's surprise, his father took the whole incident in good heart.[5]

Trotsky's concern about his father's attitude reflected a gradual breakdown in their relationship, a natural enough occurrence, but aggravated in this case by Trotsky's growing rejection of what his father represented. Returning to Yanovka after his first year at school, Trotsky noted his gradual distancing from the country.

Our house looked terribly small to me now; the homemade wheat bread seemed grey, and the whole routine of country life seemed at once familiar and strange . . . Something new had grown up like a wall between myself and the things bound up with my childhood. Everything seemed the same and yet quite different. Objects and people looked like counterfeits of themselves.

Sometimes the issues that divided him from his father were trivial – Trotsky's father considered his glasses an urban affectation, while Trotsky felt they gave him a sense of added importance – but increasingly he was disturbed by his father's kulak values. Even before the move to Odessa, Trotsky would mingle with the migrant labourers and domestic servants and note what was said about his parents as employers.

Then, in the summer breaks from schooling in Odessa, he often witnessed scenes of apparent heartlessness. He would help his father calculate the wages, and always interpreted the payment due far more generously than his father; the labourers soon sensed he was on their side, which understandably infuriated David Bronstein. One summer, after a day spent playing croquet, he witnessed his father arguing with a peasant about the damage caused by an untethered cow. On another occasion he left a field where harvesting was underway and came across a barefoot woman owed money by his father who had been forced to wait until the day's harvesting was over before being returned the money she was due. Such incidents made him feel awkward and out of place, as indeed he was, for on this last occasion he recalled that he was wearing around the farm "a freshly laundered duck suit, with a leather belt that had a brass buckle and a white cap with a glittering badge". Yet it was not just "the instinct of acquisition, the petit bourgeois outlook and habits of life" which he rejected.

While the Yanovka people were spending many weary hours trying to measure the area of a field which had the shape of a trapezoid, I would apply Euclid and get my answer in a couple of minutes. But my computation did not tally with the one obtained by "practical" methods and they refused to believe it. I would bring out my geometry text-book and swear in the name of science; I would get all excited and use harsh words – and all to no purpose. People refused to see the light of reason and this drove me to despair.[6]

What brought matters to a head was David Bronstein's decision that Trotsky should move to study in Nikolaev in order to prepare for university entrance. His father had organised some comfortable lodgings and in autumn 1895 Trotsky arrived in a nicely pressed tan suit and stylish hat; within weeks the clothes of the swell bourgeois would be exchanged for those of a worker. In Odessa Trotsky had shown no interest in politics. He had rebelled against some of the more authoritarian aspects of his school regime, but that was just at the level of bravado. In Nikolaev Trotsky discovered politics. Nikolaev was one of the towns where former political prisoners were allowed to take up residence, and it had been favoured by some of the veterans of the 1880s People's Will party. Unfortunately for David Bronstein he had chosen to lodge his son with a respectable family whose sons were captivated by revolutionary politics. After a month or so of dismissive banter about "socialist utopias", Trotsky became hooked and was introduced to Franz Shvigovskii, the key figure in a commune of revolutionary youngsters which owed its ideological allegiance to the ideas of Chernyshevsky, the radical peasant socialist or Populist of the 1860s. This link was reinforced by the fact that Shvigovskii's younger brother was also a pupil at Trotsky's school.

The South Russia Workers' Union

Trotsky soon began to neglect his studies and spend all his time in the tumbledown house and garden rented by Shvigovskii, which became a sort of debating club for Nikolaev's radical youth. In despair, Trotsky's father came down to sort things out: he was keen to expand his business and diversify into profitable sugar beet production and brewing; for this he needed not a mechanic like Greben, but a fully qualified engineer, his own son. David Bronstein berated his chosen landlady for not keeping an eye on her young ward, and told Trotsky to mend his ways or else: Trotsky responded in kind, and with great vehemence. He and his circle were, after all, preparing to build a new world. David Bronstein then cut off his allowance, forcing Trotsky to move into the revolutionary commune, dressing henceforth in blue workers' shirts and refusing to make use of "bourgeois" bedlinen. His only source of income was some private tutoring, and when he travelled to Odessa and called on the Shpentsers at this time Moishe noted he was as "gaunt and ill-clad as a tramp".[7]

The only woman associated with this commune was Aleksandra Sokolovskaya, the sister of one of Trotsky's friends. Trotsky at this stage was 17, she was 22 and had already completed a course in midwifery at Odessa University. While in Odessa she had studied the writings of Georgii Plekhanov, the founder of Russian Marxism, and was a self-declared Marxist. This made her unique among the members of the Commune, who all based themselves on the Populism of Chernyshevskii and the People's Will. Baiting Aleksandra about her Marxism was a regular pastime of the group – along with writing her love poetry – and she recalled that when she first met Trotsky she had been told by her brother that at last they had found someone who would be able to defeat her in argument. His first attack was to say: "You still think you're a Marxist? I can't imagine how a young girl so full of life can stand that dry, narrow, impractical stuff!" She replied: "I can't imagine how a person who thinks he is logical can be contented with a headful of vague, idealistic emotions." Such banter continued for weeks.[8]

Then, in spring 1896, Trotsky suddenly fainted. These fits were to occur throughout his life, but the worried revolutionaries quickly informed the family and David Bronstein was soon back on the scene, greeting the earnest young people with a cheerful, "Hello, have you run away from your father, too?" Trotsky, unwilling to patch up his quarrel with his father completely, agreed to return to Yanovka over the summer as a "guest" rather than a son. At Yanovka a compromise was hammered out. Another Odessa uncle was visiting the farm at the time; he owned a small engineering plant and was happy to look after Trotsky for a while. So it was agreed Trotsky would return to Odessa and there start attending some mathematics lectures at the university to see if such a career suited him. September saw him doing just this, discussing with tutors possible futures for those with a degree in mathematics. He remained financially independent from his father, again earning money from giving private lessons and, when money was short, staying with the Shpentsers. But politics got the better of him. He attempted to set up a political cell in the Shpentser printworks and by December 1896 was back in the Nikolaev commune and back in the company of Aleksandra Sokoloskaya.[9]

Not long after his return, Trotsky became involved in a cruel practical joke on Aleksandra. While in Odessa he had begun to wonder if there might not be something to Marxism after all, and had discussed this with Shvigovskii. Shvigovskii had countered these doubts and teased Trotsky that he was falling under Aleksandra's influence. Maybe because this touched a raw nerve, Trotsky joined with Shvigovskii in stage-managing the following humiliation. Aleksandra was invited to the Commune's New Year's party, tempted by the story that Trotsky had returned a Marxist. She, sceptical at first, was assured by the others that it was true and agreed to come, seeking out her new ally and being particularly friendly. Then, at midnight, instead of toasting the New Year, Trotsky proposed "a curse on all Marxists" and Aleksandra stormed off, swearing "never to offer my hand to that little boy again". Trotsky had no choice but to apologise.[10]

Yet within weeks the two were lovers, brought together by joint involvement in the revolutionary cause. In February 1897 Aleksandra's brother Grigorii made the acquaintance of a "real" worker. Using this contact Trotsky, Aleksandra and Aleksandra's other brother Ilya became the core of a workers' cell which adopted the rather grandiose name South Russia Workers' Union in honour of a similarly named organisation of the 1870s; they were joined by Grigorii Ziv, a medical student who returned at Easter from his studies and threw himself into the work of the union. Trotsky's revolutionary career had begun and things developed rapidly. Soon about 20 workers were gathering for secret meetings and discussions; Ziv recalled how at one of the early ones, in the forest around Nikolaev, he chickened out of speaking, but Trotsky managed to stutter something more or less convincing. Soon they had moved on to producing revolutionary literature and Trotsky set about writing proclamations and duplicating them on a hectograph. It was not long before Trotsky had moved from proclamations to a newspaper, *Our Cause*. As Ziv later recalled, this was very much Trotsky's initiative. The paper was edited by Trotsky and it was he who wrote most of the articles, penned every letter himself for the hectograph, and ransacked the newspapers in the public library for cartoons, which he doctored for his own purposes. Trotsky's inexhaustible energy kept this tiny show going – he even took the overnight steamer to Odessa, sleeping on deck under the stars, to spread the message there.

The group worked harmoniously until August 1897 when Ziv announced that he intended to resume his medical studies at Kazan University. For Trotsky this was a stab in the back; he could not imagine how the personal satisfaction of study could be more important than the revolutionary cause; in a hurtful gesture he wrote on the back of the group photograph the four conspirators – Trotsky, Aleksandra, Ziv and Ilya Sokolovskii – had had taken, "faith without action is death". Deprived of Ziv's support, Trotsky worked ever harder, producing in all three issues of *Our Cause*. It was a happy time for him. "Never in my later life did I come into such intimate contact with the plain workers as in Nikolayev . . . The principal types of the Russian proletariat impressed themselves on my consciousness forever." However the authorities pounced on 28 January 1898 when over 200 arrests were made, such had been the growth of the organisation in the course of the year.[11]

There then followed nearly two years in prison followed by trial and exile to Siberia. It was in prison that Trotsky's gradual evolution towards Marxism came to completion. Populism as a body of ideas focused on the peasantry: the South Russia Workers' Union sought to organise industrial workers. Populists had always looked to contact the peasantry through those peasants working as factory workers, but in Nikolaev Trotsky's group was most successful among skilled shipbuilders with few links to the countryside. Trotsky seems to have worried about this and at one point in spring 1897 raised with Ziv the possibility of being a Social Democrat without being a Marxist; at this time he had become fascinated with the life of the German socialist Ferdinand Lassalle, with whom Marx had repeatedly clashed. As the group spread its influence to Odessa, Aleksandra's Marxist contacts became increasingly involved and the group would eventually describe itself as Social Democratic. Ziv heard from others that Trotsky had resolved to become a Marxist on the eve of his arrest; Trotsky himself said that it was during his first days in prison that this conversion occurred, but that he clung to his old views simply from stubbornness. His first public statement on the matter to other revolutionaries came while in Odessa prison. He was, he always stressed, a bit of a self-taught Marxist at first, not having read any Marxist classics. In November 1899, after being sentenced to four years' exile, he was held in Moscow transit prison for six months and it was there that he read Lenin's *The Development of Capitalism in Russia*.[12]

In Odessa prison there was another falling out with Ziv. Ziv had become increasingly irritated with two character traits of Trotsky that would stay with him throughout his life. The first was an almost uncontrollable urge to humiliate an opponent in debate. This had already happened with the affair of the New Year's toast, but Ziv felt that, repeatedly, Trotsky went too far. Second, Ziv felt that Trotsky saw success in everything he did, identifying himself with the cause. While they were in prison Trotsky,

Ziv and other comrades organised a hunger strike to try and force the release of an innocent man. From Ziv's perspective, the strike was a complete failure since their main demand was not met. For Trotsky, however the strike had seemed a great success; although the main demand had not been met, the authorities had made a minor concession and prisoners were henceforth allowed to choose their cells. Trotsky was happy to see only the success and not the failure. It was an example of what Ziv already saw as one of his character traits, the ability to see "the revolution and his active ego as coinciding". These rows with Ziv were bitter and during one of them Trotsky experienced another of his fainting fits.[13]

Prison had a happier outcome, however. When in Kherson prison Trotsky had proposed that he marry Aleksandra. Since he was still only 20 he needed his father's permission, and David Bronstein would not hear of it. This resulted in the final rift between Trotsky and his parents and was not resolved even after a visit from his mother while in Odessa prison. However, in the transit prison in Moscow, at the start of the journey into exile, the authorities turned a blind eye to his under-age status and the two were married. Life in their first place of residence, Ust-Kut on the river Lena, was difficult to bear. It was freezing in the winter and in the summer mosquitoes made life miserable. Trotsky took the opportunity to read some Marx and later recalled how he would resort to "brushing the cockroaches off the page" as he ploughed through the first volume of Marx's *Capital*. He also studied the details of the Bernstein-Kautsky controversy within the German Social Democratic Party over the question of whether Marxism implied reform or revolution. Trotsky and Aleksandra did not stay long in Ust-Kut. They were granted permission to move further east for a while to the river Ilim, where Trotsky was given a job as a clerk; he did not take this work seriously and was soon sacked for incompetence. The couple then moved further south to Verkholensk.

From the very start of his exile Trotsky began to write articles for the *Eastern Review*, a legal newspaper started by Populist exiles. Struggling to find a pen-name, he opened an Italian dictionary at random and found the word "antidoto", this he turned into Antid Oto and it remained his pen-name for many years. Later he would jestingly explain to friends that he wanted to inject a Marxist antidote into the legal press. These articles were not political. Many were on literature, although those on the peasantry had a social edge. After two years of exile, a Social Democratic organisation called the Siberian Union was established in Siberia, and its members contacted Trotsky for help with their literary ventures; soon he was writing proclamations and leaflets once again. Among the themes he felt obliged to take up was the need for more centralism among the disparate social democratic organisations in Russia.

Thus, when in summer 1902 he first heard that Lenin, Julii Martov and other leading émigré Social Democrats had launched a new newspaper called *Iskra* (*The Spark*), and then read a copy of Lenin's *What is to be done?*, he knew what he had to do – escape from exile. While in Siberia, Aleksandra had given birth to two daughters, Zina and Nina, yet she encouraged him to escape. He recalled in his memoirs: "She was the first to broach the idea of my escape when we realised the great new tasks; she brushed away all my doubts." Although Aleksandra accepted the separation and Trotsky was essentially right to say "life separated us, but nothing could destroy our friendship and our intellectual kinship", it may be presumed that Aleksandra had hoped to meet up with Trotsky again once her own escape from exile could be arranged. By the time they did meet up two years later, however, Trotsky had found a second love.[14]

For *Iskra*, against Lenin

Trotsky's flight was almost childishly simple to arrange. He reported ill, made a figure out of straw to look like a man in bed, and then hid under a pile of hay in a peasant's cart. The peasant took him to Irkutsk, where he met Aleksandra's brother Ilya who supplied him with a passport in the name of a local man called Trotsky; from then on this was how he would be known to the world. Trotsky then travelled to the Volga town of Samara, a distribution centre for the Social Democrat newspaper *Iskra*. Here he was welcomed by the local Social Democrat organisation and given the pseudonym "Pero" or "Pen", an allusion to his journalistic skills which were already much appreciated. The *Iskra* group in Samara decided to make use of his Ukrainian background and sent him on a tour of Kharkov, Kiev and Poltava to try and negotiate with the editors of a local Social Democrat newspaper called the *Southern Worker*; the backers of this paper had stated that in principle they supported *Iskra*'s programme for centralising the Social Democratic movement, but then proved difficult to pin down. From an organisational point of view the trip was not a success; the contact address in Kharkov had proved wrong and the editors had indeed proved slippery, trying to support *Iskra* while retaining a degree of local independence, independence aimed at allowing them to continue their own policy of co-operation with the Liberals. However, Lenin, Martov and the other *Iskra* editors were extremely impressed with the report that Trotsky wrote on the tour, which brought out clearly the political issues at stake. Samara was instructed to send Trotsky abroad to the *Iskra* leadership, divided at that time between Zurich and London.

Trotsky arrived in London in October 1902 and went straight to the house where Lenin was staying. It was the start of a tempestuous relationship lasting 20 years. After discussions about the *Southern Worker* and the need for a centralised party organisation, Lenin found Trotsky a room in the house shared by his fellow *Iskra* editors, Martov and Vera Zasulich. After a brief spell reading back issues, Trotsky was put to work. First he wrote short notices, then longer political articles, and finally editorials. Trotsky did not stay in London long. He was sent on a short lecture tour of Social Democratic groups in France and Belgium, all the while promoting the *Iskra* cause. After this he was originally supposed to return to Russia, but the plan was changed and he was ordered to Paris. There, on the stairs of the building in which he had been housed, he met Natasha Sedova, a young Social Democrat activist who had been deputed first to find him a room and then to act as his guide. Natasha was a rebel in her own right: after studying at Moscow University she had moved to Switzerland and became a supporter of *Iskra*. When she met Trotsky she had already made one trip to Russia smuggling illegal literature. Natasha was taken aback when her new companion took one look at Paris and declared that it "resembles Odessa, but Odessa is better". Quite when their romance began remains obscure. Natasha was involved with someone else and Trotsky moved on to Switzerland and Germany to repeat his lecture. He and Natasha must have kept in touch, for by the time the editorial board of *Iskra* moved to Geneva in April 1903 the couple were living together. It is probable that they were already together before this in Paris, when Trotsky was visited by his parents, who brought with them things sent from Aleksandra. The following year Aleksandra succeeded in leaving Siberia herself and, placing the girls with her parents, joined the Social Democrat community in Geneva. In autumn 1904 she visited Trotsky on her way back to St Petersburg.[15]

In March 1903 Lenin decided that Trotsky should not return to Russia but stay abroad and be co-opted to the editorial board of *Iskra*. Martov backed him on this, but Plekhanov, the father of Russian Marxism, detected a ruse on Lenin's part to win control of the board and opposed the proposal. In the end Trotsky was brought into the board as an advisor. However, the issue of the future of the editorial board did not go away, and opened up the first major disagreement between Lenin and Trotsky. All *Iskra*'s efforts were geared towards calling a Second Congress of the Russian Social Democratic Labour Party which would adopt a new, centralised organisational structure. Most *Iskra* activists, Martov included, assumed that once this congress had been held and once the new centralised structure was in place, a new *Iskra* editorial board would be elected by the congress; the self-appointed group who had established the paper would bow out, their task achieved. Lenin did not accept this. In his scheme the Central Committee would be concerned only with events in Russia, not with the conduct of the editorial board. In Geneva Trotsky raised this with Lenin, who responded: "We are the stable centre, we are stronger in ideas, and we must exercise guidance from here". "Then this will mean a complete dictatorship of the editorial board?" Trotsky asked. "Well, what's wrong with that?" Lenin retorted. "In the present situation, it must be so."[16]

Although Trotsky had expressed this concern about Lenin's proposals even before the Second Congress began, like most other delegates he had not anticipated that the party would split. The Second Congress opened on 30 July and lasted until 23 August. In the early sessions Trotsky and Lenin appeared at one. Trotsky had abandoned any sense of Jewish separateness as he became an "urbanite" and therefore backed Lenin in criticising those Jews who favoured autonomy for a specifically Jewish section in the Party; from the Congress floor he explained that not all Jews backed the idea. Trotsky also supported Lenin in the debate on the agrarian question, for example. Yet behind the scenes tempers were fraying. Things came to a head over discussion of the apparently innocuous rule number one for party membership. Lenin's resolution ran: "A member of the RSDLP is one who accepts its programme and supports the Party both financially and by personal participation in one of the Party organisations." Martov's proposal read: "A member of the RSDLP is one who accepts its programme, supports the Party financially and renders it regular personal assistance under the direction of one of its organisations." Martov's formulation was broader, and aimed at allowing into the party all the many workers who were linked to it through such activities as organising strikes and distributing literature, but did not participate in the secret work of the underground cells. Lenin's objection was that Martov's formulation would not only let in workers, and not even all workers could be relied on, it also allowed opportunist intellectuals to call themselves Party members. And so the Party split, with the supporters of Lenin's formula becoming the Bolshevik faction and the supporters of Martov the Menshevik faction.

Trotsky's first contribution to the debate was relatively measured: "I fear that Lenin's formula will create a fictitious organisation, one which will merely give its members a *qualification* but will not serve as a means for party work." By the next session he had developed what was to be a consistent theme in his critique.

I did not know that one could exorcise opportunism by means of rules. I think that opportunism is produced by more complex causes. Finally, I did not realise that opportunists are organically incapable of organisation. I know the Jauresist party [in France], which is organised opportunism . . . The point is that Lenin's formula, against intellectuals' individualism, hits quite a different target . . . if statutory definitions are to correspond to actual relations, Comrade Lenin's formula must be rejected. I repeat: it misses the mark.

As the Congress first split into Bolshevik and Menshevik factions, and then degenerated into ever more vitriolic accusation and counter-accusation, Trotsky did not hold back. Indeed, his behaviour was almost disruptive. He was one of the delegates who heckled Lenin when he proposed giving the *Iskra* board the power to dictate to the Central Committee; he made loud sarcastic comments when the minutes of the crucial debate on the party rules were being discussed; and he constantly asked that the voting figures in the Central Committee elections be made public, so that it was clear that the 20 members of what was now the Menshevik faction had deliberately abstained.[17]

After the Second Congress Trotsky played a major role in the Menshevik campaign to subvert its decisions, a campaign launched after a meeting in Geneva in September 1903. The Mensheviks boycotted both the Central Committee and the *Iskra* editorial board, leaving only Lenin and Plekhanov as members. The tactic worked. Plekhanov decided to use his powers as father of the party, and chairman of the Party Council (a body charged with liaising between the Central Committee and the *Iskra* board), to co-opt the Menshevik members back on to the board; Lenin resigned in protest. Thus the Mensheviks were back in charge of *Iskra* and Trotsky was writing for it once again. Unfortunately for Trotsky, the way events had developed had given Plekhanov undue influence in the running of *Iskra*. Plekhanov believed implicitly that the party's allies in the future struggle against the Tsar would be the Liberals. Trotsky, by siding with Lenin on the agrarian question, had already challenged Plekhanov implicitly by allotting a potentially revolutionary role to the peasantry. Furthermore, in an unremarked speech early in the Second Congress, Trotsky seemed to suggest that the proletariat could actually lead the revolution: "There can be no doubt that the developed and revolutionised proletariat exercises a revolutionary effect in a purely spontaneous way upon other social classes and strata . . . Bringing this idea to the proletariat means at one and the same time *demarcating* our party from all other oppositional and revolutionary movements and also *supporting* these movements."[18]

Relations between Plekhanov and Trotsky broke down completely in March 1904. By then the Russo-Japanese War had begun and Trotsky was increasingly infuriated by what he saw as the weakness of the Liberals in opposing it. For him this weakness simply reinforced the notion that Liberal dilatoriness opened the way for what he now called "the self-determination of the proletariat". The *Iskra* article "Wise Birds", published on 16 March 1904, summed up Trotsky's stance. After a blistering attack on the Liberal "wise birds" he ended:

The working class should know that, whatever happens, these ravens will prophesy doom and it will only be the strength of the proletariat which determines whether such prophesies will snuff out the cause of freedom . . . [The proletariat] must, with unweakening energy, undertake its own political campaigns . . . with its own slogans, under its own banner of social democracy, the working class must go into battle . . . It must do this, because otherwise the results of that revolution, paid for with its blood, will be determined by those ravens of doom.[19]

Plekhanov called for Trotsky's resignation. The other editors protested. Trotsky offered to resign. Plekhanov did resign. In the end Trotsky left quietly and took no further part in *Iskra*. Instead he devoted the summer to writing a devastating critique of Lenin's views on party organisation. *Our Political Tasks* appeared in August 1904. Summing up the essential difference between the Bolshevik and Menshevik concepts of the party he asserted: "In the one case we have a party which *thinks for* the proletariat, which *substitutes* itself politically for it, and in the other we have a party which politically *educates* and *mobilises* the proletariat to exercise rational pressure on the will of all political groups and parties." In his famously prophetic insight Trotsky pointed out the logical outcome of these policies. "In the internal politics of the Party these methods lead to the Party organisation substituting itself for the Party, the Central Committee substituting itself for the Party organisation, and finally the dictator substituting himself for the Central Committee."

The theme that emerged from the combination of sarcasm and vitriol with which Trotsky assaulted Lenin was this: the working class had to learn for itself through its own self-activity; there were no short cuts, the working class could be guided but not led.

It is necessary to understand, gentlemen, that the development of a whole class proceeds surely but slowly, but it is necessary to understand that we have no other basis for political successes, except the standard of the proletarian class consciousness, nor can we find any other. It is necessary once and for all to give up the "accelerated" methods of political substitutionalism. He who has no patience, he who wants to look for other guarantees – not in the class, but in the top layer engaged in organising conspiracies – might as well leave us today.

Although the main target of Trotsky's attack was Lenin, it was also aimed at Plekhanov and those Mensheviks who looked to the Liberals. Working class self-activity should be just that, action by and for the working class and not for any other social or political group. Thus he also condemned those committees which "instead of organising the proletariat into becoming socially aware, intercede with the bourgeois-democratic movement".[20]

Here, by autumn 1904, Trotsky had already elaborated the ideas that would dominate his activity during the 1905 Revolution. Working class self-activity, under clear Social Democratic slogans rather than "liberal petitioning", would be the essence of everything he did during that revolutionary year. He moved from Geneva to Munich and in September 1904 wrote an *Open Letter to Comrades* announcing that he had left the Menshevik Bureau; in private he told Martov and Zasulich that he hoped to reach an understanding with the Bolsheviks' Central Committee. In Munich he shared lodgings with A. L. Helphand, better known as Parvus, a regular contributor to *Iskra* who, Trotsky was delighted to discover, shared his analysis of the need for independent working class leadership of the revolution.

By autumn 1904 events in Russia were developing quickly. The Tsar had finally agreed that the elected assemblies for local government (*zemstvos*) would be allowed to hold a congress. That congress inevitably raised national political issues and resolved to call on all *zemstvos* and all public bodies to petition the Tsar to grant an elected national assembly with legislative power. All sorts of public bodies responded and, in imitation of events in France on the eve of the 1848 Revolution, massive banquets were held to get around the ban on public meetings. Trotsky drafted a pamphlet in which he urged the working class to take part in this campaign as an independent entity. Revolution was in the air, "the incredible becomes real, the impossible becomes probable", and so, working class action was needed.

Tear the workers away from the machines and workshops; lead them through the factory gate out into the street; direct them to neighbouring factories; proclaim a stoppage there; and carry new masses into the street . . . Taking possession of the first suitable buildings for public meetings, entrenching yourself in those buildings, using them for uninterrupted revolutionary meetings with a permanently shifting and changing audience, you shall bring order into the movement of the masses, raise their confidence, explain to them the purpose and sense of events; and thus you shall transform the city into a revolutionary camp.[21]

The Mensheviks were still debating whether this pamphlet should be published when the Bloody Sunday massacre occurred on 9 January 1905.

The 1905 Revolution

On 9 January 1905 workers belonging to the Assembly of St Petersburg Factory Workers, led by the Orthodox Priest Father Gapon, had been doing precisely what Trotsky had called for, introducing a working class voice into the opposition to the Tsar. Carrying a working class petition calling for a national legislative assembly they had been shot down nearing Palace Square. The Tsar's immediate response to the massacre was to set up an inquiry to be chaired by senator N. V. Shidlovskii. To ensure working class grievances were heard, the Tsar agreed that 50 workers' representatives could take part in this commission, and to select them every factory employing more than 100 workers was allowed to elect a delegate on the ratio of one per 500 workers; in all 372 delegates were sent in mid February to a meeting to choose the 50 representatives. The dominant figure at this meeting was the radical lawyer G. S. Nosar, who gained admission to the meeting by posing as one of the electors from a textile factory, P. A. Khrustalev; thus for the rest of the year he was known as Khrustalev-Nosar. At this meeting roughly 35 per cent of the electors were supporters of Father Gapon, 20 per cent Social Democrats and the rest of no clear political affiliation. The authorities promptly cut the ground from under the feet of the Gaponists. In the aftermath of the massacre they had closed down the Assembly, and they now refused to reopen it. This cleared the way for the Social Democrats, and the obvious task for Trotsky and all those keen to influence the course of the revolution was to help the 20 per cent of Social Democrat electors win over the rest of the working class.

Trotsky had learned of the Bloody Sunday massacre the day after it happened in Geneva, where he had returned to give a lecture. He and Natasha decided to go back to Russia at once. They returned to Munich and from there to Vienna, where through contacts of Natasha's they prepared to make their way to Kiev. Trotsky stayed in Kiev for several months, working together with the Bolshevik activist Leonid Krasin, and it was through Krasin's contacts that he made his way to St Petersburg and the Menshevik group there. Although throughout the first half of 1905 strikes and peasant disturbances had continued, most of the political leadership had remained with liberals associated with the *zemstvos*. After a Third Zemstvo Congress at the end of May the Tsar met its leaders and speeded up work on a consultative national assembly, announced on 6 August. Trotsky persuaded the St Petersburg Mensheviks to have nothing to do with such an assembly, which some Liberal leaders were ready to accept. Meanwhile on May Day 1905 Natasha had been arrested while helping to organise a clandestine meeting in a forest, so Trotsky took safety in Finland.

Here, writing and walking, he finally formulated his view that while Russia might be experiencing a bourgeois-democratic revolution this did not mean that the liberal bourgeoisie was bound to come to power. The key in Russia was the attitude of the peasantry, which political grouping could inspire them to rebel. Trotsky was more and more convinced that only the working class could persuade the peasantry to act and that, if it gave a firm lead, Russian Social Democracy could emerge from the revolution by capturing power. Trotsky's head was still full of such ideas when at the end of September he moved deeper into Finland and settled by a lake, planning for what he believed would be an upsurge in the revolution on the anniversary of Bloody Sunday. He was thus caught completely unaware by the strike wave in St Petersburg in October 1905.[22]

The strikes in St Petersburg began on 3 October when St Petersburg printworkers came out in support of striking colleagues in Moscow. The printers' action sparked off a storm of strikes which rumbled through the capital for the next ten days, culminating in a railway workers' strike. Social Democratic activists struggled to give the movement some cohesion. Among the proposals that Trotsky had drafted in Finland was one for an elected non-party workers' organisation, like the electors to the Shidlovskii Commission but a permanent feature of working class life. In his absence this idea was taken up by the St Petersburg Mensheviks, who on 10 October issued an appeal for the formation of "a revolutionary workers' council (soviet) of self-management". They suggested using the same elective principal as the Shidlovskii Commission and in fact many of the same worker activists became involved. After issuing the appeal, the Mensheviks sent 50 agitators out into the factories and on 13 October over 30 delegates attended the first meeting of the General Workers' Committee of St Petersburg at the Polytechnical Institute. The gathering resolved to call a general strike and that a fuller meeting be summoned for 14 October; this was attended by over 100 delegates. At this second meeting Khrustalev-Nosar, now posing as a representative of the Print Workers' Union, was elected chairman. Delegates still tended to use the name council or soviet, rather than committee, and so the name Soviet of Workers' Deputies was formally adopted on 17 October.[23]

Trotsky's first meeting of the Soviet was at that second meeting of 14 October. Until his arrest on 3 December he devoted every waking hour to its work, attending as one of the agreed number of party representatives. On 14 October the Soviet had agreed both to broaden the strike call and to send a delegation to the City Council to seek its support. After much hesitation, the latter agreed to hold a "private conference" with some of the Soviet leaders. Not surprisingly the city fathers rejected requests to fund the Soviet and provide it with accommodation, but it did agree to help defend anyone arrested simply for being a member of the Soviet. Support was also sought from the Bolsheviks. Initially they had wanted nothing to do with this workers' parliament unless it accepted the principle of Party leadership. However, by October Krasin had moved to St Petersburg and, still in touch with Trotsky, he asked him to address the Bolshevik St Petersburg Committee on the nature of the Soviet and its work.[24]

The October General Strike was so total that the Tsar was forced to act. On 17 October he issued a manifesto agreeing to turn the consultative assembly he had offered into a legislative assembly. Although the Tsar issued his manifesto on 17 October, few details emerged until the following day. So it was on the morning of the 18th that excited crowds took to the streets and made their way across the River Neva to the university, the traditional venue for public gatherings. Here Trotsky addressed the crowds and demanded an amnesty for political prisoners and the withdrawal of troops from St Petersburg. He concluded with a theatrical flourish:

As for the Tsar's manifesto, look, it's only a scrap of paper. Here it is before you – here it is crumpled in my fist. Today they have issued it, tomorrow they will take it away and tear it into pieces, just as I am now tearing up this paper freedom before your eyes.[25]

It was the issue of an amnesty that the Soviet leaders took up first. Trotsky and the other Social Democrats involved in the Soviet hoped that continuing the strike might force the Tsar to make further dramatic concessions, possibly even to abdicate, but they were astute enough politicians not to make such revolutionary slogans their immediate demands. They focused on the issue of an amnesty and called on the strike to continue until the Tsar met their demands.

This tactic enabled the Soviet leadership to organise an orderly retreat. For all the reservations people had about the Tsar's manifesto, it was clear that a significant concession had been made and a new chapter in Russia's history had opened. Workers began to drift back to work. On 21 October the Soviet called for a general return to work, but its leaders could link this to a partial victory. There was to be no general amnesty, but on 22 October the Tsar did grant the decree "For the Relief of the Fate of Persons who, Prior to the Issuing of the Manifesto, had Perpetrated Criminal Acts against the State". Under this decree a large number of political prisoners were allowed to go free, including Trotsky's wife Natasha who, after serving her sentence of six months in prison, had just been released on licence to the provincial town of Tver.

This decree did not come out of the blue. The Soviet had resolved to make 23 October a day of commemoration for all those who had died during the revolutionary struggle. To accompany the funerals of victims they planned a city-wide demonstration. In order to ensure that this passed off peacefully the Soviet decided on 21 October to send a delegation to meet the Tsar's new Prime Minister, Sergei Witte. Witte himself was all smiles and did not rule out the Soviet's request that the police should be withdrawn and the demonstration controlled by Soviet-appointed marshals, but he stressed that the security of the city was exclusively the concern of the St Petersburg Governor Trepov. Trepov then informed the delegation that he could not do as they proposed since he had intelligence to suggest that right-wing Populist groups known as Black Hundreds planned to disrupt the funeral demonstration. When the delegation returned to the Soviet in the early hours of the morning of 22 October, there was a passionate debate, led by Trotsky. It was clear to many that the police were in cahoots with the Black Hundreds and that the Police Chief had brought them into the discussion simply to put pressure on the Soviet leaders. It was equally clear that the funeral demonstrations were likely to be marred by violence. So, after much soul-searching, the Soviet voted to call off the planned demonstration. The Tsar's decision to grant a partial amnesty later the same day was a gesture to encourage the Soviet's moderation.[26]

The Soviet, however, was not interested in moderation but in testing to the limit the Tsar's manifesto. The Tsar had mentioned freedom of speech, but how could this exist if censorship continued? The Soviet announced on 19 October that print workers would only work with copy that had not been sent for censorship. To enforce this, print workers remained on strike and by 22 October the censorship system had been sidelined and freedom of the press effectively won. At the same time the Soviet moved to establish its own newspaper, *Izvestiya* (*News*). Since the Soviet had no printing press of its own, workers started to produce it on plant closed down by industrial action. Sympathetic workers would occupy the printing presses of a strike-bound company, get their fellow workers to restore electricity to the plant, and print the necessary copies.[27]

The turning point for the Soviet began as early as 23 October when the Tsar began to reassert his authority. On that day a campaign began among the sailors of the Kronstadt naval base for the civil liberties promised in the Tsar's manifesto to be extended to military personnel. When on 26 October some soldiers stationed at the base presented similar demands to their commanding officers, they were arrested. As the soldiers were marched away to detention, some sailors tried to free them, the guards opened fire, some sailors reached for the weapons: in the end martial law was declared and troops brought in from St Petersburg to restore order; 1,200 sailors faced court-martial and possible execution. News of these events spread to St Petersburg and by 29 October protest meetings were being held in factories across the city. The events in Kronstadt coincided with other evidence that the Tsar had given with one hand only to take away with the other. In Poland martial law had been declared because of nationalist unrest, while peasant disturbances in Chernigov, Saratov and Tambov had prompted the authorities there to do the same. On 1 November the Soviet resolved to call a new general strike, although it did so only after the most heated discussion.

In organisational terms the November strike was a triumph. It had been called because of pressure from below and the workers were solidly behind it; more factories were involved than during October. At once Witte called for a return to work; the Soviet responded by calling on workers to stay out. On 5 November the government made a concession. The St Petersburg Press Agency reported that "we are authorised to state that ... participants in the Kronstadt events have not been and will not be judged by courts martial"; the same statement also promised that martial law would be lifted in Poland.

Should the strike continue? When the Soviet Executive met later that day, Trotsky argued powerfully that the strike had to end since the revolutionary movement throughout the country was on the wane. "Our strike, real as it is, is in the nature of a demonstration ... to show the awakening army that the working class is on its side." This, Trotsky argued, had been achieved.

If we consider that the purpose of our action is the overthrow of the autocracy, then of course we have not achieved that aim ... Events are working for us and there is no advantage for us in forcing their progress ... for tomorrow we shall be stronger than we are today ... Do not forget that the electoral campaign, which must bring the entire revolutionary proletariat to its feet, lies ahead. And who knows whether this electoral campaign will not end by blowing the existing regime sky high?

Trotsky's eloquence persuaded the Soviet to call for a return to work on 7 November.[28]

Thirty years later Trotsky was still wondering if he had made the right decision on that occasion. At one level the Soviet seemed to be at the peak of its power in early November. By then it had a total membership of 562 delegates, representing 147 factories, 34 workshops and 16 trade unions; its executive was composed of 22 worker deputies and nine party representatives with an advisory vote, three Bolsheviks, three Mensheviks and three members of the peasant-oriented Socialist Revolutionaries (SRs). It still had great authority. Khrustalev-Nosar recalled that all issues discussed were raised first in the localities, then formulated into proposals by the executive, and then discussed again in the full Soviet; only two executive decisions were taken without full Soviet approval, and both were endorsed retrospectively.[29] By November it also had significant funds; on 15 November it voted to donate 2,000 roubles to striking postal and telegraph workers. On 23 November it threatened a nationwide railway strike if the sentence was carried out on a telegraph engineer condemned to death; the government backed down, leaving Trotsky with "a vivid recollection of the memorable meeting of the Executive Committee at which a plan of action was drawn up while awaiting the government's reply".[30]

But below the surface the balance of forces had changed. Back on 26 October some delegates from one of the St Petersburg districts voted to introduce the eight-hour day "by revolutionary means", in other words, working for eight hours and then going home. The Soviet leadership was never keen on this proposal, but the idea caught on and on 31 October the Soviet agreed to endorse it. This campaign was quickly overtaken by the November strike, and after the decision on 5 November to order a return to work, the Soviet announced the following day that the campaign for the eight-hour day by revolutionary means was not a universal slogan, but one only to be implemented where there was a chance of success. This clarification had little impact. Employers were determined to retain their right to control the number of hours worked and, instead of returning to work on 7 November many workers found themselves locked out until, after four hours of passionate debate, the Soviet called off the eight-hour day campaign on 12 November.[31]

On 26 November the government decided to act and arrested the Soviet's chairman Khrustalev-Nosar. This was a blow from which the Soviet struggled to recover, since much of the organisational work had depended on him, a person described at the time by Trotsky as "a man of practical ability and resourcefulness, an energetic and skilful chairman".

Trotsky drew up the Soviet's protest at its chairman's arrest and then suggested to David Sverchkov, the Soviet's treasurer and a worker delegate, that he should take over. He declined and proposed Trotsky, who also turned the proposal down on the grounds that he was not a worker but a political advisor. Sverchkov then suggested they establish a three-person presidium, chaired by Trotsky, and this was agreed, though it caused some discussion when raised at the next full Soviet session. However, when a vote was taken, Trotsky topped the poll, 20 votes clear of his nearest rival. He remained in power only a week. He and the other Soviet leaders were arrested on 3 December.[32]

During the last days of the Soviet, Trotsky was visited by his old comrade Ziv. While not abandoning his medical studies, Ziv had continued to work for the revolutionary cause after his release and had relaunched *Our Cause*. The two revolutionaries embraced warmly, but Trotsky had to rush off to a meeting and although they arranged a second meeting, he had been arrested before it could take place. Ziv felt slighted, he had sensed an air of condescension in Trotsky's attitude. The youth who once sported workers' blouses was now elegantly dressed again, so much so that Ziv scarcely recognised him. Ziv was probably being unfair. Trotsky exaggerated in his autobiography when he declared "all the decisions of the Soviet were shaped by me", but certainly many of them were. And it was not the Soviet alone. Trotsky worked hard to bring the Bolsheviks and Mensheviks together, encouraging them to form a federative commission. Then there was his journalism. Not only was he involved in *Izvestiya*, of which ten issues came out, but he was the driving force in the Menshevik paper *New Life*, contributing to 16 issues. From mid November he was also involved in *Russian Gazette*, a paper he founded jointly with Parvus. It was a hectic schedule, as he recalled: "The fifty-two days of the existence of the Soviet were filled to the brim with work – the Soviet, the Executive Committee, endless meetings, and three newspapers."[33]

Results and Prospects

Trotsky's second spell in prison was far easier than his first. After a short time in Kresty Prison, he was moved to solitary confinement in the Peter-Paul Fortress; but from there he was soon moved again to the House of Preliminary Detention, where the regime was positively lax. In April 1906 Russia's new elected assembly, the First State Duma, started its work and the prisoners found that not only could they associate freely, but that they had access to lawyers, via whom they could smuggle out pamphlets and articles and keep in contact with the Party leadership. Trotsky would often retreat to cell 462 so that he could study and write. One of his major concerns was how the Soviet leaders should defend themselves. While Trotsky was in prison the Russian Social Democratic Party had held a congress in Stockholm, which elected a new Menshevik-dominated Central Committee. That committee advised the Soviet leaders to base their defence on the grounds that they had only acted under the terms of the October Manifesto which mentioned the right to freedom of assembly. Although the committee's motivation was simply to reduce the likely sentences passed by the court, Trotsky was furious: taking such a line would legitimise the October Manifesto and mean that, in court, the Soviet leaders would sound like the Liberal politicians he so despised. Although Khrustalev-Nosar had his reservations, all the accused resolved to use their trial as a platform for socialist propaganda. The proceedings began on 19 September 1906.[34]

The Soviet leaders were accused of preparing for an armed uprising, and when Trotsky rose to speak on 4 October he tackled this issue head on. The Soviet had never discussed as such the need for a republic or the need for an insurrection; but the Soviet was in effect a government in its own right and therefore had the authority to use force and other repressive measures. However force was not the essence of the insurrection.

To unite the proletarian masses within a single revolutionary protest action, to oppose them as enemies of the organised state power – that, gentleman of the court, is insurrection as the Soviet understood it and I understand it too.[35]

The trial was not without elements of drama. It was attended by Trotsky's parents, and his mother periodically cried throughout his speech. During interrogation Trotsky suffered one of his fainting fits and proceedings had to be suspended. The defence tried to call Trepov as a witness, so that he could tell the court about the links between the police and the Black Hundreds, and when this was refused, the defendants voted to boycott the court. In the end the verdict was handed down to an empty courtroom. That verdict was enforced settlement in exile and the deprivation of all civic rights.[36]

During his time in prison, Trotsky not only prepared for his defence, but reflected on the importance of his time working for the Soviet. It "underlined the unquestionable and unlimited hegemony of the proletariat in the bourgeois revolution". Although the Soviet did not achieve power, its achievements hinted at what proletarian power would be like.

By the pressure of strikes, the Soviet won the freedom of the press. It organised regular street patrols to ensure the safety of citizens. To a greater or lesser extent, it took the postal and telegraph services and railways into its hands. It intervened authoritatively in economic disputes between workers and capitalists. It made an attempt to introduce the eight hour day by direct revolutionary pressure . . . If the proletariat, on the one hand, and the reactionary press, on the other, called the Soviet a workers' parliament, that merely reflects that the Soviet did indeed constitute an embryonic organ of revolutionary government."[37]

Trotsky was generalising from what he had seen, but the notion that the proletariat might play a hegemonic role in the bourgeois revolution was not something that orthodox Marxists could easily accept. It was the accepted wisdom that the revolution which overthrew tsardom would usher in a period of liberal and parliamentary rule, during which the labour movement, freed from legal restrictions on its activities, would rapidly grow to the point where it would first challenge liberal rule and then overthrow it. Trotsky seemed to be suggesting that this liberal phase could be skipped and instead of being episodic, the revolution would be permanent, moving quickly to the point where the working class established its own government.

These ideas were most clearly formulated in *Results and Prospects*. In this 1906 essay written while in prison, Trotsky argued that the formation of the Soviet made it impossible to close one's eyes to the following fact.

The chief actor in this bourgeois revolution is the proletariat, which is being impelled towards power by the entire course of the revolution . . . Once the proletariat has taken power in its hands it will not give it up without a desperate resistance, until it is torn from its hands by armed force.[38]

Social Democrats should therefore consciously work towards forming a working class government.

The proletariat in power will stand before the peasants . . . [and recognise] all revolutionary changes (expropriations) in land relationships carried out by the peasants. The proletariat will make these changes the starting point for further state measures in agriculture. Under such conditions the Russian peasantry in the first and most difficult period of the revolution will be interested in the maintenance of a proletarian regime.

There was, of course, the possibility that the peasantry would not look to the leadership of the working class, but instead form its own political party. Trotsky dismissed such a danger: "Historical experience shows that the peasantry are absolutely incapable of taking up an *independent* political role." They were always forced to choose between the policy of the bourgeoisie and the policy of the proletariat.[39]

Trotsky concluded his analysis of the peasantry by gazing into the revolution's crystal ball and speculating what would happen after the working class's victory.

The proletariat will enter the government as the revolutionary representative of the nation, as the recognised national leader in the struggle against absolutism and feudal barbarism . . . [However] every passing day will deepen the policy of the proletariat in power, and more and more define its *class character* . . . The abolition of feudalism will meet with support from the *entire* peasantry . . . but any legislation carried through for the purpose of protecting the agricultural proletariat will not only not receive the active sympathy of the majority, but will even meet with the active opposition of a minority of the peasantry. The proletariat will find itself compelled to carry the class struggle into the villages and in this manner destroy that community of interest which is undoubtedly to be found among all peasants, although within comparatively narrow limits . . . The primitiveness of the peasantry turns its hostile face towards the proletariat. The cooling-off of the peasantry, its political passivity, and all the more the active opposition of its upper sections, cannot but have an influence on a section of intellectuals and the petty-bourgeoisie of the towns. Thus the more definite and determined the policy of the proletariat in power becomes, the narrower and more shaky does the ground beneath its feet become.[40]

Having raised the danger that the working class, having established its government in Russia, might end up clashing with its own peasantry, Trotsky offered a way out: revolution in Europe. The triumph of revolution in Russia would mean revolution in Russian Poland; this would in turn spark risings in German and Austrian Poland. The German and Austrian emperors would send troops to restore order, revolutionary Russia would respond by declaring war and that war would lead to revolution in both Germany and Austria. "Left to its own resources, the working class of Russia will inevitably be crushed by the counter-revolution the moment the peasantry turns its back on it. It will have no alternative but to link the fate of its political rule, and, hence, the fate of the whole Russian Revolution, with the fate of the socialist revolution in Europe."[41]

Results and Prospects expressed all Trotsky's key ideas; it was in essence a credo for life, which never changed. Friend and foe alike would later refer to this body of writing as Trotsky's theory of permanent revolution, and friend and foe alike would point to the similarities and differences with Lenin's writings at this time.

Like Trotsky, Lenin had no time for the prospect of Liberal rule in Russia. However, Lenin did not believe that the proletariat would be able to form a government alone; he preferred to talk about "a revolutionary dictatorship of the proletariat and peasantry". Trotsky was dismissive of the very idea of independent political activity on the part of the peasantry; when a peasant group was formed in the First Duma he went out of his way to stress in a footnote to *Results and Prospects* that this did not disprove his theory. Lenin on the other hand welcomed the formation of this group as the nucleus of "a strong revolutionary peasant party" which would emerge as the revolution progressed. His references to the peasantry during 1905 were quite different to those of Trotsky. When a Peasant Union was established in November he asked himself why serious Marxists had devoted so little time to the peasantry. "The moment has now come when the peasant has come forward as the conscious creator of a new structure in Russian life." Marxists had to ask what the peasantry could give the revolution and what the revolution could give the peasantry. His answer was similar to Trotsky's, that once land and liberty had been achieved not all peasants would join in the struggle against capital, but Lenin did not see a clash as inevitable, nor did he see the peasantry acting as a single block. He stressed that some peasants would "determinedly and consciously go over to the workers" if the Social Democrats were patiently to explain their policies to them. Thus Lenin sent "warmest greetings" to the Peasant Union and wrote of its delegates as "true democrats" and "allies with whom we are united in a common great struggle". Although Trotsky accepted that the Peasant Union "embraced some elements of radical democracy" – and he publicly shook the hand of the Chairman of the Peasant Union when he addressed the Soviet on 27 November – he saw little evidence of consciousness at the Peasant Union Congress. "In a folkloric sense this was one of the revolution's most interesting gatherings," he wrote. "One saw many picturesque characters, provincial 'naturals', spontaneous revolutionaries who had 'thought it all out for themselves', village politicians with passionate temperaments and even more passionate hopes, but with rather confused ideas."[42]

By the end of 1905 Trotsky had more than served his revolutionary apprenticeship. Anatolii Lunacharskii, who worked with him closely over the next two decades, recalled that when he first arrived abroad Trotsky still had a great deal of "juvenile bumptiousness" about him and nobody took him very seriously, for all that it was accepted that he could write and speak well and that "this was no chick but an eagle". Of their first meeting Lunacharskii noted: "Trotsky then was unusually elegant, unlike the rest of us, and very handsome; this elegance and his nonchalant, condescending manner of talking to people, no matter who they were, gave me an unpleasant shock, I regarded this young dandy with extreme dislike." By 1906 Lunacharskii's verdict was immeasurably more positive.

His popularity among the St Petersburg proletariat at the time of his arrest was tremendous and increased still more as a result of his picturesque and heroic behaviour in court. I must say that of all the social-democratic leaders of 1905–6 Trostky undoubtedly showed himself, despite his youth, to be the best prepared . . . [He] understood better than all the others what it meant to conduct the political struggle on a broad, national scale.[43]

Notes

1 L. Trotsky, *My Life* (New York, 1970), pp. 1, 87.

2 Trotsky, *My Life*, pp. 11, 20.

3 Trotsky, *My Life*, pp. 2, 12, 40.

4 M. Eastman, *Leon Trotsky: Portrait of a Youth* (London, 1926), p. 26; Trotsky, *My Life*, pp. 40, 44.

5 Eastman, *Portrait*, p. 34; Trotsky, *My Life*, p. 72.

6 Trotsky, *My Life*, pp. 26, 79, 82, 88.

7 Eastman, *Portrait*, pp. 46–8, 51.

8 Eastman, *Portrait*, p. 56.

9 Eastman, *Portrait*, pp. 65–9.

10 G. A. Ziv, *Trotskii: kharakteristika po lichnym vospominaniyam* (New York, 1921), pp. 14–15; Eastman, *Portrait*, pp. 77–81.

11 Eastman, *Portrait*, pp. 18–24; Trotsky, *My Life*, pp. 105–11, 183.

12 Ziv, *Trotskii*, pp. 18–20, 26; Eastman, *Portrait*, p. 128; Trotsky, *My Life*, pp. 120–2.

13 Ziv, *Trotskii*, pp. 27–32.

14 Trotsky, *My Life*, pp. 131–2.

15 Trotsky, *My Life*, p. 148; Eastman, *Portrait*, pp. 164–8.

16 Trotsky, *My Life*, p. 157.

17 *1903: Second Congress of the Russian Social Democratic Labour Party: Minutes* (London, 1978), pp. 324, 414, 433, 442, 455.

18 *1903: Minutes*, p. 299.

19 *Iskra*, No. 62, 16 March 1904.

20 L. Trotsky, *Our Political Tasks* (New York, 1979), pp. 72–7. (The passage beginning "it is necessary to understand" comes from the section "A Dictatorship over the Proletariat", which was omitted from this English edition. It can be found in English translation in Geoffrey Swain *The Bolshevik Seizure of Power* (University of Southampton, 1993), line 13098; this is a Historical Document Expert System (HiDES) software package.)

21 Cited in I. Deutscher, *The Prophet Armed, Trotsky: 1879–1921* (Oxford, 1970), p. 110.

22 Trotsky, *My Life*, pp. 168–74.

23 The founding of the Soviet is described in G. D. Surh, *1905 in St Petersburg* (Stanford, 1989), p. 328; L. Trotsky, *1905* (Harmondsworth, 1973), p. 265; and Kozovlev, "Kak voznik Sovet" in [no author] *Istoriya soveta rabochikh deputatov* (St Petersburg, 1906), p. 22.

24 Trotsky, *1905*, p. 126; Deutscher, *Armed*, p. 126.

25 Trotsky, *1905*, p. 135.

26 Trotsky, *1905*, pp. 141–6; Zlydnev, "U grafa S Yu Witte", *Istoriya*, p. 267.

27 Trotsky, *1905*, p. 172.

28 Trotsky, *1905*, pp. 185–7.

29 Khrustalev-Nosar, "Istoriya sovet rabochickh deputatov", *Istoriya*, p. 152.

30 Trotsky, *1905*, pp. 230–1.

31 Trotsky, *1905*, pp. 195–8.

32 Trotsky, *1905*, p. 233; Zvezdin, "Poslednyie dni soveta", *Istoriya*, p. 172.

33 Trotsky, *1905*, pp. 178, 181; Ziv, *Trotskii*, p. 150.

34 D. Sverchkov, *Na zare revolyutsii* (Leningrad, 1925), p. 205.

35 Trotsky, *1905*, pp. 399–400, 405.

36 Trotsky, *My Life*, 190–1; Ziv, *Trotskii*, p. 33.

37 Trotsky, *My Life*, p. 180; Trotsky, *1905*, pp. 266–7.

38 L. Trotsky, *Results and Propects* (London, 1962), pp. 191–2, 199.

39 Trotsky, *Results*, pp. 202–4.

40 Trotsky, *Results*, pp. 208–9.

41 Trotsky, *Results*, p. 241.

42 Trotsky, *Results*, p. 204; V. I. Lenin, "The Proletariat and the Peasantry" and "The Aims of the Proletarian Struggle in Our Revolution" in V. I. Lenin, *On the Revolution of 1905* (Moscow, 1955), pp. 363–4, 631.

43 A. V. Lunacharskii, *Revolutionary Silhouettes* (London, 1967), p. 61.

Chapter 2

Revitalising the Party

On 3 January 1907 Trotsky was moved to the St Petersburg transit prison before commencing exile, which this time would be for an indefinite period. Even before he left St Petersburg, he was determined to escape. In the scrummage with other prisoners to obtain clothes for the journey, he struggled to hold onto his boots for, "in the sole of one I had a fine passport, and in the high heels gold pieces". He was destined for a village 1,000 miles from the nearest railway. The first stage of the journey was under military guard by train as far as Tyumen, then by sledge along the course of the River Ob to Tobolsk, and from there north towards Obdorsk. While en route Trotsky's party stopped at the village of Berezov for a rest, because beyond that town the sleighs were to be pulled by reindeer rather than horses. A local land surveyor suggested to Trotsky that, although there were no roads in the area, the River Sosva could be followed towards the Urals, where a narrow-gauge railway serving the local mines led eventually to the main Trans-Siberian Railway at Perm, from where it was a straight journey to St Petersburg.

Trotsky feigned sciatica and escaped, found a guide willing to take him by deer sled along the Sosva and set off through the February blizzards. It was, Trotsky remembered, "a magnificent ride through a desert of virgin snow all covered with fir trees and marked with the footprints of animals." The travellers boiled snow for water, and after a week in which they covered 400 miles, they reached the Urals. Here Trotsky took a horse, and then, as planned, the narrow-gauge railway towards Perm, then St Petersburg and the relative safety of autonomous Finland. In Finland Trotsky was briefly back in the company of both Lenin and Martov. Despite the bitterness of their dispute about Party organisation, Lenin was friendly and simply taunted him about assessing 1905 in a Bolshevik way while refusing to join the Bolsheviks. After a few weeks in Finland Trotsky moved, with all the other Party leaders, to London for the Fifth Party Congress in May 1907 and a second spell of foreign exile.[1]

The Disintegrating Party

At the Congress Trotsky adopted the stance that he would be known for throughout the next decade, that of a conciliator. This meant that he supported the Mensheviks when it came to questions of party organisation, or more accurately, how the Party should be reorganised in the aftermath of 1905. On one issue, however, he made public his support for the Bolsheviks. This was the era of the Second Duma, which had opened in January 1907 and sat until it was dissolved in June the same year. Within the Duma there was a Social Democratic faction that was some 60 strong, but whether the deputies should ally themselves with the Liberals or the peasant Party of Socialist Revolutionaries (SRs) within the Duma was a matter on which Bolsheviks and Mensheviks were bitterly opposed. On the peasant issue Trotsky supported the Bolsheviks and identified the peasantry as the proletariat's natural ally: but he insisted that the Congress minutes note that he differed with the Bolsheviks in one important respect; unlike Lenin, he did not believe that the peasantry could play an independent political role.[2]

After the Fifth Party Congress Trotsky went to Berlin, where he was joined by Natasha, and the two of them set off for a holiday together in Saxony. Natasha then returned to Russia to collect their infant son Lev, while Trotsky attended the Stuttgart Congress of the Second International. Then, in October 1907, he moved to Vienna where he was rejoined by Natasha and Lev, settling first outside the city at Hütteldorf and later moving to the "more democratic" suburb of Sievering. Why did he choose Vienna when the rest of the foreign exiles were concentrated in Switzerland and Paris? Trotsky explained in his autobiography that his closest contacts he now felt were with German political life. Settling in Berlin, however, was impossible because of police persecution, so he chose Vienna, but travelled almost weekly to Berlin, thus becoming acquainted with the leading figures of both German and Austrian Social Democracy. He fell "under the spell" of the German Social Democrats. On his regular visits he would attend meetings of the Left caucus within German Social Democracy, headed by Karl Liebknecht.[3]

From his escape from exile in 1907 to his appointment as a Bolshevik commissar in 1917 Trotsky had to live off the money he earned as a journalist. In Siberia he had already established quite a reputation when writing for the *Eastern Review*; now he became a regular contributor to another regional publication with a radical reputation, *Kiev Thought*. His earnings from his journalism were, he recalled, quite enough for his family's modest living. A second son, Sergei, was born soon after the move to Vienna and the family more or less got by. An American visitor recalled:

His house in Vienna was a poor man's house, poorer than that of an ordinary working man. His three rooms in a working class suburb contained less furniture than was necessary for comfort. His clothes were too cheap to make him appear "decent" in the eyes of the middle class Viennese. When I visited his house, I found Mrs. Trotsky engaged in housework, while the two light-haired lovely boys were lending not inconsiderable assistance. The only things that cheered the house were loads of books in every corner.[4]

On the basis of this modest home-life and the intellectual ferment of German Social Democracy, Trotsky set about trying to restore the Russian labour movement to health.

While Trotsky was gathering his family around him in his new home, dramatic events were taking place in Russia. A fortnight after the Fifth Party Congress ended its work in May 1907 the Second Duma rejected the government's plans for land reform and the Tsar dissolved it on 3 June 1907. In violation of the Tsar's own constitution, the electoral law was changed in the absence of the Duma and a Third Duma was summoned, to be elected on 1 September by a completely new franchise which drastically reduced the representation of workers, peasants and other oppositional groups. The revolutionary upheaval that had begun in November 1904 was well and truly over. Although the main ideological dispute between the Bolsheviks and Mensheviks during the years 1906–7 related to the question of electoral alliances, there was a secondary issue which took on greater significance when the Third Duma was summoned, that of the trade unions. The Tsar's October Manifesto had spoken of freedom of assembly and the government's provisional regulations, under which trade unions were made legal, were made public on 4 March 1906. The workers, who had rallied to the Soviet with such enthusiasm, now put their energies into building up a trade union movement. By mid May 1907 a total of 245,555 workers had joined trade unions, 3.5 per cent of the workforce. In the country as a whole 904 unions were registered between March 1906 and December 1907. In 1907 the Social Democratic Duma deputies co-operated closely with the St Petersburg Central Bureau of Trade Unions, on which former members of the Soviet were well represented. When the government staged its 3 June coup it also launched an assault on the trade unions. In 1907, 159 unions were closed down, in 1908 it was 101, then 96 in 1909 and 88 in 1910. During the years 1907–11, 604 unions were refused registration and 206 trade union activists were either imprisoned or exiled.[5]

The combined impact of the government's assault on the Duma and the trade unions served to heighten the divisions within the Party. Despite continuing state persecution, a legal labour movement survived. More than that, as early as January 1908 it became clear that after 1905 there were other "legal opportunities" for labour activists. In January 1908 the authorities allowed the People's Universities to hold a national congress. A workers' delegation attended this gathering, headed by the leaders of the St Petersburg Metal Workers' Union and St Petersburg Textile Workers' Union; they found that the congress provided them with a platform for socialist agitation. The Party was ambivalent about this development. By the end of 1907 the Central Committee had fled abroad, leaving behind its Russian Bureau. This had been lukewarm about the policy of workers attending the Congress of People's Universities, but the success of the group meant it had no hesitation in endorsing the proposal to send a workers' group to the Co-operative Congress in April 1908. The activities of the Russian Bureau at this congress led to its arrest.

The arrest of the Russian Bureau left the Party in chaos. In July 1907 the Third Party Conference had voted to take part in the Third Duma elections, despite the narrowing of the franchise. Many Bolsheviks had accepted this decision very reluctantly and then argued that the experience of the first weeks of the Third Duma had proved how ineffective the Duma had turned out to be in preventing the assault on the labour movement, so the deputies should be recalled. This hard-line stance of Recallism spilled over into trade union work and that of labour representation at legal congresses, which Recallists equally opposed. As one noted: "The impossibility of founding legal trade unions puts us almost back in the position we were before the revolution [of 1905], puts back on the shoulders of the party the task of leading economic struggle." By summer 1908 Recallists had such a grip on the St Petersburg Committee that it had virtually ceased to work in the trade unions and it tried to disrupt the Congress of Women's Organisations, held in December 1908, where the activities of the trade union-sponsored "group of working women" were successful in giving labour concerns high-profile press coverage.

When the Russian Bureau was arrested, some Mensheviks went to the opposite extreme and proposed liquidating the Central Committee and replacing it by an "information bureau" which would simply co-ordinate the work of labour activists operating within Russia's legal labour movement. These Liquidators met with little support; a conference of St Petersburg Mensheviks countered that what was needed was not the abolition of the Central Committee and its committee structure, but a mechanism whereby those active in the legal labour movement were given a greater say in

Party affairs. Bolshevik legal activists made precisely the same point. Proposals for a joint conference of legal activists and the underground were put to the Fifth Party Conference in Paris in December 1908, but were rejected because Lenin believed that those who advanced this proposal were planning to downgrade the position of the underground committees and "liquidate" the Party through the back door.[6]

Thus, by the time Trotsky was well and truly settled in Vienna, the Party was no longer just split two ways, but four ways; there were Leninist Bolsheviks and Bolshevik Recallists, Party Mensheviks and Menshevik Liquidators. To restore the party to health Trotsky decided to launch a new workers' newspaper, *Pravda* (*The Truth*), the title later hijacked by the Bolsheviks for their legal daily paper launched in 1912. Unlike the other Social Democrat newspapers that had a clear factional line to preach, Trotsky wanted to highlight events within Russia, convinced that just as the dynamic development of the Soviet in 1905 had made factional struggle irrelevant, so a strong labour movement in Russia would help overcome disputes which he felt were accentuated by the difficulties of the emigré life.

Vienna *Pravda*

Pravda had begun life in 1905 as the organ of a group of left-wing Ukrainian Social Democrats. On the basis of Trotsky's existing links with the labour movement in Kiev, and his work for *Kievan Thought*, he was approached to take over the running of the paper. His first issue came out in October 1908, published in Lvov until issue six in November 1909, when the whole operation moved to Vienna. Once established, the paper appeared twice a month, being smuggled into Russia with the help of Black Sea sailors and long-established contacts in Odessa. As with any such newspaper, the secret correspondence concerning the administration of delivery and distribution took an enormous amount of time and effort. Funding was always a problem. There were some generous donations from wealthy associates; Trotsky was able to persuade the German Social Democrats to give him a small grant; the Latvian Social Democratic Party provided another. But the main source of funding came from Trotsky himself; *Pravda* was a labour of love.

Trotsky intended to address himself to "plain workers" rather than Party men, "to serve not to lead" his readers. *Pravda's* plain language and the fact that it preached the unity of the Party secured it much popularity. In the editorial of its first issue of 3 October 1908 *Pravda* told its readers "the workers are taking the place of the intelligentsia". Workers would have to take on their shoulders the task of reconstructing the party and the paper's editors were convinced they were ready for the task, for in establishing the Soviet in 1905 and the trade unions thereafter they had shown their capacity for self-organisation. Now, through gritted teeth, they should reconstruct the underground party. *Pravda*'s task was "not to split, but to unite". As to the Liberals, the paper's line was abundantly clear: the revolution of 1905 had shown that "the bourgeoisie has everywhere betrayed the people and done a deal with the government and the ruling classes of the old order". While the bourgeoisie and bureaucracy might jockey for position in the State Duma, the revolutionary days of the bourgeoisie were over. "Russian workers must now carry on the same struggle against both the government and the bourgeoisie that is being undertaken by the proletariat in the West", thus in November 1909 Trotsky repeated his message of *Results and Prospects* and his great lesson of 1905.[7]

Pravda put a particularly optimistic gloss on the events at the 1908 Women's Congress held in St Petersburg. Although the underground Party organisation had been partly too weak and partly too Recallist to give much support to the idea of organising a working women's group at this congress, trade unionists had taken the initiative. For *Pravda* the Women's Congress marked an important turning point because the majority of those involved in forming the group had resolved that it was now up to workers active in the trade unions and other areas of legal labour activity to take the lead in reviving the Party. Reviewing its progress in 1910, *Pravda* noted that the first issue of the paper had aroused no interest; there had been some demand for issue number two, in mid December 1908, but that it had only been with issues three, in March 1909, and four, in June 1909, that appreciable demand had been felt. By summer 1909, the paper argued, the mood had completely changed and trade union activists were pressurising the underground Party to stop squabbling and get active, a mood that by winter 1909–10 was difficult to ignore.

An important milestone in this process was the Congress of Factory Panel Doctors, held in April 1909, which saw the close collaboration between trade unionists and the Social Democratic Fraction in the Third State Duma. "There have never been so many conscious social democrats", the paper crowed over the summer of 1909, but it recognised that most of these workers had never been members of the Party underground and were dubious about joining it now because of the factional in-fighting. "The leading workers, who are now so active in the trade unions ... and attend legal congresses are almost all social democrats," *Pravda* argued, "but they are not linked to one another through the Party." Such people had to be brought into the Party. At the end of 1909 one of the paper's organisers noted that he had recently returned from making the same trip to Russia as made a year earlier and that the situation had changed dramatically. In St Petersburg 1,000 copies of *Pravda* were in circulation and underground activists were no longer shunned; in the Narvskii region of the capital local Bolsheviks had reissued *Pravda* number five as their own paper.[8]

Reports on the situation in Moscow in autumn 1909 summed up *Pravda*'s approach to the crisis in the Party. At first sight it seemed to have collapsed completely, since the Party committees which survived had no contact with the factories. But this was a false picture, fanned by political intrigue abroad and the fact that the Central Committee was only in touch with "so-called committees" which were divorced from the masses. In the factories the masses were actually more conscious than before 1905, but were cautious to have contact with underground intellectuals who called for "a struggle against opportunist trade unionism". The Central Committee needed to get back in contact with the Moscow Committee, which in turn needed to get back in contact with the factory organisations – this was the apparently simple message of *Pravda*. Part of the problem was the use made of professional revolutionaries: paid only 15–20 roubles, they were almost forced to become "expropriators", bank robbers in the Party's name, who then became easy prey for the Tsar's secret police. Provocation was scarcely known at factory level, but was rife at committee level where professional revolutionaries abounded; the solution, according to *Pravda*, was to bring workers in to the higher echelons of the party. There had actually been a general recovery in the Moscow labour movement over summer 1909. The trade unions had organised a series of meetings on social insurance, the Print Workers' Union had been successfully re-registered, and the Central Bureau of Moscow Trade Unions had been reformed and employed a paid secretary.[9] 1909 also saw a Central Bureau of St Petersburg Trade Unions re-established which, together with the Social Democratic Fraction in the Third State Duma, drew up some "Theses on Insurance" to be put before the State Duma, as it debated proposals for social insurance legislation.

Trotsky's campaign to revitalise the Party by bringing to the fore class-conscious workers was very nearly successful. During 1909 the advances made by the legal labour movement made Lenin's insistence at the Fifth Party Conference on maintaining the status quo seem short-sighted. Trotsky's opportunity came when Lenin decided it was time to deal with the Recallist Bolsheviks. In June 1909 he summoned a Meeting of the

Extended Editorial Board of the *Proletarian* in Paris. The *Proletarian*, officially the organ of the St Petersburg and Moscow Party Committees, was Lenin's underground newspaper, the cover through which the Bolshevik faction still operated within the supposedly united Party. Lenin's purpose at this meeting was to get delegates from Russia to agree to his proposal that the Recallists be expelled from the Bolshevik faction and thus prevented from airing their views in the *Proletarian*. The delegates from Russia had their own agenda. They echoed Trotsky's analysis and insisted that the only reason why Recallism survived was because it was prevalent among the student radicals who formed the core of the underground committees; and these committees only survived because they received financial handouts from Lenin. The Russian delegates insisted that Lenin's subsidies to the St Petersburg and Moscow committees should cease and that the funds thus made available should be used to launch a legal newspaper in Russia. The meeting also insisted that the *Proletarian* should be transformed into a monthly theoretical journal and called on the Bolshevik leadership to open immediate discussions with Trotsky about collaboration with *Pravda*.

The Extended Meeting of the Editorial Board of the *Proletarian* did not address the issue of the relationship between the underground party committees and the legal labour activists. However, the Menshevik proposal for a joint conference of legal activists and committee men had not been forgotten. Indeed, in September 1909 those legal activists planning to take part in the Temperance Congress, called for January 1910, held their own conference to debate the future of the party; the majority of those present, some 90 per cent, rejected the resolution put forward by those advancing the slogan "Down with the Central Committee, down with the local committees" and insisted that the way forward was to build an illegal party around the new core of working class legal activists. In November 1909 the same legal activists held a second conference, this time with representatives of some of the underground committees, which agreed to unite the new organisations of legal activists with the old underground. It really was as *Pravda* described it.

Under the burial shroud of the old party, a new one is being formed. And, our task, the task, of all the living healthy elements of Social Democracy, is to put all our forces to this end, to facilitate the birth and growth of the Social Democratic Party on this new, healthy, proletarian base.

And the obvious way forward seemed to be a joint conference of legal and underground workers, a proposal Mensheviks again endorsed in October 1909.[10]

The issue was decided at the Plenum of the Central Committee held in Paris from 2–23 January 1910. The scene of much factional bloodletting, this meeting agreed that the purely Bolshevik funds which had once funded the *Proletarian* should be handed over to the Central Committee and that *Pravda* should henceforth become an officially sanctioned Party paper, supported by a Central Committee grant of 150 roubles per month and with a Central Committee representative on its board, the Bolshevik Lev Kamenev. It was further agreed that a Party conference would be held within six months and that "Social Democratic groups in the legal sphere, which were prepared to affiliate to the party" and even "individual activists" would be invited to attend the conference. The vexed issue of the voting rights to be given to such legal activists present at the hoped-for Party conference would be resolved by the conference when it met, and not decided in advance by the plenum meeting in Paris. In preparation for this conference, joint conferences of the underground and legal activists, like the one seen in St Petersburg in November 1909, were to be encouraged.[11]

Pravda's response to the January Plenum of 1910 was positive: "conscious and independent worker social democrats" were replacing the old introverted world of factions. As Duma work and illegal work were combined, factional divisions in the localities should be supplanted and new district organisations formed, bringing together those active in the trade unions and those in underground cells. Trotsky wrote in *Pravda* for April 1910 that, if there really were two clearly defined Recallist and Liquidator factions, then members of them should indeed be expelled. The reality, however, was that both tendencies were ill-defined, certainly containing some out-and-out sectarians and opportunists, but mostly made up of activists whose stance was unclear. Expulsions would therefore only harden positions, the key was to "overcome" such tendencies on the basis of deepening social democratic work. "Not a fractional struggle against Liquidationism, but overcoming Liquidationism by attracting worker-liquidators into general Party work", such was *Pravda's* message for June 1910.

The Vienna Conference

Work in organising the planned Sixth Party Conference, which would bring together the underground and the legal activist, began at once, but immediately ran into difficulties. A new Russian Bureau of the Central Committee was chosen and empowered to set to work. The membership sought to balance legal activists and the underground. Thus Stalin, the illegal committee man from the Caucasus, was made a member, as was Roman Malinovskii, the secretary of the St Petersburg Metal Workers' Union. For the Mensheviks Sverchkov was chosen, the former treasurer of the Soviet and still a supporter of Trotsky. Unfortunately when the Russian Bureau met in Moscow in May 1910 its members were arrested. A further attempt was made to assemble candidate members in November 1910, but this was unsuccessful, and when they finally assembled in Tula in February 1911 they too were arrested.[12]

Lenin had never been happy with the January Plenum agreement and as the Russian Bureau struggled to organise itself, he decided to act unilaterally. One of the subsidiary agreements reached in Paris was that the Mensheviks would cease to publish their theoretical journal *The Voice of the Social Democrat*; in return, they would be allowed access to the official party journal *The Social Democrat*. When Lenin sought to prevent Menshevik articles appearing in that journal, the Mensheviks decided to continue publishing *The Voice of the Social Democrat*. Trotsky's response was to ignore this development as a typical squabble among emigrés which the Russian Bureau could resolve when it met. Lenin felt that Trotsky should condemn the Menshevik decision in *Pravda*; Trotsky saw this as interfering in his editorial judgement. And so in August 1910 Kamenev resigned as Central Committee representative on *Pravda* and the Central Committee subsidy ceased; shortly afterwards Lenin launched his own underground paper, *Workers' Gazette*, as a rival.

Trotsky responded in November by announcing that a fund had been established in Vienna to organise the planned Sixth Party Conference. Lenin then called for the decisions of the January Plenum to be annulled. At this point news came that the Russian Bureau was about to meet in Tula, and Lenin backed down, but news of the final arrest of the Russian Bureau persuaded him to renew his campaign. According to the Party rules, in these circumstances the Foreign Bureau of the Central Committee had either to organise another Russian Bureau meeting in Russia or to organise a plenum abroad. The Foreign Bureau, while agreeing that the wave of arrests meant that there was no choice but to organise a meeting abroad, nevertheless resolved to reconstitute a Russian Bureau and get it to agree to hold a meeting abroad. Lenin interpreted this as a delaying tactic aimed at wrecking the work of the Central Committee and ordered his representative on the Foreign Bureau to walk out, summoning his own meeting of those members of the Central Committee who felt frustrated by the impasse that had been reached. Lenin's meeting dissolved the Foreign Bureau and established first an Organising Commission and then a Russian Organising Commission to summon the planned Sixth Party Conference.[13]

Trotsky and Lenin were at loggerheads, both planning to summon a Sixth Party Conference. In his memoirs Trotsky recalled this as "the sharpest conflict with Lenin in my whole life". Things came to a head when the two men prepared to attend the Copenhagen Congress of the Socialist International in 1910. Trotsky was travelling from Vienna and Lenin from Paris, but chance meant that they ended up at the same German railway station awaiting a connection to Copenhagen. Their conversation began in a friendly enough manner, but then Trotsky mentioned that he had written an article for the theoretical journal of the German Social Democratic Party *Vorwärts* on "Russian Social Democracy" and its current state. The article was timed for the Copenhagen Congress and interpreted events from Trotsky's standpoint. Lenin reacted with fury and lobbied the Russian delegation to the Copenhagen Congress to condemn Trotsky's article, but this they refused to do. Trotsky recalled that Lenin's temper was not improved by the fact that "he was suffering from a violent toothache and his head was all bandaged".[14]

Trotsky strove to be conciliatory as 1911 developed. He was willing to recognise Lenin's Organising Commission, if the Foreign Bureau were reconstituted and agreed to endorse it. But Lenin had no intention of recreating the Foreign Bureau, for it would certainly repeat its insistence on re-establishing a Russian Bureau. Thus Trotsky ended up opposing the work of Lenin's Organising Commission and ignored the Prague Conference which was assembled by Lenin in January 1912 and was designated by the Bolsheviks alone as the Sixth Party Conference. This gathering elected a new Central Committee and expelled the Liquidators from the Party; it also resolved that the Liquidators needed to be opposed in the Duma elections scheduled for autumn 1912. Activists in the legal labour movement would be allowed to affiliate their organisations to the Party only if a special conference of underground activists agreed that this could happen.[15]

The Foreign Bureau of the Central Committee did not accept that it had been dissolved by Lenin. It met in July 1911 and summoned a conference in Berne on 20–23 August, attended by Trotsky and other prominent social democrats. This meeting agreed to establish its own Organising Commission and summon a conference in Vienna in line with the decisions of the January 1910 Plenum. Trotsky then became the key organiser of the conference. At a further meeting in Switzerland Trotsky secured agreement to attend from the St Petersburg Initiative Group, recently established by leading legal activists in the capital. The biggest underground organisation in St Petersburg was the Central Group which *Pravda* backed enthusiastically. The Central Group had no truck with the St Petersburg Committee set up at the end of October 1911 to elect a delegate to Lenin's Prague Conference. For the Central Group, this affair of the 1911 St Petersburg Committee was a classic example of Bolshevik sectarianism. For the Prague Conference to be a success, a representative from St Petersburg was essential, but anyone sent by the Central Group would have raised awkward questions about the constitutionality of what Lenin proposed; better by far for Lenin to ignore the Central Group and invent a "St Petersburg Committee", even if the delegate chosen in this way had little popular standing. The Central Group agreed to come to Vienna for Trotsky's conference, but just when things seemed to be going so well, disaster struck. N. P. Bogdanov, the secretary of the Woodworkers' Union and leader of the Central Group, was a police agent. Before delegates could be chosen for Vienna, the organisation was destroyed by arrests. No representatives of the St Petersburg underground made it to Vienna, only the Initiative Group of legal activists; and one of their two representatives was V. Abrosimov, a leading activist in the Metal Workers' Union and another police spy.[16]

Trotsky's Vienna Conference of August 1912 did not expel anybody and presumed only to establish an Organising Committee rather than an all-powerful Central Committee. As planned, it discussed the relationship between legal and illegal activists within the framework of the 1910 January Plenum. However, much to Trotsky's disappointment, the Vienna Conference made radical changes to the party programme. Not all developments in Russia were as Trotsky described. Some legal activists really had slipped into opportunism. The right-wing Menshevik editors of Our Dawn, a legal journal which appeared in St Petersburg from January 1910, really were Liquidators and were determined to encourage co-operation between the labour movement and the liberal opposition to the Tsar. During the first months of 1911 they came up with the notion of a "petition campaign". On 4 March 1911, five years would have passed since the 4 March 1906 legislation which had allowed the formation of trade unions. This could mark a suitable date to petition the Duma for a genuine law on freedom of assembly, a campaign which liberals within the Duma could support. Although the St Petersburg Initiative Group of legal activists took up the campaign, the Central Group and other underground groups in St Petersburg condemned it, as did the Social Democratic Duma Fraction and Pravda. The campaign seemed to imply that the Duma had the power to pass radical legislation on social issues, which was patently untrue; if the petitions had gone to the Social Democrat Duma deputies rather than the Duma president, the campaign might have been better focused.[17]

These tensions resurfaced in Vienna, where there were no representatives of the underground to resist them. Joint pressure from *Our Dawn* and the Initiative Group persuaded the Conference to revise the Party's electoral programme to make it more amenable to the Liberals. Elections were to take place for the Fourth Duma in autumn 1912 and for those elections Mensheviks seeking co-operation with the Liberals felt it was essential to modify the more extreme passages of the Party's election programme. Thus there was no mention of the democratic republic, only "sovereign popular representation" while land confiscation became "a revision of the agrarian legislation of the Third Duma". Trotsky was appalled. His starting point had been the betrayal of the revolution by the Liberals. All he had worked for since 1905 stood in ruins. The power of the police to manipulate representation at foreign-based conferences meant that none of the healthy experience of work in Russia encouraged through *Pravda* could be felt. The August 1912 Vienna Conference had become the power-base for Liquidator Mensheviks who wanted to reform the Party programme to make it more acceptable to the Liberals. Two years of preparation had provided a result that only Lenin could welcome, for it seemed to prove that without the careful selection of delegates the Party would fall into the hands of Reformists.

The Balkan Wars

Understandably, after the failure of the Vienna Conference, Trotsky experienced a crisis. For the first time in many years he wrote to the old comrades of his youth in the South Russia Workers' Union, Ziv and Shvigovskii. If he was looking for some support from old friends, in a world where all his new political acquaintances had turned against him, the move backfired; both were offended by Trotsky's tone, Ziv especially. Ziv had emigrated to New York in 1908 and by 1912 was a successful doctor, yet he was still hurt by Trotsky's accusation that by continuing his medical studies he had somehow deserted the revolution. He therefore reacted in fury to Trotsky's apparently innocuous comment, "I hope you have not become too Americanised". For Ziv this was to repeat that he had somehow betrayed the revolution, after spending more time in prison for his beliefs than Trotsky. So he did not reply to the letter, any more than Shvigovskii replied to his, but Ziv did concede that Trotsky was genuine in resolving to renew his old contacts, it was just that he lacked the humility to do so properly.[18]

Disillusioned with the politics of Russian labour, Trotsky took up the offer of becoming a war correspondent for *Kievan Thought*. In autumn 1912 the long threatening political crisis in the Balkans exploded. The independent Balkan states presented Turkey with an ultimatum threatening war unless certain conditions were met. When at the end of September the King of Montenegro declared war even before the ultimatum had expired, Trotsky hurried from Vienna to Belgrade, where he witnessed the hastily mobilized troops marching to the front with sprigs of green in their hats; from there he went to the Bulgarian capital Sofia, arriving on 6 October. For the next year he would devote himself almost exclusively to war reporting, basing himself mostly in Bulgaria but also returning to Belgrade. When the First Balkan War ended with the Treaty of London of 30 May 1913, Trotsky stayed on to cover the Second Balkan War, started when Bulgaria launched its surprise attack on Serbia and Greece; this conflict was ended by the Peace of Bucharest on 10 August 1913. His last articles were more in the style of travellers' tales than war reports, touring the Black Sea Coast in September 1913 and describing the life of isolated communities of Russian religious sects that had settled in the region.

The theme of much of his reporting was the "scientifically organised system of duping public opinion". He wrote about recent Balkan history; he ridiculed the visiting Russian dignitaries; he lambasted the Bulgarian censorship; but most of all he opposed the nationalism and chauvinism that encouraged war, and the myth of Slavophilism which justified it. In particular he exposed the atrocities inflicted by Bulgarian troops on wounded and captured Turks. The war was fought to liberate the Slav peoples, but that could not justify vengeful brutality. While the Tsarist press was quiet on these atrocities, Trotsky, writing again as Antid Oto, gave chapter and verse. He wrote of the shooting of prisoners, of reprisals, of the torching of Albanian villages in Kosovo, of an anti-Semitic pogrom in a newly liberated Bulgarian village. He wrote of the horror of war and the thin veneer of civilisation.

The chaotic mass of material acquisitions, habits, customs, and prejudices that we call civilisation hypnotises us all, inspiring the false confidence that the main thing in human progress has already been achieved – and then war comes, and reveals that we have not yet crept on all fours from the barbaric period of our history. We have learned how to wear suspenders, to write clever leading articles and to make milk chocolate, but when we need to reach a serious decision about how a few different tribes are to live together on a well-endowed European peninsula, we are incapable of finding any other method than mutual extermination on a mass scale.[19]

Occasionally, Trotsky raised issues of a military nature, in particular two lessons that he would later put to good use when Commissar for War.

> The war offered the masses of Bulgarian people the prospect of finishing at last with both the Turkish past and the Turkish present. This is why the Bulgarian soldiers marching to the front put flowers in their caps; this is why regiments go into attack with such enthusiasm under savage artillery bombardment; this is why detached units of cavalry carry out so successfully the tasks of partisan warfare assigned to them; and this is why many wounded soldiers apply, as soon as they have recovered, to go back to the front line. The Turkish army presents a quite different picture. It had no general aims in this war that could have inspired the masses' willing sacrifice.[20]

Later Trotsky would always insist that the Red Army soldier needed to know why he was fighting. It was the same with problems of supply.

> The medical and also (especially) the victualling services of the Bulgarian army are organised very badly indeed. Carried away by the easy capture of Kirk-Kilissa, Radko Dmitriev thought only of conducting the entire remaining part of the campaign as a sort of cavalry charge; he simply failed to take steps to ensure correspondence between the army's offensive and the movements of its supply columns.[21]

The very same problem would haunt Trotsky throughout the Russian Civil War.

The Interdistrict Group and *Bor'ba*

Trotsky might well have continued to devote himself to journalism if events in Russia had not, belatedly, moved in the direction he had always anticipated. In April 1912 striking miners had been massacred on the Lena Gold Fields in Siberia. It was a signal to the working class that little had changed since Bloody Sunday. From then on Russia experienced a strike wave that ebbed and flowed, but never disappeared until the general strike in St Petersburg on the eve of the First World War in July 1914. Against this background, workers became increasingly militant. The editors of *Our Dawn* and the leaders of the Initiative Group, governed by their desire to keep some sort of dialogue with the Liberals, were cautious about the apparent willingness of workers to go on strike at the drop of a hat; they began to urge workers to think of the consequences before they took action. The result was that members of the reformist

Initiative Group found themselves being removed from the leadership of the major trade unions in St Petersburg in late 1912 and early 1913 and replaced by more militant figures. By 1914 reformists had virtually no influence in the Russian trade union movement.

One of the last acts of the Third Duma, before the election of the Fourth Duma in autumn 1912, had been to pass legislation introducing a social insurance scheme for certain categories of workers. Although limited, it gave these workers some rights, of which the most important was the right to elect worker representatives to sit on the hierarchy of boards and councils established to administer the scheme. These representatives would be in a minority, for employers' representatives had an inbuilt majority, nevertheless the election of representatives in major factories offered social democrats considerable opportunities for agitation, even in the longer term, for the re-creation of the Soviet. These elections presented the same issue of whether or not to modify demands so as to win Liberal support and in this campaign victory again went to supporters of the militant line.

What was just as pleasing for Trotsky, however, was that the Russian labour movement, while clearly hostile to reformism, was equally hostile to Lenin's attempts to bring it under his control. At the end of 1913 Lenin made repeated attempts to bind the new militant trade union leadership to the coat-tails of his Central Committee, but was rebuffed. He tried the same with insurance council delegates early in 1914 and was again unsuccessful. Lenin had more success in trying to divide the Social Democrat Duma deputies into supporters of the Prague Conference and adherents to the Vienna Conference; yet even here there was resistance to be overcome and the split in the Duma faction was frustrated until October 1913. Equally, between 1912 and 1914 no Bolshevik-sponsored St Petersburg Committee existed in St Petersburg, despite all Lenin's efforts to establish one. The biggest underground organisation in the capital was the Interdistrict Group, formed by some of those who had cut their teeth with the Central Group a few years earlier. The Interdistrict Group was true to the programme advanced by Trotsky's *Pravda* and did not recognise Lenin's Prague Conference but claimed it was faithful to the traditional form and policies of the Social Democratic Party; this meant they rejected the Bolsheviks' organisational methods and were prepared to work with all party groups which accepted the 1908 Fifth Party Conference decision to reconstruct the Party from the bottom up.[22]

The split in the Duma faction exposed the difficulties faced by deputies like Trotsky's long-term associate M. I. Skobelev who, although a Menshevik, was not prepared to modify Social Democrat slogans to appease supposed Liberal allies. In January 1914 Skobelev visited Trotsky in Vienna, accompanied by N. S. Chkheidze, another Duma deputy unhappy with the pro-liberal stance of other Mensheviks. The result was the decision to publish a new journal sponsored by Trotsky entitled *Bor'ba* (*The Struggle*). The argument advanced by *Bor'ba* was essentially that of *Pravda*. Russia was now entering a new stage in which advanced workers were deciding issues for themselves. For this they no longer needed a workers' newspaper, but a journal for the emerging class of literate labour activists. Thus armed, a workers' intelligentsia could win sufficient confidence to replace the old intelligentsia-based leadership. By the intelligentsia Trotsky meant not only Lenin, but equally the reformist editors of *Our Dawn*. Trotsky's aim was once again "the liberation of the new forms of the workers' movement from the vice of factionalism" by articulating "a clear Marxist understanding of the conditions and methods of the proletariat's struggle".[23]

The appearance of a journal so avowedly opposed to factionalism was not welcomed by all. Some doubted the possibility of fighting factionalism by founding what could be seen as a third faction, and not even all the Interdistrict Group backed the initiative. Yet its leading members did, and among those closely associated with the journal was N. M. Egorov, one of the Social Democrat deputies to the Third Duma who had in the past been closely associated with the Central Group and was now a key figure in the Interdistrict Group. At the same time the Interdistrict Group was wooed by A. F. Buryanov, the one Duma deputy who was loyal to Plekhanov and therefore also opposed to both the Bolshevik and Menshevik factions. With Plekhanov's money, Buryanov launched a newspaper called *Unity* and the Interdistrict Group was given half the seats on its editorial board.[24]

Just prior to the outbreak of the First World War, Trotsky went to Brussels with Plekhanov and Martov to appeal for the International Socialist Bureau to intervene in Russian affairs. This it agreed to do. If war had not broken out in July 1914 Lenin could have been forced to recognise Trotsky's party, the party of the January 1910 Plenum, not the Prague Conference, a party which treated worker activists and the underground committee man on a par.[25] And even though Trotsky's party was never recognised formally in this way, the reality was that it was his strategy of welding together the legal activists and underground groups such as the Central Group and the Interdistrict Group which brought about the recovery of the labour movement in Russia. Lenin's policy would have, and almost did, drive legal activists into the arms of reformists.

The First World War

When war was declared, Trotsky was shocked at the way patriotic crowds in Vienna behaved. He left at once for Zurich and it was there that he learnt that the German Social Democratic Party had voted to support their country's war effort. Although this too shocked him, he was one of the first to notice that although the German Social Democrats had voted unanimously for war credits in the public assembly of the Reichstag, the internal debate which preceded this had ended in a much closer vote. He still had faith in comrades like Karl Liebknecht to rally opposition to the war. Even in the first days of the conflict Trotsky was convinced that the only thing that would bring peace would be "a revolutionary awakening of the proletariat", meaning that the coming years would inevitably be "an epoch of socialist revolution". These ideas were developed more fully in *War and the International* which argued that the war "would bring about a profound change in the mental attitude of the working class, curing them radically of the hypnosis of legality". He predicted "the terrible poverty that prevails during this war and will continue after its close will be of the sort to force the masses to violate many a bourgeois law".[26] On 19 November 1914 Trotsky moved to France, for *Kievan Thought* had asked him to work as a war correspondent on the Western Front. He could therefore continue his life much as before, writing some sixteen articles for the paper from the moment of his arrival until his deportation in September 1916. Although the editorial policy of the paper meant he could not oppose the war, he could raise the issue of the gap between real and propagandist motivations behind the conflict, as well as exploring the misery of war.[27] Such writing earned him enough to move the family to Paris in May 1915 and to resume his political writing for the good of the cause. The emigré community in Paris produced a thriving newspaper, *Our Word*, which Trotsky was soon helping to edit. Founded with a capital of only 30 francs, it was always produced in close association with the group of French anarcho-syndicalists led by Alfred Rosmer, who produced the working class daily *La Vie Ouvrière*.[28]

It was on the pages of *Our Word* that on 14 February 1915 Trotsky made public that he could no longer associate himself with the Organising Commission set up by his own Vienna Conference. To those in the know this was nothing new, since he had played no role in it since 1913. What motivated his public stance was the decision of many of the reformist Mensheviks around *Our Dawn* and the St Petersburg Initiative Group to support Russia's war effort. Trotsky's commitment to opposing the war was total; however, this did not bring him any closer to Lenin. Lenin still published the official Party journal *Social Democrat* and in spring 1915 it was mooted that since *Our Word* and *Social Democrat* both opposed the war, further co-operation might be possible. But Lenin insisted that Trotsky had still not done enough to distance himself from the Vienna Conference, while Trotsky argued that since many supporters of the Conference were, like Trotsky himself, having second thoughts, it made no sense to frighten them by imposing conditions for loyalty. Trotsky blamed Lenin's "terrible egocentrism" for the breakdown in these discussions.[29]

Relations became even worse as 1915 developed. At the end of May Lenin invited Trotsky to join a new Bolshevik journal, *Kommunist*. Trotsky refused because he rejected Lenin's theory of "revolutionary defeatism". According to Lenin, Russia's defeat in the First World War would be "a lesser evil" for the revolutionary movement than the Tsar's triumph. Trotsky did not write about "revolutionary defeatism" but "the struggle for peace". According to Lenin, however "the struggle for peace" was a deliberately vague slogan, used to hide the stance of principle, that of "revolutionary defeatism". Lenin therefore condemned as pro-war "social patriots" those whose opposition to the war was hazy and not grounded in "revolutionary defeatism". For Trotsky even those whose motivation for opposing the war remained hazy were internationalists at heart. In particular Trotsky defended the Social Democratic Faction in the Fourth Duma. When war broke out, the Russian Social Democrats in the Duma had condemned the war in a joint statement put out both by the deputies loyal to Prague and those loyal to Vienna. To foster divisions within the group, the government responded by arresting and exiling only the deputies loyal to Prague, the Bolsheviks, and leaving the others free and able to speak in the Duma. Lenin felt these deputies had become pro-war; Trotsky argued that most opposed the war.[30]

Trotsky went public over the summer of 1915 about the importance of the slogan "the struggle for peace", which could not, he argued, be dismissed as passivism. Late in July 1915 Lenin raised the ideological level of the attack with his insistence that "defeatism be the axiom of a revolutionary class during a reactionary war" and that "wartime revolutionary action against one's own government indubitably means not only desiring its defeat but really facilitating such a defeat". Although Lenin explained that talk of revolutionary defeatism did not mean sabotage, he did not explain precisely what it did mean. Trotsky responded in articles published in *Our Word* in August and September 1915, again stressing that defeat implied victory and that "we do not know of any European social and state organism which it would be in the interest of the European proletariat to strengthen". War was not something revolutionaries could control; it might lead to revolution, but there was no certainty that revolution would stop the war.[31]

Trotsky represented *Our Word* at the conference of anti-war socialists which took place in Zimmerwald in Switzerland from 5 to 8 September 1915. There was still no love lost between him and Lenin, and Lenin spent some time at Zimmerwald arguing the purely procedural point that Trotsky's mandate to attend the conference was not valid. Trotsky continued to work for conciliation. He wanted the anti-war alliance to be as broad as possible and put forward a resolution that was worded loosely enough to be backed by those who opposed the war from purely pacifist motives. Lenin insisted that the war could only be opposed on the grounds that it was an imperialist war, and that pacifism was merely a product of woolly thinking. To Lenin's fury, the Zimmerwald Conference passed Trotsky's resolution.[32] In the aftermath of the Zimmerwald Conference of September 1915, Lenin continued to push for "revolutionary defeatism", convinced that this was an issue which clarified the distinction between his principled anti-war stance and the "woolly" resolution drafted by Trotsky which had sought, as Trotsky had consistently done since 1905, to bring the largest possible number of supporters to adopt a revolutionary position. Lenin did not let the matter drop. With no greater success he put to the Anti-War Conference in Kienthal in April 1916 a resolution which stated in part, "it is not enough to say, as the Zimmerwald manifesto does, that . . . the workers in their revolutionary struggle must ignore their country's military situation, it is necessary to state clearly . . . that revolutionary action during the war is impossible unless 'one's own' government is threatened with defeat".

And yet, despite the intensity of this disagreement, by the start of 1916 Trotsky had determined to work for a rapprochement with Bolshevism. This change of stance was prompted by events in Russia. *Our Word* wrote on 19 January 1916: "One ought not to and one need not share the sectarian narrow-mindedness of Lenin's group, but it cannot be denied that in Russia, in the thick of political action, so-called Leninism is freeing itself from its sectarian features, and that workers connected with *Social Democrat* are now in Russia the only active and consistently internationalist force."[33] Trotsky was referring to developments which had taken place in autumn 1915 and early 1916. As part of the overall war effort, the Tsar had agreed that local chambers of commerce could establish War Industries Committees to help factories adapt to the demands of total war. Soon a hierarchical network of these committees existed all over Russia. Some of the liberals involved in establishing them were keen to involve patriotic workers in their activities, and so permission was obtained to hold elections to a "workers' group" within the War Industries Committees. In Petrograd, as St Petersburg was renamed during the war to avoid the Germanic connotations of "burg", these elections were held in September 1915 and took place in two stages; first there would be a vote at factory level to choose "electors" and then a vote of electors to choose representatives. Pro- and anti-war social democrats promptly began to organise, and when it came to the second stage of the elections, the anti-war social democrats won, a victory signified by the fact the long-standing Bolshevik activist S. Bagdatiev topped the poll. In order to get himself elected, Bagdatiev had taken on the identity of a factory worker, just as Khrustalev-Nosar had done in February 1905. The pro-war social democrats decided to denounce this well-established act of revolutionary subterfuge to the authorities and forced a second ballot. When that second ballot was held, the anti-war social democrats refused to take part, on the grounds that in the intervening weeks many of their fellow anti-war electors had been arrested.

There were other encouraging signs of growing militancy in Petrograd. The mandate of those workers elected to serve on social insurance boards had been for three years; thus in autumn 1916 new elections fell due and another field for open struggle between the pro- and anti-war social democrats opened up; again the anti-war group was victorious. Early in October 1916 elections were held to the Petrograd City Insurance Board, resulting in victory for four Bolsheviks and one SR, while a fortnight later it was the turn of the Petrograd Provincial Insurance Board, resulting in victory for three Bolsheviks and two Mensheviks. However, as in 1914 this was not a victory for what the Interdistrict Group liked to call Bolshevik sectarianism. The elected worker representatives sought to distance themselves from any resolution which might turn them into mere ciphers of an emigré-based central committee. The electors were presented with two sets of instructions, one drawn up by the Bolsheviks and one by the Mensheviks; the victorious Bolsheviks voted for the Menshevik instructions and did so because, while on the substantive issue of social insurance the instructions were identical, the Bolshevik instructions called for the new Labour Group on the Insurance Council to be responsible to the Prague Central Committee, while the Mensheviks proposed that they be responsible to those who elected them.[34]

At the same time as this campaign was underway, the Interdistrict Group had re-emerged as the dominant underground group in the capital. It was staunchly anti-war and desperate to try and launch a legal daily newspaper, for the legal Social Democratic press had been closed down when the war began. The group succeeded in producing one issue of an underground paper during the War Industries Committee elections and was engaged in talks with the Petrograd authorities about a legal newspaper which would be published in Petrograd but rely on editorial contributions from *Our Word* in Paris. True to its non-faction stance, the Interdistrict Group co-operated closely with the Bolsheviks in Petrograd at this time, for by 1915 Lenin had succeeded in establishing more or less reliable contacts with the capital. Early in 1916 both the Bolsheviks and the Interdistrict Group tried to organise a party conference in the capital which would take as its point of authority the January 1910 Central Committee Plenum in Paris.[35]

Trotsky followed these developments with close interest and used the pages of *Our Word* to criticise those unhappy with the growth of anti-war internationalism. Over summer 1916 he became especially concerned that the Duma deputies continued to associate themselves with the War Industries Committees and refused to celebrate, as he did, the victory of the anti-war groups. However, Trotsky's close involvement with these events was brought to a sudden end in September 1916 when he was expelled from France; allegedly some mutinous French soldiers had been discovered reading *Our Word*. He was deported to Spain and told to board a boat for Cuba. After a protest, the Spanish authorities agreed he could go to New York instead. Once his family had joined him, he set sail on Christmas Day 1916 and arrived during the night of 13–14 January 1917. They were soon settled in a flat in the Bronx, amazed at such bourgeois luxuries as a gas cooker, a bath, a rubbish chute, a lift and a telephone.[36]

In New York he sought journalistic work with the Russian language paper *New World*. For a few weeks it was the usual round of writing articles and addressing labour meetings on the need to oppose the war, but he also looked up his old friend Grigorii Ziv, making use of his new telephone. Ziv later recalled how the phone rang and it was Trotsky: "Is that you, Grisha, do you not recognise me?" Despite their differences, Ziv was one of the few people Trotsky addressed with the intimate word for "you" – *ty*. Ziv had become a supporter of the war, so there was no question of their friendship resuming completely, but Trotsky took his elder son round to meet his old friend and the two men played several games of chess together.[37]

Then news came of the abdication of the Tsar and Russia's February Revolution. Trotsky telephoned his wife to make immediate preparations for their return to Russia. On 27 March they set sail on a Norwegian boat, but at Halifax, Nova Scotia, the boat was stopped and the British authorities interrogated all the Russians on board. On 3 April Trotsky and the other Russian men were taken ashore and held in a German PoW camp at Amherst; Natasha and the boys were allowed to stay in Halifax. After protests from Russia's new democratic government, Trotsky was released on 29 April, put on a Danish boat and this time he and his family completed their journey back to Russia where the re-established Soviet had already been arguing and debating for more than two months.[38] He could return to Russia optimistic. His experience of the 1905 Soviet had taught him that the best way to revive the Party was to have the support of the legal activists and the events of 1916 suggested that those people had themselves put the Party on a revolutionary footing.

Notes

1 L. Trotsky, *My Life* (New York, 1970), pp. 193–200; V. Serge and N. Sedova-Trotsky, *The Life and Death of Leon Trotsky* (New York, 1973), p. 20.

2 Cited in I. Thatcher, *Trotsky* (London, 2003), p. 50.

3 Trotsky, *My Life*, p. 212.

4 Cited in I. Deutscher, *The Prophet Armed, Trotsky: 1879–1921* (Oxford, 1970), p. 183.

5 G. R. Swain, "Freedom of Association and the Trade Unions, 1906–14" in O. Crisp and L. Edmondson, *Civil Rights in Imperial Russia* (Oxford, 1989), p. 177.

6 G. R. Swain, *Russian Social Democracy and the Legal Labour Movement, 1906–14* (Basingstoke, 1983), pp. 38–54.

7 *Pravda* (Vienna), 5 November 1909.

8 *Pravda* (Vienna), 14 June 1909 and 8 December 1909.

9 *Pravda* (Vienna), 5 November 1909, 1 August 1910.

10 Cited in Swain, *Russian Social Democracy*, p. 89, from where this summary of events is taken.

11 Swain, *Russian Social Democracy*, p. 93.

12 Swain, *Russian Social Democracy*, pp. 96, 104.

13 Swain, *Russian Social Democracy*, pp. 110–14.

14 Trotsky, *My Life*, pp. 218–19.

15 Swain, *Russian Social Democracy*, pp. 141–3.

16 Swain, *Russian Social Democracy*, pp. 146–9.

17 Swain, *Russian Social Democracy*, pp. 119–23.

18 G. A. Ziv, *Trotskii: kharakteristika po lichnym vospominaniyam* (New York, 1921), pp. 57–8.

19 L. Trotsky, *The War Correspondence of Leon Trotsky: the Balkan War, 1912–23* (New York, 1980), p. 148.

20 Trotsky, *Balkan War*, p. 195.

21 Trotsky, *Balkan War*, p. 273.

22 The trade union movement 1912–14, the social insurance elections of 1913 and the relationship of both to Lenin's leadership abroad is discussed in Chapter Six of Swain, *Russian Social Democracy*.

23 I. Thatcher, "*Bor'ba*: a Workers' Journal in St Petersburg on the Eve of the First World War", *English Historical Review*, 1998, No. 450, pp. 100–4.

24 I. Yurenev, "Mezhraionka, 1911–17", *Proletarskaya revolyutsiya*, No. 1, 1924, pp. 120–5.

25 Deutscher, *Armed*, p. 213.

26 I. Thatcher, *Leon Trotsky and World War One* (Basingstoke, 2000), pp. 9–10, 46.

27 Thatcher, *World War One*, p. 25.

28 Serge and Sedova, *Life and Death*, p. 28.

29 Thatcher, *World War One*, pp. 46–7; 50–3.

30 Thatcher, *World War One*, pp. 55–60.

31 B. Pearce, "Lenin versus Trotsky on 'Revolutionary Defeatism'", *Sbornik*, 1987, No. 13, p. 18.

32 Deutscher, *Armed*, p. 225.

33 Pearce, "Revolutionary Defeatism", p. 18; Deutscher, *Armed*, pp. 233–5.

34 G. R. Swain, "Late Imperial Revolutionaries" in I. Thatcher (ed.), *Late Imperial Russia: Problems and Prospects* (Manchester, 2005), pp. 163–4.

35 Yurenev, "Mezhraionka", p. 116.

36 Trotsky, *My Life*, 258–71.

37 Ziv, *Trotskii*, pp. 75–6.

38 Trotsky, *My Life*, pp. 277–85.

Chapter 3

Insurrection

Trotsky arrived in Petrograd on 4 May 1917 and, as soon as he had found some lodgings for his family, he set off for the Smolny Institute, the former young ladies' academy whose buildings had been allocated to the Petrograd Soviet. For Trotsky the prospects for the revolution were quite straightforward: workers should take up where they had left off in 1905 and use the power they exercised via the Soviet to establish a working class government. As he understood it, during February it had been the workers who had ensured the success of the revolution by seizing control of the post and telegraph services, the wireless office, all the railway stations and the printing works; and if they were prepared to act in this way again political power could be theirs. He was therefore delighted to discover that Lenin too favoured the principle of the Soviet taking power, and had abandoned the hesitations on the matter which had marred co-operation in 1905.

Joining the Bolsheviks

Trotsky's late arrival in Petrograd meant he had a poor understanding of events within the Bolshevik Party during March and April 1917 when the issue of Soviet power had first been raised. When the Tsar was overthrown, the first Bolsheviks to emerge from underground to establish a temporary Bureau of the Central Committee opposed the Provisional Government being established by the Liberals and demanded "a revolutionary provisional government". When Kamenev and Stalin returned from exile in Siberia in mid March they pulled the Central Committee away from this radical stance and called for a dual strategy of close supervision of the Provisional Government combined with moves gradually to develop the Petrograd Soviet into "the beginnings of a revolutionary power". When Lenin returned to Petrograd on 3 April, he condemned this caution and called for Bolsheviks to campaign for a Soviet Government. However, events soon convinced Lenin that it was premature to launch such a programme.

In mid April the Provisional Government and the Soviet clashed over the Liberal Foreign Minister's determination to continue pursuing the war aims of the Tsar. Soviet protest demonstrations were called, and the Bolshevik Petrograd Committee, echoing Lenin's radicalism, issued leaflets calling for the overthrow of the Provisional Government and the immediate establishment of soviet power; the key figure in producing this leaflet was Bagdatiev, who had played such a prominent role in the campaign against the War Industries Committee. On 24 April, during the Seventh Party Conference, Lenin condemned the launching of this slogan at the present time as "adventurist"; "we cannot now overthrow the government", he stressed. Thus, just as Stalin had moved to discipline those Bolsheviks keen to seize power in March, so Lenin too criticised those calling for insurrection in April.[1]

On his arrival, Trotsky's reception at Smolny was rather lukewarm. After the initial confusion of the Tsar's overthrow, the leadership of the Soviet had fallen into the hands of pro-war Mensheviks. These were the political associates of the two organisations which had had a legal existence during the First World War, the non-Bolshevik deputies to the Fourth Duma and those pro-war Mensheviks who, despite the clear vote of the factories in 1915 not to establish a Workers' Group within the War Industries Committee had nonetheless gone ahead and established just such a group. These leaders of the legal labour movement, already used to co-operating with the Liberals and SRs represented in the Duma, had almost inevitably come to dominate the Soviet in its first weeks of existence. At the moment Trotsky arrived, far from urging the Soviet to seize power, its leaders were negotiating with the Liberals about forming a Coalition Government. Because of his role in 1905, Trotsky was given a non-voting seat on the Soviet Executive, but his views were completely out of tune with the Soviet leadership.

Thus on 5 May Trotsky's first political act of 1917 was to join with the Bolsheviks and vote in the Soviet against the formation of a Coalition Government. His message was simple: do not trust the bourgeoisie, control your own leaders and rely on your own force. This stance did not go down well. To quote his own *History of the Russian Revolution*, "he left the hall amid far less applause than had greeted his entrance" and for the next few weeks Trotsky showed little interest in attending Soviet Executive meetings. As Trotsky stressed in his memoirs, he argued his case for revolution "on the basis of my own premises and my own revolutionary experience", but he was now proposing "the same line of strategy as Lenin" and that caused him to reassess his relationship with the Bolshevik leader: joint activity was clearly essential to rally opposition to the established Soviet leadership. Trotsky immediately re-established contact with the Interdistrict Group, which had survived the wartime persecution more or less intact and retained a good following in the factories, and urged them to consider uniting with the Bolsheviks.[2]

Talks between the Interdistrict Group and the Bolsheviks about a possible merger began almost at once. On 7 May the two organisations hosted a joint meeting to mark Trotsky's return and the talks proper began on the 10th. Trotsky found himself face to face with his old protagonists Lenin and Kamenev, joined now by Lenin's closest associate from the years of emigration, Grigorii Zinoviev. Trotsky was wrong-footed by Lenin's determination to be conciliatory: Lenin had wanted to make Trotsky editor of *Pravda*, but his Central Committee colleagues would not agree; nevertheless Trotsky and his supporters were offered seats on the paper's editorial board as well as on the Central Committee. The talks stalled because of fears that, despite Lenin's apparent generosity, the Interdistrict Group was being taken over rather than offered a genuine merger. Trotsky was keen that the new merged organisation should have a new name rather than inheriting the Bolshevik title, and he had to consider the views of those rank and file Interdistrict Group activists who felt that there was no evidence to show that the Bolshevik faction was now truly democratic and had abandoned the old sectarian practices of the Bolshevik committees.[3]

Some of the Interdistrict Group leaders, notably Anatolii Lunacharskii, felt that the discussions with the Bolsheviks should be put on hold. He believed that the Interdistrict Group should associate itself with the left-wing Menshevik newspaper *New Life*, which was critical of the formation by the Soviet of the Coalition Government, but without going so far as calling for its replacement by a Soviet Government. For Trotsky the issue of a workers' government was fundamental. On 25 May he attended a formal meeting of *New Life*'s editorial board; but when it became clear that the editors would not support calls for a Soviet Government, Trotsky stated "it remains for me and Lenin to make our own newspaper", at which point any lingering association with the Mensheviks on Trotsky's part ended. And yet the merger talks with the Bolsheviks remained stalled. Lunacharskii's opposition to the merger was supported by others, and so the Interdistrict Group put its editorial energies into establishing a short-lived newspaper, *Forward*.[4]

Trotsky had always argued that Bolshevik sectarianism was a product of the backwardness of the Russian working class movement and would be outlived only by practical activity within the grassroots. Events of May–June 1917 seemed to bear this out, for increasingly over these weeks, whatever issues still divided them, the Interdistrict Group and the Bolsheviks co-operated closely in co-ordinating their opposition to the Coalition Government with its policy of supporting the war. On 13 May the Soviet at the naval base in Kronstadt clashed with the Provisional Government. The issue at stake was the power that should be exercised by the commissar, appointed by the Provisional Government, to oversee the naval base and its level of support for the forthcoming military offensive. To the fiercely anti-war Kronstadt sailors, the man appointed as commissar, a Liberal, had counter-revolutionary connections and so they rebelled through their Soviet, which declared itself sovereign and arrested both the commissar and several unpopular officers. The Coalition Government asked the Petrograd Soviet to intervene and help resolve the crisis by arranging for the arrested commissar to be released. Their intervention failed, and in fact made things worse when the Soviet leaders tried to put the representatives of the Kronstadt Soviet on trial. Trotsky took up their defence, while at the same time underlining the powerlessness of the Soviet leadership by successfully arranging himself for those who had been detained in Kronstadt to be released. This combination of advocacy and diplomacy was backed up by a steady round of public meetings addressed by Trotsky, Lunacharskii and Bolshevik agitators.[5]

When the First Congress of Soviets assembled at the start of June, co-operation between the Interdistrict Group and the Bolsheviks became even closer. On 4 June the Bolshevik faction at the Congress read out a statement on the Provisional Government's planned military offensive which had been written by Trotsky. When called upon to speak, he took the same line as Lenin, predicting that the offensive would end in disaster and urging the Soviet to establish its own government able and willing to spread revolution to Europe: "The Russian revolutionary army and Russian democracy will find allies in Europe . . . if Germany does not rise, or if she rises too feebly, then we shall move our regiments not in order to defend ourselves but in order to undertake a revolutionary offensive." As the Congress proceeded, so did the level of Interdistrict Group–Bolshevik co-operation. Although Lenin faced opposition from within his Central Committee and Trotsky faced opposition from Lunacharskii and more cautious colleagues, the two organisations agreed to organise a massive demonstration on 10 June under the slogan "Down with the ten capitalist ministers"; the Provisional Government banned the demonstration. Both organisations accepted that they had no choice but to cancel the action, but how to explain this to their supporters without losing face. Lenin drafted a statement, but was unhappy with it, as were other Bolshevik leaders; Trotsky, who had delivered a similar speech in 1905, submitted a draft which the Bolsheviks accepted and was read out in the name of the whole opposition.[6]

Very little now separated Lenin and Trotsky, but nuances could be detected. During the First Congress of Soviets, stung by a Menshevik challenge that there was no socialist party ready to take power into its own hands, Lenin had asserted that there was and it was the Bolsheviks. Trotsky's emphasis was different: he always referred to a Soviet Government, with the implication both that it might have a non-Bolshevik composition and, given the then composition of the Soviet, the formation of such a government was some way off. Such differences would be important for the future, but the rank and file of the Interdistrict Group were already calling for the merger with the Bolsheviks to be speeded up. On 2 July a special conference of the Interdistrict Group took place and the result was a foregone conclusion. Trotsky still faced some opposition from leading figures within the organisation but decided to pre-empt them by publishing a statement in *Pravda* to the effect that "there are in my opinion at the present time no differences either in principle or tactics between the Interdistrict and Bolshevik organisations; accordingly there are no motives which justify the separate existence of these organisations".[7]

The July Days

The official merger of the two organisations would take place only in late July at the Sixth Party Congress. However, collaboration continued at once, since the two organisations adopted the same stance in the crisis known as the July Days. As Trotsky had predicted, the Provisional Government's June Offensive had been a disaster. Preparations for the offensive had been the one thing that had kept the unstable Coalition Government together and, as it faltered, the Liberal ministers decided to bring down the government by resigning, taking as their pretext the latest disagreement about whether or not to allow a limited degree of regional autonomy to Ukraine. In the absence of a secure government Trotsky and the Bolsheviks resolved to organise mass demonstrations under the slogan "All Power to the Soviets". Although in the Petrograd Soviet as a whole the Bolsheviks were still in a minority, the Soviet had both workers' and soldiers' sections and in the workers' section Trotsky and the Bolsheviks had a clear majority by July. The workers' section thus supported the idea of a demonstration by endorsing a resolution proposed by Kamenev and seconded by Trotsky; the demonstrators would lobby the meeting of the Soviet Executive called to decide how the Soviet should respond to the collapse of the Coalition Government. The meeting of the Soviet Executive was to take place at the Tauride Palace.

The idea, once proposed, rapidly got out of hand. Crowds rallied outside as, in the early hours of 4 July, the Soviet Executive held preliminary discussions, resolving that any decision taken should be binding on all members, something which prompted Trotsky and his supporters to walk out. Many workers wanted to protest with Trotsky at the way the Soviet Executive planned to force through a decision in favour of forming a Second Coalition Government, but this anger soon intermingled with a separate but related issue. Throughout the June military offensive the First Machine Gun Regiment, stationed in Petrograd, had resisted orders that its units be sent to the front. By the end of June rumours were rife that the whole regiment would either be sent to the front or disbanded, and activists were determined to rebel rather than suffer either fate. Some offered the Bolshevik Military Organisation enough machine guns to seize power, but the Central Committee stamped on such wild schemes. However, the Bolshevik Military Organisation did start to encourage the machine-gunners to take part in the planned demonstration and by the evening of 3 July some had begun to take control of strategic positions in the capital. Trotsky only learned of the machine gun regiment joining the demonstration on the evening of 3 July. The news took him by surprise, particularly when it became clear that the Kronstadt sailors were also determined to join in. When the Bolsheviks and the Interdistrict Group met before dawn on 4 July they had to decide whether to try and cancel the demonstration, which seemed to be getting our of hand, or stand at its head and try to keep it within bounds; they opted for the latter and Trotsky, on the telephone to the Kronstadt sailors, appealed to them to attend the demonstration unarmed.

The Kronstadt sailors landed at about ten in the morning and marched straight to the Bolshevik headquarters at the Kshesinskaya mansion. Lenin addressed them from the balcony, before handing over to Lunacharskii, who was a much better orator. Their message was the same, however. Despite the revolutionary rhetoric there was no call on the sailors to seize power. Instead Lunacharskii led the demonstrators to the city centre, where he linked up with workers who had marched in from the industrial suburbs. The angry demonstrators were then marched along the main thoroughfare, Nevskii Prospekt, and on to the Field of Mars. En route there was some shooting, but a heavy downpour of rain calmed the mood a little. After this tour of the city the demonstrators arrived at the Tauride Palace at about five in the afternoon, where they were joined by workers from the Putilov Factory.[8]

When the Kronstadt sailors arrived at the Tauride Palace they demanded to speak to one of the socialist ministers who had been in the Coalition Government. The most left-wing of their number, the leader of the SR party Victor Chernov, the former Minister of Agriculture, agreed to speak to them. He made a short speech, blaming the Liberals for precipitating the crisis, and then a voice from the crowd called for the nationalisation of the land. The throng surged forward and angry demonstrators grabbed Chernov and pushed him into a nearby car, declaring he was under arrest. When news of the incident was brought to the Soviet Executive by a group of workers, Trotsky was the first to intervene; pushing people aside he rushed to Chernov's rescue. His initial plan was to accompany the arrested Chernov out of the square and then quietly negotiate his release, but he was persuaded that the crowd's indiscipline needed to be confronted. He climbed onto the bonnet of the open car and began to speak. He struggled to make himself heard, the sailors refused to shake his hand, for a while he was lost for words, but in the end he persuaded the sailors to release their captive and Trotsky was allowed to take Chernov by the arm and bring him back to the Tauride Palace.[9]

Despite this attempt by Trotsky to defuse the situation and keep the demonstration within bounds, the violence displayed on that day played into the hands of the Provisional Government. During the night of 4–5 July units loyal to the Soviet Executive and Provisional Government began to arrive and by midday on the 5th these troops were in full control of the capital. At the same time the Provisional Government announced that it had evidence that Lenin and the Bolsheviks were funded by the Germans and their plans to seize power and surrender the country had only just been thwarted. On the morning of 5 July Trotsky met Lenin, who was in a gloomy mood: "Now they will shoot us down, one by one", he said. With a warrant out for his arrest, Lenin felt he had no choice but to go into hiding; Zinoviev and Kamenev had already been taken into custody. Trotsky was not on the wanted list and did not abandon Soviet work. The Bolshevik group in the Soviet was now leaderless after Kamenev's arrest, so approached Trotsky to address them and give them leadership even though, strictly speaking, he was not yet a member of the Bolshevik faction; this he did willingly. On 10 July he decided to go further. Lunacharskii had made some statements after the July Days which had been seized on by the press as a sign of division between the

Interdistrict Group and the Bolsheviks. Trotsky defended the action of the Bolsheviks during the July Days both on the floor of the Soviet and in the Executive, and published an Open Letter to the Provisional Government in which he stressed that the Interdistrict Group had supported the Bolsheviks fully. With rhetorical flourish he ended: "you can have no grounds for exempting me from the action of the decree by virtue of which Lenin, Zinoviev and Kamenev are subjected to arrest". The Provisional Government called his bluff and arrested him on 23 July.[10]

Towards October

Trotsky was released from prison on 2 September without having to make use of the penknife that his wife had carefully smuggled to him on a family visit under the eyes of his excited sons.[11] By then the political situation in revolutionary Russia had changed completely. While he was in prison a Second Coalition Government had been formed, but it proved to be even less stable than the first. The new Prime Minister, Alexander Kerensky, appointed as Commander-in-Chief of the Army General Lavr Kornilov, whose troops on the South-west Front had achieved some success during the ill-starred June Offensive. Kornilov, however, was an inveterate plotter against the revolution, having first considered restoring order by force in April 1917. His summer campaign for the restoration of discipline in the rapidly disintegrating army through the restoration of the death penalty made him the rallying point for all counter-revolutionary forces. On 13–14 August a State Conference was held in Moscow to try to rally to Kerensky's side groups of all political shades, from the Soviet on the left to the former Duma deputies on the right. By then plans were already well advanced for Kornilov to seize power and arrest the Soviet. Kerensky discovered the threat to his position on 26 August, but he could only resist Kornilov by appealing to the Soviet to mobilise its forces in the defence of the revolution. This he did and the Soviet saved both Kerensky and the revolution.

Trotsky went straight from the Kresty Prison to a meeting of the Committee for the Defence of the Revolution which had been established by the Soviet. Within the Soviet itself Kornilov's attempted putsch had prompted a radical turn to the left, particularly among the soldier delegates. Just before Trotsky's release, on 1 September, the Soviet had supported a Bolshevik resolution for the first time. The Menshevik and SR leaders of the Soviet decided to test whether this vote had been a "one off" or marked a complete change of direction, and so called a vote for

9 September. It was Trotsky's first public appearance at the Soviet since his release and the vote was won; two days later there was an even more convincing Bolshevik victory after another display of Trotsky's oratory. While Trotsky was in prison the Bolshevik Central Committee, despite the formal merger of the Bolsheviks and the Interdistrict Group, had rejected a proposal that Trotsky join the editorial board of *Pravda*; this decision was reversed on 6 September, for all Bolsheviks could appreciate his ability to influence the Soviet.[12]

With Lenin still in hiding and Trotsky's oratorical skills plain for all to see, he was to dominate the public face of Bolshevism for the next six weeks. The issue facing the country in the aftermath of Kornilov's attempted putsch was whether to follow Kerensky and form a new Third Coalition Government with the Liberals, or whether the time had come to form a Soviet Government, the policy of the Bolsheviks. To win popular backing for his proposal for a Third Coalition Government Kerensky summoned an assembly known as the Democratic Conference made up not only of the soviets that now existed throughout Russia but also of other democratically elected organisations such as trade unions, co-operatives and local town and provincial councils. The Democratic Conference opened on 14 September and Trotsky read the official statement made in the Bolshevik Party's name. After a series of rather contradictory votes, Kerensky won support for his proposal that a Third Coalition Government be formed; however the majority of delegates to the Democratic Conference insisted that this government should be held responsible to a temporary popular assembly so that the government and its policies could be monitored until elections to a national Constituent Assembly were held in mid November. The proposed temporary assembly was given the name of the Preparliament and the key issue of debate at the Democratic Conference then became – would all political parties be willing to take part in the work of the Preparliament, which would be comprised not only of those social groups represented at the Democratic Conference but also representatives of property owners and their organisations.

The Bolsheviks discussed the issue of participation in the Preparliament on 20 September 1917 at a conference which included delegates to the Democratic Conference, members of the Petrograd Committee and members of the Central Committee. Trotsky called for the Preparliament to be boycotted. He was already thinking in terms of an insurrection, having made clear in the Party's opening declaration to the Democratic Conference that the only real bulwark against counter-revolution was to arm the workers. However, the majority of those present were not agreed that the time was right to abandon parliamentary struggle. No agreement could be reached in the Central Committee, and so it was left to the Democratic Conference delegates themselves to decide and they voted to participate. On 22 September the Bolsheviks informed the Democratic Conference that they would take part in the Preparliament.[13]

Trotsky's call for a boycott of the Preparliament meant that he and Lenin were on the same wavelength. From his place of hiding in Finland, Lenin had briefly favoured what might be termed the parliamentary way forward. The turn of the Petrograd Soviet in favour of the Bolsheviks in the immediate aftermath of Kornilov's failed putsch had suggested that the Bolsheviks could well be in a position to dominate any sort of socialist coalition government which might emerge from a body like the Democratic Conference. However, even as the Democratic Conference assembled and Kamenev called on it to establish a new government that very day, Lenin changed his mind and rejected such a way forward. Thereafter he bombarded the Bolshevik Central Committee with a series of letters ever more urgently urging them to prepare to seize power through an armed uprising. When he heard of Trotsky's stance on boycotting the Preparliament, he sent back the message, "Bravo Comrade Trotsky!"[14] However, although both Lenin and Trotsky were calling for an armed uprising to establish a workers' government, their visions of how this was to be achieved were far from identical. Lenin favoured a coup staged by the Bolshevik Party and its Military Organisation of radicalised soldiers. Trotsky favoured action through the soviets.

At the very close of the Democratic Conference it had been decided to summon a Second Congress of Soviets to take place in Petrograd on 20 October; Trotsky assumed that this would be the occasion for action and he made sure he took the Soviet firmly under his control. Ever since the pro-Bolshevik vote of 9 September, which had forced the resignation of the Soviet's Menshevik and SR leadership, negotiations had been underway about forming a new Soviet Executive. These negotiations were finally completed on 25 September and Trotsky knew where he stood. The new executive comprised 13 Bolsheviks, six SRs and three Mensheviks and its first act was to endorse Trotsky as president. The very first resolution passed set Trotsky's agenda: it called for the Third Coalition Government to resign and announced that the forthcoming Second Congress of Soviets would create a genuinely revolutionary government.[15]

As a result of Lenin's interventions, including a threat to resign, the Bolshevik Central Committee re-opened the question of participating in the work of the Preparliament. On 5 October it was decided that the Bolsheviks would stage a demonstrative walk-out on the first day. Thus it was Trotsky who, on 7 October, was given permission to make a special announcement during the opening ceremony and used it to denounce the Preparliament as a "council of counter-revolutionary connivance" in cahoots with "this government of treason to the people". His peroration ended:

The revolution and the people are in danger. The government is intensifying this danger, and the ruling parties are helping it. Only the people can save themselves and the country. We address the people: Long live an immediate, honest, democratic peace. All power to the soviets, all land to the people. Long live the Constituent Assembly.

With this the Bolshevik delegates walked out.[16]

Although Trotsky was committed to Soviet insurrection, the precise agent of that insurrection was still unclear at this time. He was certain that it could not be the Bolshevik Party as such, but that was all. Ironically it was the Mensheviks who resolved this conundrum. With the German Army apparently preparing to march on the capital, and the government drafting plans to evacuate the seat of government to Moscow, the Mensheviks introduced into the Soviet on 9 October a proposal that a Committee of Revolutionary Defence be formed to help defend the capital. To the surprise of many, Trotsky and the Bolshevik faction backed the proposal. As Trotsky noted in his *History of the Russian Revolution*, while the Bolshevik Military Organisation had begun to draft plans for a possible uprising "the one difficulty they had not yet got over was that of reconciling an instrument of insurrection with an elective and openly functioning soviet, upon whose benches, moreover, sat representatives of the hostile parties; the patriotic proposal of the Mensheviks, therefore, came up most appropriately". A military committee of the soviet, rather than the Military Organisation of the Bolshevik Party, was in Trotsky's mind the perfect instrument to carry out an insurrection.[17]

On 10 October the Bolshevik Party met to debate the issue of insurrection. Lenin put the case for an immediate putsch using forces assembled at Minsk for the Congress of Soviets of the Northern Region. Evidence suggested, he argued, that a second Kornilov coup was in preparation, and so prompt action was needed. As Trotsky noted: "The task of insurrection he presented directly as the task of the Party; the difficult question of bringing its preparation into accord with the soviets is as yet not touched upon; the All-Russian Congress of Soviets does not get a word." Kamenev supported by Zinoviev put the case against insurrection, which he had been arguing since the opening of the Democratic Conference. Both argued that events were moving in the Bolsheviks' favour: they would secure a majority at the Second Congress of Soviets; they could win a third of the seats in the Constituent Assembly when elections were held in mid

November; and the SRs were so riven with dissension because of their support for Kerensky that there was bound to be a split and the Left SRs would be bound to support the Bolsheviks in the Constituent Assembly because of their commitment to radical land reform. The Bolsheviks were therefore likely to be the dominant party in a democratically elected socialist coalition government without having to resort to the gamble of seizing power.[18]

Neither Lenin's views, nor those of Zinoviev and Kamenev, were accepted. The Central Committee voted in favour of the principle of insurrection, but sketched out no plan, however tentative, of how it might take place. Not even a clear time-scale was established in the resolution, although Trotsky recalled that it was informally agreed that, as a guide date, something should happen by 15 October, in other words in associa- tion with the Congress of Soviet of the Northern Region which was scheduled for 11–13 October. However, things did not work out as anti- cipated by Lenin. On 12 October Trotsky guided through the Soviet the draft resolution establishing the Soviet's Military Revolutionary Committee (MRC), as the Committee for Revolutionary Defence was rechristened; on 13 October it was endorsed by the Soldiers' Section of the Soviet. Trotsky then moved to the Congress of Soviets of the Northern Region where he subtly subverted Lenin's plans. Although the resolution he put to the Congress was, in his words, "an almost undisguised summons to insurrection", it was a summons to insurrection on 20 October when the All-Russian Congress of Soviets was due to meet; it had nothing in common with Lenin's plan that the Congress of Soviets of the Northern Region should act as the cover for the Bolshevik Military Organisa- tion immediately sending troops to Petrograd in support of a Bolshevik insurrection. The Latvian Riflemen who rallied to Trotsky's call made clear they would "defend the Congress of Soviets"; they said nothing about supporting a Bolshevik coup. Trotsky had co-opted the leaders of the Congress of Soviets of the Northern Region to his policy, rather than Lenin's, and several of them joined Trotsky on the MRC.[19]

When the Bolshevik Central Committee next met on 16 October Kamenev could rightly point out that almost a week had passed and noth- ing had been done. There was no apparatus for an insurrection, all the resolution of 10 October had done was to warn Kerensky what was afoot and give the government time to prepare a crackdown on the Bolshevik Party. This was an expanded meeting of the Central Committee, including representatives of the Petrograd Party Committee, the Military Organisation and members of the Soviet. Its purpose was to try to get more consensus on the issue of the insurrection. Again Kamenev and Zinoviev called for the policy of insurrection to be dropped, and again Lenin wanted an immediate insurrection. He therefore interpreted as shilly-shallying on Trotsky's part the statement made by the representative he sent to the meeting from the MRC. This made clear that insurrection should remain on the agenda, but that no precise date should be set. "Our task is to bring armed force to support an insurrection if one flares up anywhere", and it was likely that any move by the government on the question of troop movements could spark such a crisis. In the elliptical phrase of the Central Committee minutes, Trotsky's representative stated, "it is not necessary to worry about who shall begin, for the thing is already begun".[20]

Lenin wanted the Bolsheviks to seize power before the Second Congress of Soviets assembled. Trotsky believed that defending the Congress from possible government attack was likely to present the opportunity for a seizure of power. He would be proved right, even though the Congress itself was postponed from the 20th to the 26th. In any event, the idea of the Bolsheviks staging a coup on their own behalf had been moved off the agenda by the decision of Kamenev to resign from the Central Committee and publish in the left Menshevik press an explanation of why he and Zinoviev opposed an insurrection; by 18 October the press was full of comment on Bolshevik plans for insurrection. Trotsky recognised that Lenin's idea of unilateral action by the Bolsheviks was so unpopular that rumours of it had to be denied. As he recalled later, alarm "penetrated even the workers' sections and still more the regiments; to them, too, it began to seem as though a coming-out were being prepared without them". So he resolved to make a statement both to the Soviet and on its behalf in which he outlined his strategy for revolution.

The decisions of the Petrograd Soviet are published for public information. The Soviet is an elective institution; every deputy is responsible to his electors. This revolutionary parliament cannot adopt decisions that would be withheld from the knowledge of all the workers and soldiers ... They want at this time to clear Petrograd of its garrison. This is perfectly understandable, because they know that the Congress of Soviets will definitely pass a resolution transferring power to the Congress, for the immediate conclusion of truces on all fronts, and for the transfer of land to the peasants. The bourgeoisie knows this and, therefore, wants to arm all the forces that are subordinate to it against us. This lie and slander is, in fact, the preparation for an attack against the Congress ... We have not set a date for the attack. But the opposing side has, evidently, already set it. We will meet it, we will repel it duly, and we will declare that at the first counter-revolutionary attempt to hamper the work of the Congress we will answer with a counter-offensive which will be ruthless and which we will carry out to the end.

To Trotsky's fury, Kamenev, sitting next to him, jumped to his feet and stated that he endorsed Trotsky's statement fully, implying that the statement was a rejection of the insurrection rather than a rather tortuous explanation of how the insurrection would take place. Immediately after the incident, Trotsky met with Lenin and tried to reassure him that he was still committed to insurrection and that if they were patient, the opportunity to act would yet present itself.[21]

Lenin was worried that the Bolsheviks would be caught napping and his concerns were understandable. Although the MRC had been established in principle on 9 October and endorsed by the Soldiers' Section a few days later, it was whole week after the 9th that a full plenary session of the Soviet endorsed the initiative and a further four days before its composition was agreed; the Mensheviks and SRs refused to work in this committee they had first proposed when it became clear that the Bolshevik majority believed that the only way to defend the capital was to overthrow the government. Only the Left SRs, in the process of separating themselves from the SR majority, were prepared to work with the Bolsheviks on the MRC, and to underline its non-party status Trotsky insisted that a Left SR took the chair of the ruling bureau. These delays meant that it was only on 20 October that the MRC began to function fully.

When the Bolshevik Central Committee met on 20 October it was not planning insurrection, but squabbling about the behaviour of Kamenev and Zinoviev. Trotsky, still smarting at the way Kamenev had outmanoeuvred him on the 18th, insisted on clarifying the meaning of his statement to the Soviet and called for Kamenev's behaviour to be put to a Party court; this did not happen, but Trotsky was one of the majority who insisted that Kamenev's resignation letter be accepted. Stalin, who had agreed to a statement by Zinoviev being published in *Pravda* and had tried to smooth over the disagreement between Lenin and his comrades, also felt duty-bound to tender his resignation, but this was not accepted. It was only on 21 October that any real progress was made towards the insurrection.[22]

Uprising

Despite Lenin's concern, below the surface Trotsky's strategy was beginning to bear fruit. Not only had he got the Soviet to establish the MRC, but it had agreed to call a conference of the Petrograd garrison which took place on 18–21 October. This made clear that the garrison had no confidence in the Provisional Government and would be prepared to take armed action in defence of the revolution if called to do so by the Petrograd

Soviet or the Congress of Soviets. With garrison support for the policy of the MRC, late in the night of the 21st Trotsky sent three of the MRC bureau members to talk to General Polkolnikov of the Petrograd District Military Headquarters and ask him to accept that, henceforth, all orders would have to be countersigned by the MRC. The proposal was turned down and the MRC reported to the Soviet that it had broken with Head-quarters. A gauntlet had been thrown down, but it was still unclear how things would develop. Sunday 22 October had been designated "Soviet Day", a day of peaceful meetings and demonstrations, and Trotsky spent it addressing public meetings. His performance at the People's House was observed by Nikolai Sukhanov, a Left-Menshevik journalist. When he arrived, he saw Trotsky "flying along the corridor towards me on to the stage".

Trotsky at once began to heat up the atmosphere, with his skill and brilliance . . . "the Soviet government will give everything the country contains to the poor and the men in the trenches" . . . All round me was a mood bordering on ecstasy . . . the crowd of thousands, as one man, raised their hands . . . Trotsky rapped out the words: "Let this vote of yours be your vow – with all your strength and at any sacrifice to support the Soviet which has taken on itself the glorious burden of bringing to a conclusion the victory of the revolution and of giving land, bread and peace!"[23]

Speeches like this had their effect. During the 22nd the MRC was approached by representatives of Petrograd Headquarters looking for a possible compromise. As Trotsky later explained by the time these proposals were discussed on 23 October it was already too late. "On Saturday those conditions of semi-honourable capitulation would have been accepted. Today, on Monday, they were already too late. Head-quarters awaited an answer which never came." Not only had the popular mood changed, but by the 23rd the MRC had got down to drafting a detailed plan of operations. As Trotsky recalled it was basically very simple; chosen detachments were allocated to seize strategic points of the capital when a signal was given. The key to success was to win over as many garrison units to support the MRC, or to ensure that they remained neutral in the forthcoming struggle. A key moment came on the afternoon of the 23rd when Trotsky addressed the garrison of the Peter-Paul Fortress, at the very heart of the capital, and persuaded its members to follow the MRC. Later in the day the troops responsible for the arsenal also came out in support of the MRC.

What made Lenin nervous was that all this activity was being under-taken not in the name of a seizure of power but of defending the Second

Congress of Soviets from possible government attack. As Trotsky recalled, "that word insurrection was not spoken by anyone of the leaders". When the MRC reported to the Soviet on the evening of the 23rd it listed those units which now stated that they would obey the orders of the MRC rather than the untrustworthy government, but the logic that crowding out the government implied its overthrow was never spelled out. The Soviet backed the actions of the MRC in the spirit that they were measures to defend the Congress of Soviets, and it was up to Kerensky to attack. As Trotsky commented: "the political set-up of the revolution was so favourable that frankness itself became a kind of camouflage".[24]

Kerensky acted on the morning of the 24th and closed down the Bolshevik and Soviet press; at the same time he cut the Smolny telephone lines, resolved to prosecute members of the MRC and demanded the removal of all MRC commissars. Trotsky sent troops to reopen the Bolshevik press, but by reopening the presses had embarked on an insurrection: as he noted later: "although an insurrection can win on the offensive, it develops better the more it looks like self-defence".[25] When the Central Committee met on the 24th its task was to try to give organisational form to a process that was already underway. And yet the central ambiguity of what was taking place remained. Was power actually being seized or was all this military activity simply intended to ensure the Second Congress of Soviets met and had the opportunity to resolve the political future of the country? Trotsky dared not come clean, even with the Bolshevik caucus gathering for the opening of the Second Congress of Soviets "it was still impossible to throw off the defensive envelope of the attack without creating confusion in the minds of certain units of the garrison". When a delegation from the Petrograd City Council approached the Petrograd Soviet on the afternoon of the 24th for an explanation as to what was going on, Trotsky reassured them that "the question of power is to be decided by the Congress of Soviets . . . if the Congress declines power, the Petrograd Soviet will submit".[26]

During the morning news had come in that the Bicycle Battalion of the Peter-Paul Fortress, which had not attended Trotsky's meeting on the previous day, was still loyal to Kerensky. The MRC cut the telephone connection to the battalion and at four in the afternoon Trotsky dashed to a meeting and persuaded them to abandon Kerensky. But, as he still explained afterwards to an extraordinary session of the Petrograd Soviet, the MRC had been established not to carry out an insurrection but to defend the revolution. Trotsky's speech at this session shows clearly the full ambiguity, or camouflage to use Trotsky's later assessment, of what was going on. The MRC, he insisted, was not afraid to shoulder responsibility for maintaining order and believed in the principle of "all power to the soviets", but the issue of power would be decided by the Congress. "At the forthcoming sessions of the All-Russian Congress of Soviets, this principle ought to be put into effect; whether this will lead to an insurrection or to any other form of action depends not only and not so much on the soviets as on those who, in defiance of the people's unanimous will, still hold governmental power." Yet, having on the one hand suggested that the Second Congress of Soviets would decide whether or not there was to be an insurrection, he went on, "Tomorrow the Congress of Soviets opens. It is the task of the garrison and of the proletariat to put at its disposal the power they have gathered, a power on which any governmental provocation will founder. It is our task to carry this power, undiminished and unimpaired, to the Congress." Here the clear implication was that power had already been seized and would be offered to the Congress of Soviets, which in theory could reject it. Finally he stated: "If the illusory government makes a hazardous attempt to revive its own corpse, the popular masses will strike a decisive counter-blow." This suggested once again that an insurrection might precede the Congress of Soviets, if the government were to act.[27]

During the day, Kerensky was not inactive. In the afternoon he addressed the Preparliament, hoping to persuade it to endorse the moves he had made to challenge the Bolsheviks; but the Preparliament refused Kerensky the vote of confidence he requested. Unabashed, he ordered that the railway stations be occupied by loyal troops, checkpoints established at major road intersections and the bridges across the river Neva be raised. The MRC responded by asking the crew of the battleship *Aurora* to restore movement on the Nikolaevskii Bridge, thus re-establishing traffic between the city centre and the large working class district on Vasilevskii Island. The captain of the battleship refused to implement the order, but agreed that he could be "arrested", and then dutifully brought the ship towards the bridge, prompting Kerensky's guards to flee; then the sailors lowered the bridge. At about the same time MRC commissars gained access to the telephone exchange and restored the phone connections to Smolny. Government authority was being challenged, but power was not yet being seized. In Trotsky's words, "right up to the evening of the 24th, the umbilical cord of 'legality' was not conclusively severed".[28]

Around six in the evening of the 24th Lenin wrote a letter to the Central Committee urging the Party to end the ambiguity and seize power before what he called the wavering vote of the Second Congress of Soviets. Fearing that this, like other letters, was being ignored, he donned a disguise and made his way to Smolny about midnight. His arrival acted as a catalyst. The Bolshevik Military Organisation dusted off its plans for the seizure of key installations and the operation began about two in the morning of the 25th. According to Trotsky's account, small groups "usually with a nucleus of armed workers or sailors under the leadership of a commissar" occupied strategic sites such as the railway stations, the electricity network, bridges, the State Bank, big printing plants and the telegraph office. It was the work of "a few thousand Red Guards and two or three thousand sailors". Many were briefed by Trotsky, who could still hardly believe what he was saying: "If you fail to stop them with words, use arms."[29]

While these forces were being deployed, Trotsky was also called on to address a preliminary meeting of delegates to the Second Congress of Soviets that had been called by the Executive elected at the First Congress of Soviets, i.e. by the Menshevik and Right SR leadership. The meeting began about midnight and continued until four in the morning. At it the Menshevik leader Fedor Dan denounced the Bolshevik insurrection as paving the way to counter-revolution; lunatics were leading the revolution to ruin, he suggested, just as had happened in 1905 "when this same Trotsky stood at the head of the St Petersburg Soviet". At about three in the morning Trotsky was called on to reply, in the name of the MRC and the Bolshevik Party. Finally the ambiguity was ended. Trotsky made clear that an insurrection was underway in which the Bolshevik Party was leading the masses. He dismissed the danger of counter-revolution: "If you do not weaken there will be no civil war, for the enemy is already capitulating, and you can assume the place of master of the Russian land which of right belongs to you." Sukhanov described it as a brilliant speech, but noted that it failed to arouse much enthusiasm from its tired audience.[30]

With his men on the street and the Soviet meeting over, Trotsky was left alone in the early hours of 25 October. In his memoirs he recalled this decisive moment in the Smolny Institute.

Later on, Kamenev came in. He was opposed to the uprising, but he had come to spend that deciding night with me, and together we stayed in the tiny corner room on the third floor [where the MRC was based], so like the captain's bridge on that deciding night of the revolution . . . "Give me a cigarette," I say to Kamenev. I take one or two puffs, but suddenly, with the words, "Only this is lacking!" I faint . . . As I come to I see Kamenev's frightened face bending over me. "Shall I get some medicine?" He asks. "It would be better," I answer after a moment's reflection, "if you got something to eat." I try to remember when I last had food, but I cannot. At all events, it was not yesterday.[31]

Either he had collapsed from hunger, as he clearly believed, or he had experienced another of those fainting fits which accompanied moments of drama in his life.

Trotsky recalled that at this stage "the revolution was still too trusting, too generous, optimistic and light-hearted; it preferred to threaten with arms than really to use them." When dawn broke on the 25th, the insurrection seemed to stall. By seven in the morning Supreme Army Headquarters, Petrograd Military Headquarters and Kerensky's government in the Winter Palace had no working telephones; but there was no sign that they were on the point of surrender. At ten in the morning Smolny broadcast that the Provisional Government had been overthrown, but this was still not the case. By midday troops had persuaded the Preparliament to disperse, but the government remained inside the Winter Palace. In the early afternoon both Lenin and Trotsky addressed an emergency session of the Petrograd Soviet; but Trotsky's declaration that the Provisional Government had been overthrown was quickly followed by a clarification that the Winter Palace had still not been taken. The Bolsheviks were desperate that the overthrow of Kerensky's government should be complete by the time the Second Congress of Soviets was due to open at eight in the evening; but still the Winter Palace was not in their hands. A wrangle with the Mensheviks delayed the opening of the Congress until well after 10 p.m., but as Trotsky paced backwards and forwards between the Congress hall and the room where Lenin was based, the continuing sound of artillery fire confirmed that the Winter Palace remained in government hands. It only surrendered after two on the morning of the 26th.[32]

Trotsky claimed in his memoirs that it was as he and Lenin awaited the opening of the Congress of Soviets that Lenin became reconciled to the strategy of the insurrection adopted by Trotsky. Lenin was clearly glad that the insurrection had taken place before the Congress of Soviets, but that had not in fact been Trotsky's intention. In his *History of the Russian Revolution* he wrote that "the insurrection began earlier and ended later than had been indicated". He had assumed, as he stated repeatedly in public, that the insurrection would be a product of the Congress of Soviets and take place when it was in session, but Kerensky's action had prompted the MRC to act earlier, unexpectedly bringing the timing closer to that called for by Lenin. However, by acting before the Congress of Soviets had assembled, the veil of constitutionality had to be dropped, resistance by Kerensky's government was more stubborn and the Winter Palace, unlike some of the earlier targets, held out much longer than expected.[33]

Thus the Second Congress of Soviets opened with street fighting still underway. It was hardly surprising, therefore, that when the first speaker, Martov, called for an end to civil war and a negotiated solution to the current crisis his speech was greeted with tempestuous applause. Sukhanov noted that this applause came from all over the hall and concluded "it was manifest that a very great many Bolsheviks, not having assimilated the teaching of Lenin and Trotsky, would have been very happy to take precisely this path". It was therefore up to Trotsky to rally his forces. Making perhaps his most famous speech, he asserted that revolutionary might was right.

An instrument of the popular masses needs no justification . . . Our insurrection has conquered, and now you propose to us: renounce your victory; make a compromise. With whom, I ask . . . No, a compromise is no good here . . . To all who made like proposals, we must say – "You are pitiful, isolated individuals; you are bankrupts; your role is played out. Go where you belong from now on . . . into the dustbin of history."[34]

Sukhanov had been right to suspect that not all Bolsheviks shared Trotsky's vision. Lunacharskii followed Trotsky to the platform of the Second Congress of Soviets and explained that the Bolsheviks were not insisting on Trotsky's resolution against compromise, and were in fact ready to reach an agreement about the formation of a government with other parties represented in the Soviet. Unable to agree on whether or not to form a new government, the Congress of Soviets decided on a half-hour recess at two in the morning. When it reconvened, news had come through that the Winter Palace had fallen and Kerensky's ministers were under arrest. Only now did the Congress resolve under Kamenev's guidance to form a new Soviet government, a "provisional workers' and peasants' government, to be called the Council of People's Commissars", to administer the country "until the meeting of the Constituent Assembly".

Just as the Bolsheviks had failed to agree about whether or not to stage an insurrection, they were not agreed about what sort of government to form. During the day of 26 October Lenin and Trotsky called an informal meeting of those Central Committee members who happened to be around and resolved to form a government comprised only of Bolsheviks. Trotsky described this as "the only thinkable" proposal. However, later in the day the Central Committee invited three representatives of the Left SRs to a more formal meeting and proposed the formation of a coalition government. The Left SRs turned this down, and so Kamenev was forced to read out only Bolshevik names as he listed the new People's Commissars. There were immediate protests from the Left SR and remaining Menshevik delegates. Trotsky again spoke for the intransigents. In an extraordinary statement given his repeated attempts to "camouflage" the insurrection, he claimed that "openly and before the face of the whole people we raised the banner of insurrection". Slightly more honestly he commented: "They tell us – you did not await the Congress of Soviets with your uprising; we thought of waiting, but Kerensky would not wait." Although Bolshevik delegates were convinced by this bravado, the Left SRs were not. They controlled the Railwaymen's Union *Vikzhel* and as the session closed on the morning of 27 October a *Vikzhel* delegate announced that no trains would move on the country's railway network until a negoti-ated settlement had been reached.[35]

The *Vikzhel* negotiations lasted from 28 October to 4 November. Those Bolsheviks like Kamenev and Zinoviev, who had opposed an insurrection, were keen to see their success; Trotsky and Lenin, who saw their purpose as simply removing the Bolsheviks' monopoly of power, and indeed they themselves personally from power, consistently sought to wreck them. While the talks proceeded, *de facto* power was in the hands of the MRC, and that power was used in two directions. To the horror of moderate socialists, the MRC behaved quite arbitrarily and targeted for repression not representatives of the bourgeoisie, but those moderate socialists associated with the Kerensky administration. The other target of the MRC was the army of Cossacks assembled by Kerensky after he had fled the city. Jointly Lenin and Trotsky appointed the Left SR Colonel Mikhail Muraviev to lead those forces rapidly assembled to confront the Cossacks at Pulkovo Hill on the outskirts of Petrograd on 30–31 October; Trotsky observed the proceedings from the sidelines, issuing wild orders that for every revolu-tionary soldier killed, five enemy soldiers would be shot in their place. While the Cossacks posed a threat, Lenin and Trotsky were prepared to let the *Vikzhel* talks continue as a way of buying time; when the Cossacks were sent packing, they saw no point in the discussions going on.

Trotsky informed *Vikzhel* by telegraph on 31 October that he was not opposed to the idea of a Coalition Government formed from the Bolsheviks and the Left SRs, confirming that this had been proposed on 26 October, but he insisted that in his view the *Vikzhel* negotiations were just being used as a cover while Kerensky rallied counter-revolutionary troops: "Talks are being held with democratic organisations and parties, but we will not allow negotiations with a bunch of Kornilovites." The next day he told a session of the Petrograd Committee that the negotiations would lead nowhere. Here he spelled out ideas implicit in *Results and Prospects*, independent action by the peasants, the petty bourgeoisie, was impossible: "We shall be able to draw the petit bourgeoisie behind us only by showing that we have in our hands a material fighting force." Peasant radicalism had to be given a lead and "there was no point in organising the insurrection if we do not get the majority". The Bolsheviks needed three-quarters of the seats in any government, and the government had to be headed by Lenin. The talks should be presented with an ultimatum – back the decrees issued by the Bolshevik Government or break up the talks. After what he later described as "an incredible effort", Kamenev was able to persuade the Central Committee to agree to a continuation of the *Vikzhel* talks, but the issue was raised again in the Central Committee on 2 November.[36] Lenin demanded that the Central Committee "confirm that there can be no repudiation of the purely Bolshevik Government without betraying the slogan of soviet power". Trotsky agreed and signed the "ultimatum from the Central Committee majority to the minority" drawn up by Lenin on 3 November and presented to the Central Committee meeting of the 4th. At that meeting Lenin and Trotsky got their way, prompting Zinoviev and Kamenev to resign in protest.[37]

Brest Litovsk

In *Results and Prospects* Trotsky had argued that in the first stage of rule by a workers' government virtually the whole nation would support it, but as its socialist agenda began to be implemented the individualist aspirations of the peasantry would be offended and soon the workers' government would be under peasant attack; the only way out of this dilemma was to spread the revolution to Europe. Two months before the October insurrection Trotsky had written, "a lasting, decisive success is inconceivable for us without a revolution in Europe", and as the newly appointed Commissar for Foreign Affairs that is what he sought to achieve. Trotsky had little time for conventional diplomacy. When the crisis over the formation of a Bolshevik Government had passed, Trotsky made his first foreign policy statement to the Soviet Executive on 8 November. Bolshevik policy, he said, was rooted in the peace decree adopted by the Congress of Soviets. He was confident that the Bolshevik Government was now strong enough for foreign powers to reckon with it as a fact; whether they liked it or not, there were day-to-day practicalities like the issuing of visas which forced foreign powers to enter into normal relations, even with the Bolsheviks. Despite some attempts to frustrate his work, officials from the former Ministry of Foreign Affairs had shown him the secret treaties agreed between Imperial Russia and Britain and France, allocating Russia substantial territorial gains in the Balkans and elsewhere;

these treaties would be published in full so that the world was clear about the imperialist nature of the First World War. The Bolsheviks were serious about peace and the Allied ambassadors had all been informed that the new Council of People's Commissars had instructed the Commander-in-Chief of the Russian Army to begin armistice discussions. At the same time he had sent a radio appeal to both the Allied Powers and the Central Powers inviting them to conclude a general peace.

It took time for the armistice to be implemented. The Commander-in-Chief of the Russian Army informed Lenin that he did not recognise the Bolshevik Government, while the Allies' response was to reject Trotsky's proposal for a general armistice and warn the Commander that any separate talks with the Germans could have "the gravest consequences". The Commander-in-Chief was called on to resign and transfer authority to someone loyal to Lenin; when he queried on what authority he should do this, he was murdered in a bloody confrontation on 21 November. The Russian and German armistice delegations had first met two days earlier and during the four days of talks Trotsky tried to persuade the Germans to agree not to transfer troops to the Western Front; this proved impossible. The truce was finalised on 22 November. Still hoping for a general rather than a separate peace, a further appeal was made to the Allies, but when no response was forthcoming the Bolsheviks had no choice but to consider a separate peace. Trotsky appeared before the Soviet Executive on 8 December to justify this stance and in his speech outlined his personal agenda for the next six months.

The armistice has made a breach in the war. The gunfire has ceased and everyone is nervously waiting to see how the Soviet Government will deal with the Hohenzollern and Habsburg imperialists. You must support us in treating them as foes of freedom, in ensuring that not one iota of this freedom is sacrificed to imperialism . . . We are becoming more and more convinced that peace talks will be a powerful weapon in the hands of other peoples in their struggle for peace. If we are mistaken, if Europe continues to be silent as the grave, and if this silence gives Wilhelm the chance to attack us and to dictate his terms to us, terms which would insult the revolutionary dignity of our country, then I am not sure whether, given our shattered economy and the general chaos (the result of the war and internal strife), we could fight. I think, however, that we could do so. For our lives, for our revolutionary honour, we would fight to the last drop of our blood . . . [raising] an army of soldiers and Red Guardsmen, strong in its revolutionary enthusiasm.[38]

The talks at Brest Litovsk got underway on 9 December but progress was slow. After the formal opening there was an adjournment, followed by postponements, and it was only on 25 December that the German demands became clear; on 29 December the Soviet delegation returned to Petrograd bringing with it what Trotsky called the monstrous demands of the Central Powers. After a brief discussion among the Bolshevik leadership it was agreed that the only thing to do was to play for time in the hope that a European Revolution materialised. The negotiations had to be spun out for as long as possible, and Lenin insisted that "to delay the negotiations, there must be someone to do the delaying": Trotsky was ordered to head the delegation and set off "as if being led to a torture chamber".[39] No sooner than he had arrived, than he asked for an adjournment, arriving back in Petrograd on 7 January 1918. While en route, there had been dramatic developments in the capital. The Constituent Assembly had met and been dissolved on 6 January and its place taken by the Third Congress of Soviets. On 8 January the Bolshevik Central Committee and leaders of the Bolshevik delegation to the Third Congress met to consider what to do, and Trotsky proposed a tactic of neither peace nor war; the Bolsheviks would simply not sign the treaty proposed by the Germans, but nor would they resume hostilities. This tactic presupposed that the German proletariat would rise up in fury when it saw how outrageously its imperialist government was behaving.

The meeting accepted Trotsky's suggestion, but this was just an advisory vote; when the Central Committee resumed its discussion on 11 January, without the participation of extraneous delegates, Lenin and Trotsky clashed. Lenin felt they had no choice but to accept the German terms: "what comrade Trotsky suggests is political showmanship", he argued, if the Germans attacked the Bolsheviks would be forced to sign a worse peace. By nine votes to seven the meeting endorsed Trotsky's policy.[40] Before returning to the negotiations, Trotsky put an optimistic gloss on the situation when he addressed the Third Congress of Soviets.

They cannot threaten us with an offensive, as they cannot be sure the German soldiers will take part in one . . . and if German imperialism attempts to crucify us on the wheel of its military machine, then . . . we shall appeal to our elder brothers in the west and say: "Do you hear?" and the international proletariat will respond – we firmly believe this – "We hear!"

Just prior to Trotsky's departure, he and Lenin came to a private understanding, which modified the "no peace, no war" decision of the Central Committee. Trotsky promised to sign the peace if Lenin's fears were realised and the Germans resumed hostilities.[41]

However, before "no peace, no war" became an issue, there remained the tactic of spinning out the negotiations. There were several ways of delaying the talks. Technical communications with Petrograd were poor: Trotsky insisted he had to be in regular correspondence with Petrograd, yet the direct wire communication system constantly broke down. Then there were the details to be explored: Trotsky protested about Russian PoWs being subjected to German propaganda; the Germans responded in kind. Sometimes such points of detail were personal. Members of the Austro-Hungarian delegation were keen for the release of two personal friends held by the Russians and offered Trotsky in return the contents of the library he had left in Vienna at the start of the war. The gaps between sessions could be extended, Trotsky made a short visit to Warsaw and spent many hours dictating a history of the October insurrection to the bored stenographers who had previously worked for the State Duma.

Initially both sides were interested in such time-wasting. The German tactic was to propose a democratic peace in line with President Woodrow Wilson's talk of the self-determination of nations. They would effectively break up the Russian Empire allowing the Bolsheviks to control the Russian heartland but establishing in the Baltic lands and in Ukraine German-sponsored independent regimes. The Germans needed time to persuade Ukrainian politicians to back this scheme, while the Bolsheviks needed time to put an end to the growing Ukrainian autonomy movement and establish Soviet power in Ukraine by force. The crisis came when the Germans had their Ukrainian delegation ready. Trotsky tried to argue that a revolution had occurred in Ukraine and that local Bolsheviks, supported by Russian Red Guardsmen, had established a Soviet Ukraine which had voluntarily formed a federation with Soviet Russia on the basis of a shared foreign policy. The Germans countered that Soviet Ukraine had been established by Russian force, and Trotsky was himself rather embarrassed by reports of the arbitrary way Colonel Muraviev, the same commander who had defeated the Cossacks at Pulkovo Hill, had subjugated Ukraine. On 21 January, when Muraviev captured Kiev, Trotsky notified the Central Powers that he did not recognise the Ukrainian delegation; at the same time he informed Lenin that the negotiations could not be spun out much longer and the "no peace, no war" declaration would have to be made soon.[42]

On 28 January, the day after the Central Powers signed a separate treaty with the Ukrainian delegation, Trotsky made his final statement.

In expectation of the approaching hour when the working classes of all countries seize power . . . we are withdrawing our army and our people from the war and issuing an order for full demobilisation . . . At the same time we declare that the terms proposed to us by the governments of Germany and Austro-Hungary are in fundamental conflict with the interests of all people . . . We cannot put the signature of the Russian revolution under a peace treaty which brings oppression, woe and misfortune to millions of human beings.[43]

With this the Russian delegation left. Trotsky was convinced that there was a disagreement within the German delegation between the military and political representatives, and that the political representatives were getting the upper hand. He therefore ignored the head of the Austro-Hungarian delegation who came to see him secretly to warn him that the Germans were preparing an offensive. He also ignored the views of the three Russian military advisers who had accompanied him to Brest. Back in the capital he told the Petrograd Soviet on 16 February (the Gregorian calendar was introduced in Russia at the start of February 1918, so 1 February became 13 February):

I regard an advance by German troops against us as extremely unlikely, and if you reckon it in percentages, then it would be ninety against, ten for . . . to send German troops to Russia now, when Russia has publicly declared that it has left the state of war, would unquestionably mean provoking a mighty revolutionary protest by the German workers.[44]

Trotsky was terribly wrong. The Germans resumed hostilities on 18 February. Under the terms of the tacit agreement between Lenin and Trotsky, this was the point at which Trotsky should have agreed to sign the treaty. However, he had changed his mind. Lenin insisted that the Bolsheviks should offer to sign the treaty at once, Trotsky argued that the offensive should be allowed to begin "so that the workers of Germany would learn of the offensive as a fact rather than as a threat". When the Central Committee met on 17 February he voted for the principle of peace, but on the 18th refused to vote for the despatch of the necessary telegram to the Germans. He reported that the German offensive had indeed begun with an aerial bombardment of the city of Dvinsk, but he argued "the masses are only just beginning to digest what is happening . . . we have to wait and see what impression all this makes on the German people". Later that day, Trotsky informed the reconvened Central Committee that Dvinsk had now fallen and it was time to make a direct appeal to the civilian politicians in Berlin and Vienna. Trotsky was behaving recklessly. He was seeing what he wanted to see, just as he had done during the hunger strike in Odessa prison. Lenin insisted that the time had come to sign and Trotsky finally backed down. On 19 February the Bolsheviks sued for peace and put Trotsky in charge of a Committee for Revolutionary Defence.[45]

Declaring a willingness to sign the peace treaty was one thing, persuading the Germans to stop their advance quite another. Fighting had begun and until the Germans agreed to resume talks, they had to be resisted. Allied representatives had responded to the "no peace, no war" declaration by offering to aid Russia should hostilities resume. On 18 February Trotsky was visited by the British representative in Russia, Bruce Lockhart, who offered British military support. Lockhart found Trotsky surprisingly optimistic: "even if Russia cannot resist, she will indulge in partisan warfare to the best of her ability". However, when on 20 February Trotsky met with his key military advisers, they persuaded him that partisan operations could not hold back a modern army; the only thing to do was to retreat to a defensible line and hope to build up reserves; in the first instance every effort should be made to hold the strategic town of Pskov.

By 21 February a Russian delegation had reached Brest Litovsk, only to discover that the terms now offered by the Germans were, as Lenin predicted, far worse than the original ones. At first even Lenin thought there was no choice but to fight for survival. Given this bleak scenario it was not surprising that Trotsky continued to keep in contact with the Allies, not only with Lockhart but with French representatives as well. On 22 February he persuaded a sceptical Central Committee to accept a French offer of military aid. But the military situation was worsening all the time. On 23 February news came of the fall of Pskov and a crisis meeting of military advisers predicted that Petrograd would soon fall too. When the Central Committee met later in the day Lenin insisted that "this is where the policy of revolutionary phrase-mongering ends". Trotsky did not agree. He insisted that the Party could "tackle the task of organising defence"; even if Petrograd and Moscow were surrendered, "we could hold the whole world in tension". The problem was, he said, that the Party was not united, and "we cannot fight a revolutionary war when the Party is split". Reluctantly he would therefore resign as Commissar of Foreign Affairs and abstain in the forthcoming vote; on his abstention Lenin's policy of signing the new German proposals was passed. Reflecting the tensions within the ruling group at this time, Stalin queried whether it was possible for someone to resign from the government yet remain a Party member, but Lenin would have nothing of such vindictiveness and insisted that Trotsky not only remain in the Party but in the government as well.[46]

Rebuilding the Army

Trotsky resigned as Commissar for Foreign Affairs, but his responsibilities for co-ordinating the defence of Petrograd continued. Although a Bolshevik delegation set off to sign the new treaty on the morning of 24 February, the fighting continued. Indeed, at this time the Russian Army staged a small recovery and recaptured Pskov, holding the town for a couple of days. The treaty had still not been signed, and in these circumstances Trotsky's contact with the Allies continued; on 29 February Lenin met Lockhart and informed him that "so long as the German danger exists, I am prepared to risk co-operation with the Allies". The next day a message was received requesting a train to bring back the Russian peace mission; fearing the Germans had decided not to sign the peace treaty after all, Lenin held further talks with Lockhart and instructed the soviet in Murmansk to co-operate with the British in moving military supplies. It was only on 3 March that the Treaty of Brest Litovsk was signed and the German advance halted.

No sooner had the peace been signed than on 4 March the Bolsheviks established a Supreme Military Council and made Trotsky its chair. Trotsky had told the Soviet Executive before the Brest Litovsk negotiations started that if terms were dictated to them which "insulted the revolutionary dignitary of our country" then they would raise an army of soldiers "strong in its revolutionary enthusiasm". That is precisely what he now set out to do. At the Extraordinary Seventh Party Congress held on 6–8 March to endorse the signing of the Brest Treaty, Trotsky followed a justification of his actions with a prediction that would guide his movements over the next few weeks: "The present breathing space can be reckoned to last no more than two or three months at best, and most likely only weeks and days."[47] War with Germany would resume, and it was imperative to have a capable force ready for that day by disbanding the disintegrating army and building a new one.

During the Extraordinary Fourth Congress of Soviets, 14–16 March, which ratified the Treaty of Brest Litovsk, Trotsky was appointed Commissar of War. Trotsky's closest advisor in his campaign to construct an army capable of confronting the Germans by summer 1918 was General M. D. Bonch Bruevich who had been among those who advised Trotsky against partisan warfare when the German advance began in February. Together they began to draft a plan in the event of renewed German aggression for a fighting retreat beyond the river Volkhov, to be co-ordinated with the construction of defensive "screens" to protect Petrograd and Moscow. Allied representatives were closely involved in these preparations. Talks between Trotsky and Lockhart continued throughout March 1918; indeed when Trotsky travelled to Moscow after the decision to move the capital away from the German threat, he and Lockhart shared a railway compartment. There were other examples of collaboration; Captain Hicks of the British Mission was attached to the Supreme Military Council and once the move to Moscow had taken place, Trotsky formally asked the French Military Mission to co-operate in constructing a new army. By the end of March, 40 Allied officers were attached to the new army.

Trotsky was also keen to keep in Russia the Czechoslovak Legion. Formed by the Provisional Government from Austro-Hungarian PoWs of Czech and Slovak ethnicity, the Legion had been stationed near Kiev when the armistice with the Germans was signed. When Colonel Muraviev captured Kiev, the Legion and Muraviev's army formed a temporary alliance and together harried the German Army as it marched into Ukraine under the terms of the Brest Litovsk Treaty; at the Battle of Bakhmach on 15 March the German advance was significantly delayed. Once back in the Russian heartland the Czechoslovak Legion announced it planned to leave Russia for the Western Front, but Trotsky could see the advantage of keeping such a battle-hardened force at hand to fight alongside his newly constructed Russian Army. To help persuade the Czechoslovak Legion to stay, on 20 March he temporarily forbade any of their units proceeding further east towards Vladivostok.

Trotsky was equally clear that his new army had to be a professional army. In a speech to a session of the Moscow Soviet on 19 March, immediately after his arrival in the city, Trotsky stated that a properly and freshly organised army meant using military specialists from the old army and imposing discipline. The message was repeated to a conference of the Moscow City Communist Party on 28 March: "I have had occasion several times already to say at public meetings that in the sphere of command, of operations, of military actions, we place full responsibility upon military specialists and consequently give them the necessary powers." He also dismissed the principle of elected officers and soldiers' committees: "Given the present regime in the Army – I say this here quite openly – the principle of election is politically purposeless and technically inexpedient, and it has been, in practice, abolished by decree." To the surprise of many, on 30 March Trotsky appointed to the Supreme Military Council Admiral D. V. Verderevskii, the Navy Minister in Kerensky's last government.[48]

By April 1918 Trotsky's discussions with Lockhart had reached the point where both sides envisaged a major British intervention at the moment when the "breathing space" with Germany was over. The British would persuade the Czechoslovak Legion to stay in Russia, where they would be reinforced by an Allied expeditionary force which would land in Archangel. Trotsky backed the scheme, but pointed out that Count

Mirbach, the German ambassador, would arrive in Moscow on 26 April, making close relations between Trotsky and the Allies more problematic. Yet even after the arrival of Mirbach, such contacts continued. They did so because on 29 April the Germans revealed their true hand in Ukraine. Until then the Germans had worked with a democratically elected government in Ukraine, but because of the commitment of that government to land reform, the Germans decided to overthrow it and establish a dictatorship. For many Bolsheviks this revealed the true face of German imperialism and on 4 May Russian troops were instructed to resist any German violations of their new border. The Central Committee then went into a crisis session which lasted the best part of the week, from 6 to 13 May. Lockhart believed that a rupture with Germany was possible at any minute, but when Trotsky outlined to the Central Committee what he and Lockhart were proposing Lenin spoke out against "the English ultimatum" and, despite winning the support of key members of the Central Committee, the scheme was dropped.

Trotsky's eyes were still on Germany, however, and the threat it posed. The German Army had steadily encroached on the initially agreed demarcation line between Russia and Ukraine; they did so usually to take control of strategically important railway junctions. Cherkovo Station was captured by the Germans after some fighting on 9 May because they saw it as essential for communication with Rostov on Don; Bataisk railway junction was taken by the Germans on 2 June. They justified their actions on the grounds that the Russians had not yet scuttled the Black Sea Fleet as agreed at Brest Litovsk. While Lenin urged Trotsky not to over-react to such actions Trotsky was less conciliatory: "It needs to be clearly and firmly stated that the truce and the demarcation line can only be observed on the condition of there being some minimum degree of trust on both sides ... The artificially indeterminate position created by the German Command evokes extreme exasperation."[49] It was because of incidents such as these that Trotsky and his military commanders were taken unawares by the SR uprising and mutiny of the Czechoslovak Legion which occurred in the last week of May and the first week of June and started Russia's Civil War.

Notes

1 A. Rabinowitch, *Prelude to Revolution* (Bloomington, 1968), pp. 42–7.

2 L. Trotsky, *The History of the Russian Revolution* (London, 1965), Vol. I, p. 340; N. Sukhanov, *The Russian Revolution: a Personal Record* (Princeton, 1984), p. 359; L. Trotsky, *My Life* (New York, 1970), p. 329.

3 I. Deutscher, *The Prophet Armed, Trotsky: 1879–1921* (Oxford, 1970), pp. 257–8; N. Allen (ed.), *Leon Trotsky: the Challenge of the Left Opposition, 1923–5* (New York, 1975), p. 257, from the essay "Lessons of October".

4 Sukhanov, *Russian Revolution*, pp. 376–7; Trotsky, *History*, Vol. I, pp. 444–5.

5 Trotsky, *History*, Vol. I, p. 401.

6 Deutscher, *Armed*, pp. 266–7.

7 Sukhanov, *Russian Revolution*, pp. 383–4; Trotsky, *History*, Vol. II, p. 296.

8 Sukhanov, *Russian Revolution*, pp. 432–9; Trotsky, *History*, Vol. II, pp. 40–2; Trotsky, *My Life*, p. 311.

9 Sukhanov, *Russian Revolution*, pp. 444–7; Trotsky, *My Life*, p. 312.

10 Trotsky *My Life*, p. 316; for the July Days generally, see Rabinowitch, *Prelude*.

11 Trotsky, *My Life*, p. 317.

12 Trotsky, *History*, Vol. II, pp. 289–90; Deutscher, *Armed*, p. 288.

13 Sukhanov, *Russian Revolution*, p. 544; Trotsky, *History*, Vol. II, p. 325; for the Preparliament more generally, see G. R. Swain, "Before the Fighting Started: a Discussion on the Theme of the 'Third Way'", *Revolutionary Russia*, No. 2, 1991.

14 Trotsky, *My Life*, p. 339.

15 Trotsky, *History*, Vol. II, p. 329.

16 R. P. Browder and A. F. Kerensky, *The Russian Provisional Government 1917: Documents* (Stanford, 1961), Vol. III, p. 1729.

17 Trotsky, *History*, Vol. III, p. 90.

18 Trotsky, *History*, Vol. III, pp. 140–3; for the differing tactics of Lenin and Trotsky at this time, see J. D. White, "Lenin, Trotsky and the Arts of Insurrection: the Congress of Soviets of the Northern Region, 11–13 October 1917", *Slavonic and East European Review*, No. 1, 1999.

19 Trotsky, *History*, Vol. III, pp. 81, 483.

20 *The Bolsheviks and the October Revolution: Central Committee Minutes* (London, 1974), pp. 101–2.

21 Browder and Kerensky, *Documents*, p. 1767; Trotsky, *History*, Vol. III, p. 102.

22 *Central Committee Minutes*, p. 110.

23 Sukhanov, *Russian Revolution*, p. 584.

24 Trotsky, *History*, Vol. III, pp. 114, 116–17.

25 Trotsky, *History*, Vol. III, p. 195.

26 Trotsky, *History*, Vol. III, p. 198.

27 Deutscher, *Armed*, pp. 308–9.

28 Trotsky, *History*, Vol. III, p. 208.

29 Trotsky, *History*, Vol. III, pp. 209–12; Trotsky, *My Life*, p. 323.

30 Trotsky, *History*, Vol. III, pp. 213–14; Sukhanov, *Russian Revolution*, p. 617.

31 Trotsky, *My Life*, p. 325.

32 Trotsky, *My Life*, p. 324; Trotsky, *History*, Vol. III, pp. 284–5.

33 Trotsky, *My Life*, p. 324; Trotsky, *History*, Vol. III, p. 205.

34 Sukhanov, *Russian Revolution*, p. 636; Trotsky, *History*, Vol. III, p. 289.

35 Trotsky, *History*, Vol. III, pp. 299, 314; *Central Committee Minutes*, p. 138.

36 Swain, "Third Way", p. 224; L. Trotsky, *The Stalin School of Falsification* (New York, 1971), p. 122; *Central Committee Minutes*, p. 129.

37 R. Pipes, *The Unknown Lenin* (New Haven, 1998), p. 41; *Central Committee Minutes*, pp. 138–43.

38 J. Keep (ed.), *The Debate on Soviet Power* (Oxford, 1979), p. 187.

39 Trotsky, *My Life*, p. 363.

40 *Central Committee Minutes*, pp. 175–80.

41 D. Volkogonov, *Trotsky: the Eternal Revolutionary* (London, 1997), p. 109; Deutscher, *Armed*, pp. 375–6.

42 A more detailed account of events in Ukraine at this time can be found in G. R. Swain, *The Origins of the Russian Civil War* (London, 1996), pp. 92–118.

43 Deutscher, *Armed*, p. 381.

44 Volkogonov, *Trotsky*, pp. 111–12.

45 Trotsky, *My Life*, pp. 387–8; *Central Committee Minutes*, p. 204.

46 Swain, *Origins*, p. 133; *Central Committee Minutes*, pp. 218–25.

47 Volkogonov, *Trotsky*, p. 116.

48 L. Trotsky, *How the Revolution Armed* (New York, 1979), Vol. I, pp. 23, 43–7; for Trotsky's contacts with the Allies, see Swain, *Origins*, pp. 132–48.

49 J. M. Meijer (ed.), *The Trotsky Papers* (Hague, 1964), Vol. I, p. 55.

Chapter 4

Saving the Revolution

Trotsky's prediction that a workers' government would lose the support of the peasantry if revolution did not spread to Europe, and soon face the danger of peasant insurrection was borne out by events. After the Second Congress of Peasant Soviets in November 1917 the Left SRs did decide to support the Bolshevik Government despite the collapse of the *Vikzhel* talks. The key commissariat they were allocated was that of land, and by February 1918 it had begun to implement a land reform which broke up the noble estates and divided land among individual peasant families. It was largely because the Left SRs were so determined to implement this land reform that they had gone along with the Bolshevik decision to dissolve Russia's Constituent Assembly. The Left SRs did not stay in the government long. The Party was absolutely opposed to the Treaty of Brest Litovsk and resigned all government posts once it was signed. The Left SRs did not, however, resign from the Supreme Military Council, for they were prepared to go along with Trotsky's conviction that the Brest Litovsk breathing space would last only a couple of months and a new army needed to be established as quickly as possible. It was only in mid May, after the Bolshevik Central Committee had rejected the "English ultimatum" and Trotsky's plan for joint action with the British had been abandoned that the Left SRs began to reconsider their position.

The SR Party itself also turned on the Bolsheviks in May. The SRs had won the Constituent Assembly elections held in mid November 1917. However, they had not responded when the Constitutional Assembly was dissolved because the peace talks with Germany were at a delicate stage and any sign of internal dissension would only encourage German aggression. They too had been prepared to back the idea of a two-month breathing space and co-operation with the Allies, but once the "English ultimatum" had been rejected, the SRs called for an anti-Bolshevik insurrection. Peasant support for this insurrection was predicated on growing peasant hostility to Bolshevik policies. When the Bolshevik Central Committee rejected the ultimatum it was on the understanding that the Party was pressing ahead to build socialism. No longer held back by the Left SRs, they would build socialism both in the town and in the countryside. Left SR policy had relied on collecting grain from the countryside by free-market trading. Bolshevik policy was to abolish the market in favour of planning and to introduce class war into the countryside. In their view the February land reform had rapidly led to a situation where some peasants had become very rich and some very poor. Trade had fallen into the hands of rich peasants or kulaks, and the only way to break their stranglehold on grain prices was to encourage poor peasants to rise up against them. From May onwards the Bolsheviks began to encourage the formation of Poor Peasant Committees, which favoured ending the free market in grain and delivering it instead at low fixed prices to their working class allies in the town. In reality, the policy quickly degenerated into the forced requisitioning of grain.

Uprising on the Volga

The SR Party had always been particularly strong on the river Volga and here SR deputies elected to the Constituent Assembly began to prepare actively for insurrection at the end of May. In their search for allies, they contacted units of the Czechoslovak Legion. By May 1918 units of the Legion were strung out along Russia's railway network from the Volga to the Far East. They were subject to conflicting pressures. At the start of May it was still assumed that those units west of the Urals would become the core of an Allied intervention force based at Archangel which at Trotsky's signal would end the two-month breathing space and resume the fight against Germany. The decision to reject the "English ultimatum" had ended all that. Trotsky had no choice but to agree with the German ambassador Count Mirbach that the presence of an armed Allied Army on Russian soil violated the provisions of the Treaty of Brest Litovsk and that the Legion should be disarmed of its heavy weapons. The Legion, faced with orders to disarm and to regroup towards Archangel, feared it was being sent into a trap that would end in internment and resolved to ignore all orders and resume its journey eastwards, fighting its way there if necessary.

The Czechoslovak units outside Samara, therefore, faced the prospect of fighting their way through the city at the very moment the local SRs were drawing up their plans for an insurrection there. The logic of the situation brought them together and on 8 June Samara was captured in a joint SR–Czechoslovak operation, setting a pattern of co-operation which spread like wildfire along the railway network into Siberia. Trotsky, however, with his eyes still on the threat from Germany and still unwilling finally to break off his contact with the Allies, was very slow to appreciate its seriousness. The first Red Army commander sent to deal with the situation was a junior officer who set off for the Volga on 29 May accompanied by the 4th Latvian Regiment; it had been one of the units that had resisted the German advance into Ukraine earlier in the year and so was battle-hardened, but also exhausted. The force was quite inadequate.

Once in control of Samara, the SRs established their own People's Army and declared the formation of a new government, the Committee of the Constituent Assembly. By 17 June the Latvian units sent to confront them had been forced to abandon their original base, the Volga town of Syzran. Four days before this Lenin and Trotsky discussed the situation on the Volga and decided that the situation was serious enough to appoint a new commander, Colonel Muraviev, who had served them so well at Pulkovo Hill and in Ukraine. However, Muraviev soon found it was almost impossible to make clear to Trotsky and General Bonch-Bruevich just how serious the situation on the Volga was. With their eyes firmly fixed on the need to establish defensive screens for Petrograd and Moscow in the event of a German attack, they were quite unwilling to allocate extra resources to the Volga; Muraviev was allowed to reorganise existing forces, but not to establish a formal Eastern Front with all that meant in terms of the allocation of supplies.[1]

Trotsky's blindness to the rapidly deteriorating situation on the Volga was understandable. The First All-Russian Conference of Military Commissars took place in Moscow from 7 to 11 June and he had had to devote much time and energy to this. As he candidly told the delegates: "The military property of our state is scattered chaotically all over the country and has not been registered; we do not know precisely either the number of cartridges, of rifles, of heavy and light artillery, of aeroplanes, of armoured cars." The manpower problem was not much better; Trotsky had appealed for volunteers for his new army, but only a third of the anticipated number had come forward. Muraviev could demand fresh troops, but Trotsky was still trying to assess the military forces at his disposal. Soon, however, the situation on the Volga would deteriorate dramatically as the Left SRs joined the SR rebellion.[2]

In response to the SR insurrection, the Bolsheviks had excluded the SR Party from the soviets on 14 June. However, the Left SRs were not affected by this ban and they still hoped to remove the Bolsheviks from power democratically at the Fifth Congress of Soviets due to be held in

Moscow during the first week of July; their support among rank and file peasants, they argued, should assure them of victory. To prevent this happening, the Bolsheviks decided to change the electoral rules and allow representation at the Congress not only from peasant soviets but also from the Poor Peasants' Committees set up by Bolshevik sympathisers in the villages to undertake grain requisitioning. This gerrymandering gave the Bolsheviks a majority at the Congress and the Left SRs felt cheated; tension between the two parties was therefore high.

On the opening day of the Congress, 6 July, Trotsky made an emergency statement to condemn the Left SRs for deliberately encouraging troops to carry out border violations in an attempt to provoke a war with Germany: to great applause he insisted that, if war was called for, then the Bolsheviks were quite capable of embarking on such a war and were constructing an army and recruiting officers and specialists from the old Army for this very purpose.[3] The Left SRs had lost patience with Trotsky and decided to resort to direct action. A party member, Jacob Blumkin, assassinated the German ambassador Count Mirbach as the Congress proceedings got underway in the hope that this would reignite the war with Germany. At the same time the Left SRs staged an insurrection in Moscow, taking control of the telegraph building and much of the centre of the city. It was not until the following day that the Bolsheviks managed to regain control of the city when the commander of the Latvian riflemen Joachim Vācietis, to whom the Party had turned for support, brought heavy artillery to the Bolsheviks' defence.

The rebellion of the Left SRs was not the only anti-Bolshevik uprising at this time. Once it was clear to the British that Trotsky had abandoned his policy of a breathing space, the role to be played by the British Expeditionary Force sailing to Archangel changed dramatically. It would no longer be welcome by Trotsky, but, on the contrary, would give backbone to the anti-Bolshevik forces. It would land, seize the railway line and advance to Yaroslavl, where it would gain access to the river Volga and from there co-ordinate its activity with the Czechoslovak Legion and the SR insurgents. To smooth its path, Lockhart arranged that SR sympathisers would stage an insurrection in Yaroslavl. Poor communications meant that when the British decided to delay their landing for a month it was too late to stop the planned Yaroslavl insurrection which began on 4 July; nevertheless, it took the Bolsheviks two-and-a-half weeks to reconquer this strategic town.[4]

Even more devastating for the Bolsheviks was the rebellion by Colonel Muraviev. Muraviev's organisational skills had enabled Bolshevik forces to stage a small recovery and on 8 July the 4th Latvian Regiment recaptured

Syzran. However, that very day Muraviev, who was a member of the Left SRs, decided to follow Moscow's lead and head his own rebellion against the Bolsheviks. He left his headquarters in Kazan and on arrival at Simbirsk seized control of the telegraph and radio station and other strategic points. Local SR armed groups had been tipped off in advance, and rallied to meet him. In a heady atmosphere telegrams were sent out announcing that war had been declared on Germany and that an alliance would be reached with the Czechoslovaks to this effect. Addressing rank and file soldiers he read out the Left SRs Moscow declaration of 6 July and assured them that, like Garibaldi, he would lead a People's Army against the occupier; he deliberately kept from his audience that the Bolsheviks were back in the saddle in Moscow and that they had been restored to power by the commander of the Latvian Riflemen. It was when this news was broken to the soldiers that confusion broke out and local Bolsheviks were able to regain a degree of initiative, forcing Muraviev to attend a public confrontation at which he was gunned down.[5]

On 10 July Trotsky summoned Vācietis and ordered him to replace Muraviev as commander in the east; but the seriousness of the situation on the Volga still had not been fully understood. When Vācietis went to call on Bonch-Bruevich to receive detailed orders, he was amazed that he was asked to wait while Bonch-Bruevich concluded discussions with the French Military Attaché about the German threat. Bonch-Bruevich had no detailed plans and simply told him to take whatever troops could be spared: "There is nothing serious on the Volga; take your Latvians, arrest the Czechoslovak bandits, put them in a prison camp, and that will be the end of the matter." With great difficulty Vācietis won permission to take with him his old regiment, the 5th Latvian Regiment, but once in Kazan, where he arrived on 16 July, he found, like Muraviev before him, that he was deprived of troops and constantly refused permission to establish "a front territory". He argued that he had to have more troops and that this meant conscripting regular forces from the locality, but he was firmly told that there were to be no changes in military organisation. On 1, 2 and 3 August Vācietis sent daily appeals for reinforcements, but to no avail. Instead he was accused by Bonch-Bruevich of insubordination because he refused to accept the official position that all troops raised in Kazan were to form part of the anti-German screens to defend Petrograd and Moscow. Moscow was so out of touch that on 6 August, the day Kazan fell to the People's Army and its Czechoslovak allies, Vācietis received a nonsensical order to advance towards Ekaterinburg.

Meanwhile Vācietis found low morale and insubordination everywhere. On 9 July the 4th Latvian Regiment unilaterally withdrew from recently reconquered Syzran: when ordered to advance towards Simbirsk to defend the town, they refused; by 23 July the regiment's commander had been forced to disarm a quarter of his men for refusing to obey orders. Simbirsk fell on 22 July. The People's Army began its assault on Kazan on 5 August, by the 6th it had captured the station, and at ten in the evening of the 7th Vācietis only controlled the upper storey of his head-quarters building; his escape with five comrades, by seizing a car and posing as Czechoslovaks, was the stuff of a *Boy's Own* adventure.[6]

Trotsky first addressed the situation on the Volga in a speech to an Extraordinary Session of the Soviet Executive on 29 July. He proclaimed Soviet Russia in danger, noted that people had been slow to appreci-ate what was happening, and reassured his audience that substantial forces were in the process of being transferred to the Volga so that the Czechoslovaks would soon be outnumbered. It was at this time that the Central Committee decided he should travel to the Volga, partly to get an up-to-date assessment and partly to end the growing feud between Bonch-Bruevich and Vācietis. Trotsky found himself carrying out a difficult balancing act, rejecting the criticisms made of Bonch-Bruevich but at the same time promising that reinforcements really were on the way.[7] He began to prepare the special train which, although it was initially staffed on the assumption he would be out of Moscow for just ten days, became his home for two-and-a-half years. As he recalled: "No one knew where to find anything; the simplest task became a complicated improvisation." The armoured train, so heavy it needed two engines to pull it, included a secretariat employing several secretaries and telephonists, a printing press, a telegraph station, a radio station, an electric power station, a library, a garage with trucks and light cars, a petrol tank, two aircraft and 20 to 30 handpicked riflemen and machine-gunners, mostly Latvian, all dressed in identical leather uniforms. The train pulled out of Moscow on the night of 7–8 August with Trotsky unaware that his destination, Kazan, was no longer in Bolshevik hands.[8]

Sviyazhsk

As Trotsky recalled in his memoirs, when he got to the front line, the town of Sviyazhsk, on the other side of the Volga from Kazan, no one knew where Vācieitis was, there was panic everywhere, "the situation looked hopeless . . . the fate of the revolution was hanging by a thread". Trotsky's assessment was confirmed by Larissa Reissner, a radical journalist who had volunteered to fight on the Volga. "The situation was understood by everyone as follows: another step backward would open the Volga to the enemy down to Nizhny and thus the road to Moscow. Further retreat meant the beginning of the end; the death sentence on the Republic of Soviets." For Reissner, the situation improved as soon as Trotsky arrived: "Every new day that this God-forsaken, poor railway siding held out against the far stronger enemy, added to its strength and raised its mood of confidence in a struggle which seemed so hopeless at the outset." The situation was indeed desperate. During his first inspection of the Red artillery, Trotsky found himself diving for cover as his position came under bombardment. No sooner had he returned to his carriage than it came under attack from an enemy airplane; in those early days "planes came and went, dropping their bombs on the station and railway cars". Trotsky's first report to Moscow was full of self-criticism: reinforcements had been promised, they had not arrived and this had created "a state of psychological collapse"; everything was needed, gunners, engineers, agitators; given the shaky state of morale, officers needed revolvers for "there [was] no hope of maintaining discipline without having revolvers".[9]

Morale was worst in the 4th Latvian Regiment. Trotsky recalled in his memoirs that "of all the regiments of the Latvian Division that had been so badly pulled to pieces, this was the worst; the men lay in the mud under the rain and demanded relief, but there was no relief available." The commander and chairman of the regimental committee demanded a period of rest and recuperation lest there be "consequences dangerous to the revolution". Summoned by Trotsky to his train, the two men repeated their statement, at which point Trotsky had them both arrested by the communications officer. But as he recalled: "There were only two of us on the train staff; the rest were fighting at the front; if the men arrested had shown any resistance, or if their regiment had decided to defend them and had left the front line, the situation might have been desperate; we should have had to surrender Sviyazhsk and the bridge across the Volga."[10]

Supplies were clearly the key to the situation, but obtaining supplies meant challenging Bonch-Bruevich's assessment that the events on the Volga were a sideshow. As soon as Trotsky arrived he reminded Bonch-Bruevich that it had already been agreed in principle that troops could be moved from quiet spots in the screen's defences to other duties; such troops would now be moved to the Volga; it was not a matter of creating new regiments, just redeploying forces where there was slack. On 13 August he informed the Supreme Military Council that it had been a mistake not to establish a War Commissariat for the Volga, and immediately began a series of organisational changes to set one up. Troops and supplies were what he was after. On 11 August he requested horses and aviation fuel from Moscow; the next day he learnt of "a huge quantity of supplies" in Nizhny and demanded its transfer; the day after that he demanded that sailors with artillery experience be sent to him; by 22 August it was field telephones and field guns, both inexplicably delayed up the supply chain in Nizhny.[11] Reissner noticed the impact of these actions.

The rainy August days thus passed one by one. The thin, poorly equipped lines did not fall back; the bridge remained in our hands and from the rear, from somewhere far away, reinforcements began to arrive . . . Real telephone wires began to attach themselves, some kind of enormous, cumbersome, lame apparatus began to operate . . . Here all of Trotsky's organisational genius was revealed, he managed to restore the supply lines, got new artillery and a few regiments . . . Newspapers arrived, boots and overcoats came . . . Trotsky was able to show this handful of defenders a calmness icier than theirs.[12]

It was not just a question of hustling for supplies, Trotsky was ready to improvise to get things done. The ability of the enemy to bomb his headquarters at will had convinced him of the importance of air power. "It was necessary to organise an aviation service; I called up an engineering pilot, Akashev, who, though an anarchist by conviction, was working with us; Akashev showed his initiative and quickly rounded up an air squadron." It was improvised, the planes were old and the pilots had no proper clothes, but it worked. After a week Trotsky could tell Lenin, "We have concentrated substantial forces of aviation here, which are terrorising bourgeois Kazan by dropping large quantities of dynamite on it; air intelligence has started to yield fruitful results." The use of airplanes enabled Vācietis both to gain an overall picture of the deployment of enemy forces and to make contact with isolated Red Army units operating to the north-east of Kazan. As he noted, "When our regiments were still too weak, with little fighting capacity, the detachments of airmen who were operating before Kazan did literally everything to substitute for our infantry, cavalry and artillery; they took off in all kinds of weather, circled over Kazan and over the enemy's flotilla, they dropped heavy bombs." On 25 August Trotsky called for the transfer of the Pskov air group to the Kazan Front to reinforce his makeshift units.[13]

Trotsky was determined to restore morale. Supplies would help, but more was needed. To improve the welfare of his soldiers he sent for both a dentist and a good band.[14] However, morale was also to be restored by reimposing discipline. The commander and regimental committee chairman of the 4th Latvian Regiment were accused of treason and brought before a Revolutionary Tribunal; to avoid provoking a mutiny they were not sentenced to death, but the Tribunal made clear this would be the last case of clemency.[15] Trotsky was as good as his word, for the next case of treachery was dealt with determinedly. The Red Army launched an offensive on 11 August which, while unsuccessful did forestall enemy action and restore a degree of stability to the front. Trotsky decided to move his headquarters from his exposed position in the Sviyazhsk railway siding to a steamboat on the Volga. However, the arrival of this steamer on 14 August prompted some of the reinforcements newly sent from Petrograd to seek an escape route; they seized control of the boat and tried to sail up river to the safety of Nizhny. Trotsky had the ringleaders, the commander and the commissar, brought before a tribunal and executed. Trotsky insisted that there could be no compassion shown to the communist commissar Panteleev, since he had made no attempt to prevent the mutiny and had participated fully in it.[16]

Discipline was also restored by employing "special mounted squads, ten men strong", about which Trotsky informed Lenin on 15 August. A week later he wrote a more detailed report on these units, recommending that they be generalised throughout the army to cope with incidents of flight and panic. Initially they had developed a 50-strong unit made up of ten soldiers each, but the experiment had proved so successful that they were now organised as "hundreds", ten units of ten men. Each of the "tens" was headed by a reliable communist and assisted by two other communists; the remaining seven were made up of either communists or "good, reliable" soldiers. Most "tens" were mounted, although some were infantrymen with wheeled machine guns. At the head of each "hundred" there was a communist cavalry officer. Everywhere, Trotsky said, such "hundreds" "will play a healthy and organising role" by confronting those ready to flee and forcing them back to the front.[17]

For Trotsky discipline simply meant that orders once given should be implemented. He had to put a stop to the situation where everything was discussed and debated. At Sviyazhsk he was furious that what he saw as "a well conceived operation" was wrecked by the wilful refusal of two divisional commanders to obey orders; the officers concerned got together with their commissars and started criticising the tactics Vācietis was using. Trotsky recalled: "I had both divisional commanders arrested; five commissars, Party members, came to see me to give explanations and to obtain protection; I handed them over to the courts for abandoning their posts without permission." After this the conclaves of commanders and commissars against higher authority came to a stop.[18]

Despite all Trotsky's efforts, the situation on the Volga remained precarious. On 28 August the People's Army staged a surprise offensive. In a long-range outflanking manoeuvre its elite forces crossed the Volga, circled round Sviyazhsk and cut the railway line to Trotsky's rear; Sviyazhsk was isolated and the armoured train sent to break the encirclement was captured. Panic followed. Troops rushed to the river to try and escape by steamer, the enemy's armoured train advanced almost into Sviyazhsk station, only Vācietis' staff stood firm, along with the staff of Trotsky's train. Larissa Reissner was convinced that the only thing that saved the Bolsheviks on that day was that the enemy was exhausted after its long march and simply did not appreciate that "opposing them was only a hastily thrown together handful of fighters". Trotsky did not see panic but a deliberate decision not to remove units from "the already shaky front": however, he too recalled a desperate eight-hour battle in which even his cook was mobilised to take up arms.

After such a close shave, the question of discipline had to be addressed one more time. When order was restored the next day 20 deserters were shot, among them several communists. Reissner justified the execution of "good comrades" on the grounds that "the whole army was agog with talk about communists . . . [who] could desert with impunity". As the official account of the executions put it: "The first to go were commanders and commissars who had abandoned positions entrusted to them; next, cowardly liars who played sick; finally, some deserters from among the Red Army men who refused to expiate their crime by taking part in the subsequent struggle." However, disloyal communists were not the only target. On the same day Trotsky decreed that in view of the albeit rare incidents of betrayal by officers, the families of unreliable officers should be detained as hostages.[19]

The reliability of former officers was something that caused Lenin increasing concern. It was not a concern Trotsky shared. There had been incidents of disloyalty but by and large Trotsky was full of praise for "the young General Staffers" who helped him construct the army; he said as much in a report to Moscow dated 11 August. So when Lenin raised with Trotsky the question of excluding general staffers from the high command, Trotsky replied on 23 August in fury.

It is essential to make the entire military hierarchy more compact and get rid of the ballast by means of extracting those General Staff officers that are efficient and loyal to us and not on any account by means of replacing them with Party ignoramuses.[20]

This spat between Lenin and Trotsky about the reliability of General Staff officers had arisen as part of a broader discussion about the future organisation of the army and its relationship to the Bolshevik Party. By

27 August Soviet Russia had finalised a trade deal with Imperial Germany; this minimised the danger of a German advance and brought into question the future role to be played by Bonch-Bruevich. On 20 August Trotsky decided to abolish the distinction between those troops which were part of the anti-German screen's defence, until now Bonch-Bruevich's responsibility, and those that were not; all troops were henceforth brought under the control of the Supreme Military Council. Bonch-Bruevich did not want to be associated with civil war rather than a war of defence and resigned on 21 August. Lenin and Trotsky agreed that the Supreme Military Council should be reconstituted as the Revolutionary Military Soviet (RVS) and that Bonch-Bruevich should be replaced with Vācietis once Kazan had been recaptured. Trotsky, however, argued that if Vācietis, who was not a Bolshevik, was made Commander-in-Chief, then he should have a free hand to appoint other non-Bolshevik officers; Lenin thought rather the reverse, that his choice should be constrained to politically reliable officers.[21]

Before this dispute could develop, Lenin was felled in an attempted assassination on 30 August. Trotsky set off for Moscow the next day, but, once it was clear Lenin would recover he hurried to return to Sviyazhsk staying in Moscow only long enough to finalise the formation of the RVS on 2 September. By the time of his return preparations for the reconquest of Kazan were well underway. After the near disaster of 28 August, reinforcements had started to flood in. The assault was to be carried out by torpedo boats transferred from the Baltic Sea. Trotsky took part in the attack which began on the night of 7–8 September and recalled how his boat was hit and the steering gear shot to pieces. On the eve of the assault Trotsky was supremely confident:

Propaganda, organisation, revolutionary example and repression produced the necessary change in a few weeks. A vacillating, unreliable and crumbling mass was transformed into a real army. Our artillery had emphatically established its superiority. Our flotilla controlled the river. Our airmen dominated the air. No longer did I doubt that we would take Kazan.[22]

It was not, however, an easy victory. Larissa Reissner recalled that "hundreds of soldiers lost their lives" in the battle, while Trotsky remembered "great losses". But Lenin summed up the situation accurately when Trotsky visited him to report his triumph in person, commenting "the game is won".[23]

The pattern of events at Sviyazhsk was to be repeated many times during the Civil War. Looking back Trotsky commented, "I almost never had occasion to accompany a victorious army . . . I retreated with troops but never advanced with them." Trotsky's great ability was to turn around the retreating soldier.

Even after defeats and retreats, the flabby, panicky mob would be transformed in two or three weeks into an efficient fighting force. What was needed for this? At once much and little. It needed good commanders, a few dozen experienced fighters, a dozen or so of communists ready to make any sacrifice, boots for the barefooted, a bath-house, an energetic propaganda campaign, food, underwear, tobacco and matches. The train took care of all this. We always had in reserve a few zealous communists to fill the breaches, a hundred or so of good fighting men, a small stock of boots, leather jackets, medicaments, machine-guns, field-glasses, maps, watches and all sorts of gifts.

When the rout had stopped, it was just a question of supply, but with nothing left in central depots after spring 1919 constant improvisation was needed to keep supplies coming, and Trotsky proved a past master at organising improvisation.[24]

Tsaritsyn

After the capture of Kazan, the Red Army advanced steadily against the People's Army, opening up an Eastern Front. It approached Samara on 19 September, but bitter fighting meant that the People's Army did not abandon the town until 6 October. As the Red Army advanced towards Ufa, its progress slowed still further and by the end of the month the People's Army had staged a counter-offensive, forcing the Red Army to begin a rather panicky retreat in early November. Political develop- ments then completely changed the nature of the fighting on the Eastern Front. On 18 November, acting in the spirit of General Kornilov, with whom he had first discussed counter-revolution in April 1917, Admiral Kolchak staged a coup against the SRs and their Czechoslovak allies who owed allegiance to the Constituent Assembly and established a right- wing dictatorship. Henceforth the Bolsheviks would not be fighting the SRs, whose democratic mandate as victors in the Constituent Assembly elections was impeccable, but White generals, hell-bent on restoring the old order, with or without the Tsar. Kolchak's coup and his subsequent persecution of the SR Party in Siberia ended serious fighting in the east until the end of December. The Red Army could resume its advance and capture Ufa, leaving Trotsky free to look to other fronts.

Fighting in southern Russia predated the SR insurrection and Czechoslovak rebellion, but until October 1918 it had been desultory and never seriously threatened the survival of the Bolshevik regime. In the first months after the Bolshevik seizure of power General Kornilov and other leading counter-revolutionary generals had headed south to the Don and Kuban regions; but their attempt to break out of this isolated peripheral region had been frustrated by Red forces and by the end of February 1918 they were confined to the remote Kuban steppe. German occupation of Ukraine, and then parts of Russian territory not at first envisaged by the Treaty of Brest Litovsk, meant that these White forces were protected on one flank and able to regroup, and from August 1918 they began a series of assaults on Tsaristyn. The first assault made little impact, and the second in September was similarly ineffective; however, the third assault, in early October, nearly succeeded. Don Cossacks surrounded the city and fighting took place in the outskirts before Red reinforcements arrived in the nick of time, after a forced march of 500 miles undertaken mostly at night to avoid Cossack patrols. Stalin, who had been sent to the town on 7 June, took the credit for this victory, although others asked why, since the Reds had overwhelming superiority in artillery, the Whites had ever come as close to success as they did.

Relations between Trotsky and Stalin had been perfectly amicable over the summer. Trotsky had had no problem with Stalin being sent to Tsaritsyn, and was quite happy that a month after his arrival his duties were expanded from ensuring Moscow's oil supplies to organising the defence of the region and taking charge of the local railway network. Problems developed between them only after the abolition of the Supreme Military Council and the appointment of Vācietis as Commander-in-Chief. Stalin's forces in Tsaritsyn had been entirely independent from the Supreme Military Council but its abolition and the decision to bring all military forces under the control of the new RVS meant that Stalin's forces were to be subjected to a new hierarchy of military regulation. In particular Stalin had to accept the deployment of "military specialists", the term used for officers from the old army. Stalin was suspicious of them. As soon as he arrived in Tsaritsyn he discovered a counter-revolutionary plot involving military specialists, prompting him to put all his faith in bringing on young pro-Bolshevik non-commissioned officers to form a new officer corps. At the same time, Stalin had institutionalised a system whereby Bolshevik political commissars were able to influence decisions on purely military matters, a form of collective decision-making which contradicted Trotsky's promise that officers would have absolute authority in military matters. Stalin distrusted military specialists and had already written to Trotsky in mid July criticising their work.[25]

A row began on 2 October. Having established an RVS at national level, designated the Republican RVS, Trotsky envisaged a series of subordinate RVSs on the individual fronts. Similarly, having appointed Vācietis Commander-in-Chief, he had designated a series of front commanders. But Stalin seemed to be in no hurry to establish an RVS for the Southern Front or even, when it was established on 17 September, to co-ordinate his actions with its new commander. Although talks had taken place with Stalin, nothing had been tied down in a formal decision. On top of this, routine requests for intelligence reports had been systematically ignored. Trotsky left the Eastern Front, had a hasty meeting in Moscow on 3 October, and then travelled on south, explaining his standpoint in a message sent from his train on the 4th. He informed Sverdlov, the *de facto* secretary of the Bolshevik Party at this time, that he would of course "be careful with the Tsaritsyn people", but the essence of the conflict was this: Stalin "had established a collective command, which we have categorically rejected and which, independently of the personality of the commander, leads to a dissipation of command and anarchy; here is the crux of the matter".[26]

He was equally blunt in a letter to Lenin sent the same day which attacked not only Stalin but Klim Voroshilov, one of the non-commissioned officers Stalin was so keen to promote.

I categorically insist on Stalin's recall. Things are going from bad to worse on the Tsaritsyn Front, despite the superabundance of military forces. Voroshilov is able to command a regiment, but not an army of 50,000 men. Nonetheless, I will retain him as commander of the 10th Tsaritsyn Army on condition that he places himself under the orders of the Commander of the Southern Front, General Sytin . . . [Because autumn is approaching] there is no time for diplomatic negotiations. Tsaritsyn must either obey orders or get out of the way. We have a colossal superiority of forces but total anarchy at the top. This can be put right within 24 hours given firm and resolute support your end.

To reinforce the point Trotsky forwarded to Lenin the next day a telegram from Vācietis demanding "Stalin's military order no. 18 must be countermanded since the actions of Stalin are destroying all my plans."[27]

Stalin had written to Lenin about Trotsky's behaviour in a similarly forthright manner on 3 October.

The point is that Trotsky, generally speaking, cannot get by without noisy gestures. At Brest he delivered a blow to the cause by his incredibly "Leftist" gesturing . . . Now he delivers a further blow by his gesture about discipline, and yet all this Trotskyist discipline amounts to in reality is the most prominent leaders on the war front peering up the backside of military specialists from the camp of the "non-party" counter-revolutionaries and not preventing them from wrecking the front. (Trotsky calls this not interfering in operational matters.) . . . Remove Trotsky, since I am afraid that his unhinged commands, if they are repeated, will put the front into the hands of so-called military specialists who merit no trust at all.[28]

On 5 October Stalin insisted in a message to Sverdlov that Trotsky had been insulting and had suddenly broken off the talks aimed at reconciliation. The problem was that there had been a series of contradictory and confusing orders sent by Trotsky, some sent openly rather than in code, and that while "accepting that centralisation was essential" it was impossible to submit to just anyone. The issue should be shelved until Stalin had a chance to come to Moscow.[29]

Trotsky had clearly resolved to use party channels to have Stalin withdrawn from Tsaritsyn and military channels to have Voroshilov subordinated to the Commander of the Southern Front. He got his way and Stalin resigned from the Southern RVS on 9 October.[30] Stalin's recall demanded some diplomacy on the Party leadership's part. Sverdlov was sent in a special train to bring Stalin back and en route Sverdlov suggested on 23 October that Trotsky and Stalin should meet. Stalin, he explained, was very willing to compromise and had persuaded Voroshilov to comply with orders from the centre. Stalin was also now ready to work with Sytin on the Southern Front RVS, where the knowledge he had gained over the last six months could be put to good use. Sverdlov urged Trotsky to "put aside former differences and arrange to work together as Stalin so much desires". When the meeting took place Stalin raised the future of Voroshilov and his associates: "Do you really wish to dismiss them all, they are fine boys?" Trotsky retorted: "Those fine boys will ruin the revolution, which cannot wait for them to grow out of their adolescence."[31] When Trotsky arrived in Tsaritsyn he informed Lenin on 27 October that Voroshilov was a conscientious worker who needed to be put within the framework of a definite system of operations. The situation at Tsaritsyn then eased when on 1 November Vacietis decided that Sytin was not, after all, the best man to be Commander of the Southern Front and had him replaced.[32] Stalin's reappointment to the Southern RVS seemed to mark the end of the crisis.

In reality, however, the row had only been postponed. With Allied victory in the First World War and the signing of the armistice on 11 November, the future of German-occupied Ukraine suddenly came to the fore. The arrival less than a fortnight later of Allied ships off the coast of Novorossiisk showed that Britain and France were determined to influence the outcome of events. The Bolsheviks were determined to re-establish a Soviet Ukraine, and this task was allocated to Stalin, who established a government in waiting at Kharkov. There, he was joined once more by Voroshilov. As plans were laid for the reconquest of Ukraine so, from Trotsky's perspective, "Stalin, Voroshilov and Co." had simply regrouped in Kharkov.[33] Trotsky complained about this to Sverdlov on 10 January 1919, stressing that "the Tsaritsyn way of conducting matters which resulted in the collapse of the Tsaritsyn Army cannot be permitted in Ukraine". This time he did not get the degree of support he had received three months earlier. Lenin replied and urged him to make peace: "I think that it is necessary to make every effort for joint work with Stalin." Trotsky's response made few concessions: "Compromise is of course necessary, but not a rotten one; the fact of the matter is that all the Tsaritsynites have now congregated at Kharkov . . . I consider Stalin's patronage of the Tsaritsyn tendency a most dangerous ulcer, worse than any treason or betrayal by military specialists." The crux of the matter, he said, was that "in a month's time we shall have to bear the consequences of the Tsaritsyn muddle, this time opposed not by Cossacks but by the Anglo-French".[34]

The Military Opposition

By the time of the Eighth Party Congress on 18–23 March 1919 the supporters of Voroshilov had formed themselves into a political faction determined to challenge what they saw as Trotsky's undue reliance on military specialists. To many Bolsheviks Trotsky's support of the military specialist could seem cavalier. Although on 2 October he learnt of the betrayal of a certain Lebedev and ordered the arrest of his family, it was more usual for Trotsky to intervene to get arrested officers released. On 4 October he asked the Tver security police (*cheka*) to release a certain Sulimov who he argued was needed at the front. A week later he wrote two telegrams on the subject of arrested specialists: the first was to Zinoviev, responding to the arrest of 16 communication officers and asking for the release of those "for whom there were not individual charges"; the second was to Dzerzhinsky, the head of the *cheka*, asking for the release of the Tver Aviation Group commander, who had been arrested "just because he was a former officer". On 16 October he complained about the action of the Nizhnyi *cheka*, which persecuted army officers in the town while going about their legitimate business of touring barracks and bases; the *cheka*'s duty, he reminded them, was not to interfere with the work of military officers, but to keep tabs on the families of those suspected of being unreliable and arresting those families should the need arise. A few days later he was again contacting Dzerzhinsky asking for the release of officers. Early in November he took up the case of an officer arrested by the Tsaritsyn *cheka* while Stalin was in charge.[35] He even proposed that in those cases where there was no direct, serious charge against the arrested officers, they be put at his disposal if they agreed to serve the Red cause. He also asked that "General Staff officers held as hostages" should be put at his disposal.[36]

Those opposed to Trotsky began to argue that he was not only soft on officers, but also persecuted Bolshevik commissars. Trotsky's decision to execute Panteleev while in Sviyazhsk suddenly became important. Documents from the RVS of the 5th Army, which his critics had studied, revealed that no individual charges had been brought against Panteleev. Trotsky was forced to explain to Lenin that Panteleev had not been executed because his regiment had deserted, but because he too had fled and tried to seize a steamer and escape to Nizhny; there were no individual charges because there was nothing individual about his conduct, he was just another deserter. It was not only those close to Voroshilov and Stalin who made such claims. Zinoviev too had concerns, and a commissar close to him, M. M. Lashevich, protested at the end of October when Trotsky put the blame for the way the Red Army had faltered and then retreated on the Eastern Front at this time on poor work by commissars; not surprisingly the commissars blamed disloyal officers.[37]

In these rows Trotsky did not back down, and neither did his opponents. At the end of December he issued a special appeal "To Commissars and Military Specialists", noting recent clashes and criticising the attitude adopted by some commissars; the military were to have full freedom of action in the sphere allocated to them and commissars should show them due respect and deference. On 30 December he expressed the hope that he was turning to this issue "for the last time" and protested at the "wholesale and frequently unjustified attacks on the military specialists". But a member of Voroshilov's staff attacked him publicly in *Pravda* on 25 December and Lashevich insisted on raising the Panteleev case in the Politburo. On 11 January Trotsky wrote a long exposition of the Panteleev case, sending it to Sverdlov and the editorial board of *Pravda*.[38]

Under insistent criticism from the Military Opposition, Lenin began to doubt whether Trotsky was right. He decided to back Trotsky only towards the end of February. Trotsky returned to Moscow for the opening of the Eighth Party Congress and during a government meeting Lenin passed Trotsky a note saying, "What if we fire all the specialists and appoint Lashevich as Commander-in-Chief"; Lashevich had some military experience, having been a sergeant during the First World War. Trotsky passed back a note with the words "infantile nonsense". When Lenin later asked him why he had been so dismissive, Trotsky asked him how many former officers were serving in the Red Army. Lenin confessed he had no idea and was astonished when Trotsky explained that 76 per cent of officers had served in the Tsar's Army and only 12.8 per cent were "fledgling Red commanders". From that point Lenin backed Trotsky on the issue of military specialists.[39]

Lenin, however, offered no support when it came to commissars. In an order issued on 2 March Trotsky noted that the internal service regulations of the Red Army made no mention of the rights and duties of commissars. Trotsky explained that this was completely logical since it was clear that "the institution of commissar is not a permanent institution"; sooner or later, he believed "one-man management in the sphere of administration and command" would be established.[40] Although the Eighth Bolshevik Party Congress defeated the Military Opposition to the extent that it put an end to the baiting of military specialists, it reinforced the position of the military commissars rather than bringing their role to an end. Moves by both Stalin and Zinoviev ensured that Trotsky should be instructed to pay more attention to communist opinion in the army.

Zinoviev sent Trotsky a copy of the minutes of the Central Committee meeting of 25 March which made clear that unanimity at the Congress had only been achieved by passing resolutions which were not made public. These were to reorganise the General Staff; to clarify the role played by Field Headquarters; and to establish regular monthly meetings between Trotsky and leading commissars. Trotsky's response was one of incandescent rage. Did this decision mean he should stop touring the fronts and direct the war from Moscow, he demanded of Lenin? Trotsky also rejected Zinoviev's view that the Military Opposition had accepted Trotsky's stance on military specialists. According to Trotsky, the Military Opposition still represented "a plebeian protest at the 'wooing' of military specialists" which expressed the political attitude "not of a triumphant class become its own master and its own builder" but merely reflected "instinctive hatred towards a stratum which used formerly to occupy a leading position in society".[41]

The Kolchak Offensive

Trotsky did not attend the Eighth Party Congress; he was called back to the front in mid March because of the dramatically worsening situation in the East. The collapse of the Eastern Front was largely the consequence of the Bolsheviks' agrarian policy. When the fighting against the SRs and Czechoslovaks had begun in May 1918, Trotsky, like all the Bolshevik leaders, had linked the unrest to the activities of the kulaks. The kulaks were "beasts of prey, exploiters of hunger and misfortune", while the armed Moscow proletarians engaged in grain requisitioning were taking part in "a crusade against the kulaks".[42] However, towards the end of November 1918, Lenin began to have doubts about this peasant policy. If in the first week of that month he had been talking about advancing towards large-scale socialised farming with the support of the poor peasant, by the end of the month he was identifying middle peasants as the Party's main ally and even hinting that kulaks could be managed: "For the middle peasant we say – no force under any circumstances; for the big peasant we say – our aim is to bring him under the control of the grain monopoly and fight him when he violates the monopoly and conceals grain." By December 1918 Lenin had gone still further and taken it on himself to resolve a number of incidents where local soviets had gratuitously antagonised the middle peasants, incidents which had occurred in Yaroslavl, Tver and Vologda. On 4 December 1918 a decree was signed quietly abolishing the Poor Peasants' Committees.

In mid December 1918 Kolchak, having settled scores with the SRs, began to advance and on 24–5 December he captured Perm. When Stalin was sent to investigate why this strategically sensitive town had fallen with such ease, he focused on the failings of the Poor Peasants' Committees; the key lesson of Stalin's report was that peasants opposed the agrarian policies of the Bolsheviks. Trotsky had found the same. In late November 1918 he faced a widespread peasant rebellion in the rear near Voronezh; it was followed in late December by a rebellion of peasant troops further to the south and west in Valuiki, Urazovo and Kupyansk. Trotsky had not yet taken on board Lenin's views about the middle peasant and condemned the rebellion as the work of "Left SRs, Anarchists and Counter-revolutionaries". He brought in loyal troops, surrounded the insurgents, and on 27 January issued the following proclamation:

I have come to the front in order to put an end to your shameful and dishonourable mutiny . . . I have instructed the Soviet authorities to place your families under temporary arrest and to seal all your property in villages and towns. On behalf of the Council of People's Commissars I order that all instigators, traitors, self-seekers are to be crushed, shot, wiped off the face of the earth. There is to be no quarter for anyone . . . Whoever remains in the ranks of the mutineers twelve hours after the publication of this order will meet with ruin and death.

It was perhaps not surprising that, in the popular view, Lenin gained a reputation for being pro-peasant, whereas Trotsky was branded anti-peasant. On 6 February 1919 Trotsky wrote a *Letter to the Middle Peasantry* to counter the rumours that Lenin favoured the middle peasants, whereas he was their irreconcilable enemy. He expressed regret for a number of cases where peasants had been mistreated by soldiers with a low level of political consciousness and stressed that "the middle peasant, provided he has not been duped by kulak lies, ought to be our friend". He then denounced most stories about the Red Army's misbehaviour as Left SR slander. "The wretched clique of adventurers and political rogues who call themselves Left SRs are now the principle centre from which come lies and slanders for duping the more backward sections of the population," he said. "They are spreading false stories about the Red Army being formed to fight the middle peasants."[43]

As the worst of the winter weather eased in early March 1919 Kolchak renewed his offensive, and the speed of his advance was linked to the continued hostility of the middle peasant to Bolshevik agrarian policy. As Kolchak advanced, so peasant disturbances broke out on the Volga, in Syzran, Simbirsk and Samara. In addition, many of Kolchak's advance guard were soldiers recruited into the People's Army by the SRs, who had then retreated to Siberia in autumn 1918 and now looked forward to going home. No wonder Trotsky took up the cause of the middle peasant with renewed enthusiasm. On 15 March 1919 he wrote of justified complaints at the behaviour of the Red Army and reminded soldiers that "the kulak is our enemy; but the middle peasant, the labouring harvester, should be our friend and brother worker". Its impact was limited; as Trotsky travelled east, his train was delayed when peasant insurgents blew up the track. On 21 March he wrote to Lenin and Stalin calling for a special inspection team to be sent from the centre: peasant unrest had been caused by the poor functioning of the local soviet and Party administration and the centre had to be seen to be putting things right. "An inspection team of the highest authority for work in the rear of the Eastern Front is essential for calming the peasant elements . . . the middle peasants are exasperated by the manifest malpractices of official institutions."[44]

It was not difficult to counter Kolchak's offensive. Kolchak had absolutely no intention of giving land to the peasantry in the areas he controlled, and once this became clear the peasant insurrections ceased. The other reason for Kolchak's dramatic advance was also easily addressed. Trotsky informed Lenin on 25 March: "The system of slackness, grumbling and criticism implanted from above undoubtedly constituted the most important reason for the falling off in the Army; instead of an order being immediately executed, it became a subject for discussion." Orders, such as the one for retreating soldiers to blow up the bridge at Ufa, had been ignored. The lessons of Sviyazhsk simply had to be learned once more and when discipline had been restored by the team on Trotsky's train, the situation began to improve. Only a month after Trotsky left Moscow, he could return for a Central Committee meeting on 18 April and report that the situation had improved dramatically. Vācietis could report on 1 May that "the Eastern Front has been reinforced and strengthened; we are holding the enemy's attack and on certain sectors have begun to go over to the offensive ourselves". The Kolchak danger was over.[45]

Disintegration of the Southern Front

A fortnight after the start of offensive operations against Kolchak, Trotsky completed work on a report about a different crisis he faced, the Don Rebellion. He had intended to bring this report to a meeting of the Politburo in Moscow in mid May, but he turned back to Kharkov on 16 May because the situation had become so grave. Lenin and Trotsky's message about wooing the middle peasantry had not been taken on board by the Don Bureau of the Communist Party. It had one aim, to destroy the power base of the Cossacks who had for so long been a symbol of the Tsar's repressive regime. Although military commanders on the Southern Front saw the value of co-operating with those Cossacks sympathetic to the new regime, of which there were quite a number, the Don Bureau did not. Calling at the end of January for "the wholesale destruction of upper elements of Cossack society", the Don Bureau introduced a reign of terror as Cossacks were disarmed, their grain surpluses seized and their land confiscated in preparation for the introduction of collective farms. Those who resisted were subjected to terror; in what was possibly the worst incident 260 Cossacks were killed in one village.

By 10 March resistance to this policy had become open rebellion and by the end of the month much of the Don region was "liberated" from Bolshevik control. Instead of having numerical advantage over the enemy, the Red Army was soon outnumbered, a situation made worse when a typhus epidemic broke out. The Bolsheviks' response was to send in an expeditionary force, responsible for at least another 8,000 executions; not surprisingly some Red Army units, especially those composed of peasants, defected rather than be associated with such crimes.

The rebellion simply got worse. Initially these Don rebels fought completely independently of the White generals still confined to the Kuban. However, on 9 May General Denikin sent an emissary in one of his British-supplied biplanes to the rebels. Soon they were receiving regular air drops. By contrast, reports on the state of the Red Army described barefoot men refusing to fight until they were properly clothed; Vācietis informed Trotsky on 7 May that the Southern Front was only getting 40 per cent of the supplies it needed. Not surprisingly, by 8 June the rebels and Denikin had linked up and the Whites had escaped from their confinement in Kuban and gained access to Ukraine.[46]

What made this doubly disastrous for the Bolsheviks was that they had effectively also lost control of Ukraine. Trotsky had been keen for the Bolsheviks to re-establish a Soviet Ukraine as the German Army withdrew and had appointed Antonov-Ovseenko to lead the Ukrainian Red Army. However, the liberation of Ukraine from German rule was not the achievement of the Bolsheviks alone; in the south-west and south it had been the achievement of the Left SRs and their anarchist allies. Nevertheless, when the Bolsheviks formally established the Ukrainian Soviet Government on 6 March 1919 they not only took power alone but also ignored Lenin's appeals to conciliate the middle peasantry, drawing up instead plans for collective farming. The peasant response was immediate: revolts broke out on a wide scale, 93 in April with a further 26 in May. Lenin, happy to see a change in land policy, rejected out of hand Antonov-Ovseenko's view that the situation had become so severe that in Ukraine the Left SRs needed to be brought into a coalition government.

Trotsky was also concerned at the military implications of what Antonov-Ovseenko was proposing. Conciliating the Left SRs and anarchists meant, in the military sphere, co-operating with their partisan guerrilla forces. These might have been effective in harrying the retreating Germans and their Ukrainian nationalist allies, but they would be no match for Denikin with his Allied supplies. Just as it had been essential to create a centralised professional army in Russia in summer and autumn 1918, so in spring 1919 it was essential to create a centralised Red Army in Ukraine, an army which would recognise its historic duty and concentrate its forces against Denikin. On 1 May Trotsky sent a detailed memorandum to the Central Committee outlining Antonov-Ovseenko's failings in this regard. Instead of making concessions to these partisan leaders, "the moment has now arrived when it is necessary to state, firmly and clearly, that the Revolution has derived all that can be derived from improvised insurgent detachments, and that henceforth these detachments become not only dangerous but positively disastrous to the cause of the revolution." These units should be "purged of their openly criminal units" to establish firm discipline and end the system of electing officers.[47]

However, Antonov-Ovseenko actively sought concessions, heading a delegation in person to the two main partisan leaders, the Left SR sympathiser Ataman Grigoriev and the anarchist Makhno. Antonov-Ovseenko's talks with both these leaders convinced him that collaboration was possible, the sticking point was political representation in the Ukrainian Soviet Government. But before further progress could be made, on 7 May Ataman Grigoriev rebelled against the Bolshevik Government. The rebellion was quickly suppressed, but its outbreak reinforced Trotsky's hand. He responded by calling on 17 May for Antonov-Ovseenko's dismissal and demanding "an implacable liquidation of the partisan movement of separatism and left-wing hooliganism" combined with a complete reorientation of forces towards the Denikin front. On 22 May he ordered the formation of a special *cheka* battalion "to discipline Makhno's anarchist bands" and placed Voroshilov in charge of combating the partisan tendency in the Second Ukrainian Army.[48]

The strategic problem for Trotsky was that Makhno, based in the town of Gulyai Polye in southern Ukraine, was the first to confront Denikin's forces as they emerged from Kuban. By the end of May Makhno's forces were in steady retreat, but that did not prevent him from continuing with his political agenda. Makhno wanted to call a congress of soviets from the area he controlled for 15 June to debate why there was no peasant representation in the Ukrainian Soviet Government; for the Bolsheviks this was tantamount to organising an insurrection. Trotsky argued it was impossible for Makhno to talk of accepting local soviet power while refusing to recognise the central government, especially when, under the arrangements introduced by Antonov-Ovseenko, the central government had helped to arm him. As Denikin advanced and Makhno retreated, so Trotsky railed against Makhno. It was time, he said on 2 June, "to finish with this anarcho-kulak debauchery". When Gulyai Polye was captured by Denikin on 6 June – Makhno himself was rescued by Voroshilov – Trotsky's fury knew no bounds. His order of 8 June entitled "An End to Makhnovism" denounced "corrupted regiments which do not obey military orders" which would be "wiped off the face of the earth with their commanders the first to suffer punishment".[49]

Given Trotsky's hostility to Antonov-Ovseenko's policies and the whole Makhno affair it was ironic that Lenin became convinced at this time that Trotsky was not fulfilling Party decisions with sufficient vigour. Lenin had long been worried that the existence of a separate Ukrainian Soviet Government, especially one with its own Commissariat of War and its own Red Army, was producing a dangerous division of authority. Antonov-Ovseenko's behaviour seemed to prove it, and he feared that events had drifted towards Ukrainian separatism. Lenin wrote angrily to Trotsky on 2 June: "I am extremely surprised, and to put it mildly, distressed, that you have not put through the directive of the Central Committee and removed Antonov-Ovseenko"; meanwhile, he went on, "Voroshilov is making off with military stores and there is complete chaos, with no effective aid being given to [confront Denikin in] the Donbas." Trotsky replied on the 3rd insisting that the "reproaches are unfounded": he had carried out the decisions of the Central Committee, but before they were finalised he had been forced to move to the Don, from where communication with both Moscow and Kiev had been difficult; as soon as a replacement could be found, Antonov-Ovseenko would go, there was no other reason for the delay in carrying out the Central Committee decision. Lenin's response was brusque: now Trotsky was back on the spot the issue should be resolved at once, ignoring Trotsky's view that the Army could not be left without a commander.[50]

Thus, at the very moment when the double disaster of the Don Rebellion and the collapse of the Ukraine had enabled Denikin to advance into southern Russia, relations between Lenin and Trotsky had been soured by Trotsky's apparent, and it was only apparent, unwillingness to accede to Central Committee decisions, even though the Eighth Party Congress had called on him to ensure that he made every effort to co-ordinate his actions more fully with the Party leadership. This helps explain why Lenin sided with Stalin when the issue of military specialists again came to the fore.

In May 1919 a new front suddenly opened up in Russia's Civil War. From newly independent Estonia, formed after the withdrawal of German troops from the Baltic, General Yudenich sent a force against Petrograd. This surprise attack very nearly succeeded. Stalin was ordered to Petrograd on 17 May and from the moment of his arrival on the 19th instigated a number of desperate measures to save the former capital. At once he sensed that counter-revolutionary intrigue was part of the problem, something he had long suspected and had raised with Lenin before. Stalin sent Lenin a long report on 4 June which detailed his suspicions and confirmation came a few days later when on 13 June two forts which protected the approaches to Petrograd rebelled; their action was supported by British motor launches operating from Finland called in by the British spy Paul Dukes, who had access to all the decisions made by the Northern Front RVS. It was a close shave for the Bolsheviks, but the loss of the forts proved to be the worst of the crisis; two days later the forts were recaptured and Stalin could return to Moscow.

Stalin had claimed in his report of 4 June that "it is evident that not only the Chief of Staff of 7th Army [based near Petrograd] works for the Whites", but "also the entire Staff of the Republican RVS", in particular those responsible for assigning reserves. It was, he insisted, "now up to the Central Committee to draw the necessary inferences – will it have the courage to do it!" Among the suggestions he made was that "Party workers who urge the military specialists on against the commissars" should be assigned to other duties since they "demoralise the vital core of our army". The Petrograd affair had produced ample evidence of treachery among the Petrograd command, Stalin's allegation that it extended further into the Republican RVS was more difficult to substantiate, but as he commented, "the analysis of evidence is continuing and new 'possibilities' are opening up". Thus by June 1919 not only had a combination of the Don rebellion and the collapse of Ukraine enabled Denikin to enter southern Russia, but a combination of genuine misunderstandings on Lenin's part and deliberate stirring on Stalin's part had reopened the issue of Trotsky's conduct of the war and the absence of close Party control.[51]

Command Crisis and Victory

Although Vācietis had first suggested as early as 7 May that it was time to concentrate on the danger posed by Denikin, at the start of June 1919 it was still the common currency of all Bolsheviks that Kolchak and the Eastern Front remained the more important. There were, however, differences of emphasis even before the crisis on the Southern Front forced a reassessment of this conviction. In a telegram of 1 June Trotsky made clear that, since it was "clear we cannot at present advance to Vladivostok", the offensive should continue only until an agreed defensive line was reached. This was not the view of the Eastern Front Commander, S. S. Kamenev, who on 6 June submitted plans for an immediate advance on Krasnoufimsk en route for Ekaterinburg. Vācietis shared Trotsky's assessment and considered an advance on Krasnoufimsk as quite unrealistic, given the pressure on the Southern and Petrograd Fronts. On 12 June he ordered Kamenev to establish a defensive line on the Kama and Belaya rivers, where his troops were currently deployed. Kamenev, however, was supported in his plans by his military commissars, in particular Lashevich who had clashed with Trotsky the previous autumn; Lashevich believed that, since plans for an insurrection in Kolchak's rear were already well advanced, the admiral really could be annihilated within a few weeks. So he decided to take up Kamenev's case when the Central Committee held a plenary session, in Trotsky's absence, on 15 June. This lobbying worked and Vācietis was instructed "to continue the offensive against Kolchak". Vācietis appeared to accept this, but on 22 June ordered Kamenev to shift the direction of his advance from due east to south-east, towards Zlatoust, away from Ekaterinburg and towards the railway network leading back to the Volga and the south. To Trotsky's fury, on 3 July Vācietis was dismissed by the Central Committee for failing to support its policy in the east and replaced by Kamenev.

By then the utter irrelevance of the dispute about the east was clear for all to see. The Party's attempt to impose its direction of the war meant that it sacked the Red Army's Commander-in-Chief for remembering the importance of the Southern Front, and ordering troops to march to a railway line linked to the south, just when Denikin's advance was accelerating alarmingly. Kharkov fell on 25 June, with Ekaterinoslav and Tsaritsyn following on the 30th. The removal of Vācietis was absurd, but this was not the only decision taken by the Central Committee at this fateful meeting. An issue left unresolved after the Eighth Party Congress was the location of the Field Headquarters of the Republican RVS; this was now moved from its base at Serpukhov to Moscow. At the same time the composition of the RVS itself was changed, reducing its size, removing some of Trotsky's allies and bringing in supporters of the campaign for an eastern offensive. Opposed to all these moves, and supported by no Politburo colleagues, Trotsky resigned, left the Central Committee meeting, slammed the door and took to his bed complaining of ill health.

The Central Committee did not accept his resignation when it met again on 5 July and in a series of conciliatory gestures made clear that it would continue to supply the Southern Front where Trotsky was urged to concentrate his efforts. Back there on 8 July Trotsky learned that Stalin's vendetta against Vācietis had succeeded and that the former Commander-in-Chief had been arrested on charges of counter-revolutionary activity. The charge was ludicrous. Trotsky commented in his memoirs that "perhaps before going to sleep, the chap had been reading Napoleon's biography and confided his ambitious dreams to two or three younger officers", for the only "evidence" against Vācietis, as Lenin informed Trotsky on 9 July in response to the latter's query, was that Vācietis had shared lodgings with a General Staff officer who had allegedly been linked to a conspiracy of other General Staff officers within Field Headquarters.[52] Trotsky immediately went onto the offensive to prevent a new assault on military specialists. On 9 July 1919 he announced:

In connection with the treacherous conspiracy by a section of the commanding personnel on the Petrograd Front articles have appeared in the press which are being interpreted as a sign of a change in Soviet policy in military matters, particularly where the military specialists are concerned . . . giving rise to feelings of alarm and uncertainty. I therefore consider it necessary to make clear Soviet policy in military matters remains unchanged.

When a Kharkov paper put the collapse of the Southern Front down to the treachery of officers who had gone over in droves to Denikin, Trotsky set the record straight. At a series of rallies on 11 and 14 July Trotsky pushed through resolutions stressing that policy towards military specialists should not and would not change.[53]

Tension between Trotsky and the rest of the Bolshevik Party leadership heightened as Kamenev turned his attention to the Southern Front. Saved by the last minute decision of Vācietis to divert forces to Zlatoust, he now proposed an assault on Denikin which would make use of these forces assembled on the Volga. He wanted a two-pronged assault, one on the right flank to the east of Kharkov, but the other more major attack on the left flank down the lower Volga and then, to Denikin's rear, into Kuban. Trotsky, supported by the discredited Vācietis, argued that Denikin had to be tackled head-on in the Donets Basin, where there were large industrial towns that could be expected to rally to the Bolshevik side and where the Red Army would not find itself surrounded by hostile Cossacks. The Central Committee backed Kamenev on 23 July and called for the offensive to begin three weeks later.

It was hardly surprising that the Southern Front Commander was unimpressed with the plan drawn up by the new Commander-in-Chief. When on 27 July he told Trotsky he was not happy to implement the plan, Trotsky informed Lenin and proposed the appointment of a new Southern Front Commander, prepared to be more co-operative. Lenin, apparently assuming Trotsky was making mischief, ignored the request; he did, however, appoint a former commissar on the Eastern Front to the Southern Front RVS to limit Trotsky's freedom of movement, prompting an immediate protest from Trotsky. Unable to challenge openly a plan endorsed by the Central Committee, Trotsky complained that the supplies promised him on the Southern Front were not in place and "the entire operation may come to grief over the issue of small arms ammunition". On 1 August he was even blunter, telling Lenin, "Neither agitation nor repressive measures can make an unshod, unclothed, famished, lice-infested army combat fit; the necessary turning point can only be attained after supplies have been received." Angry disagreements continued during

Trotsky's tour of the western edge of the Southern Front in the first week of August. Trotsky's motives were by now suspect in Moscow. He wrote angrily to the Central Committee on 7 August: "You have again got things wrong as a result of your careless reading of telegrams . . . in future it will be a case of my having to express myself at greater length, so as to avoid misunderstandings with the Politburo, such as have been so frequent of late." Writing two days later Trotsky complained: "I strongly request Moscow to give up its policy of fantastic apprehensions."[54]

When the Kamenev offensive opened on 14 August the right flank thrust east of Kharkov soon faltered. Although Kupyansk was briefly captured, the Red Army was driven back to its starting point by early September. The outflanking assault down the Volga was more successful, and by 5 September the Red Army was approaching Tsaritsyn, but they were unable to consolidate their position. This was largely because of stiff opposition from Denikin's British tanks and aircraft, but partly because the Bolsheviks had to divert troops to combat a daring raid by the White General Mamontov, who cut behind the Red lines and briefly captured Tambov. By mid September the Red offensive had petered out and Denikin had resumed his advance, even though the Red Army was beginning to outnumber Denikin's forces. In August Trotsky read a detailed report on the Don rebellion which concluded that the Red Army had failed to quell the region because it had not developed independent cavalry units, but had dispersed mounted troops among infantry battalions. This lesson, combined with the spectacular success of Mamontov's raid, convinced Trotsky of the need for agile cavalry formations. At the start of September he launched the slogan "Proletarians to horse!" If cavalry regiments were the way forward they needed within them a firm proletarian core "if only in the role of commissars".[55]

Relations with Moscow, however, continued to be poor. On 6 September the Politburo expressed its astonishment at Trotsky's "attempts to revise the basic strategy plan decided upon"; Trotsky had written to Kamenev urging him to reconsider his priorities. Trotsky refused to be put down, replying the same day to the whole Central Committee that the plan was disintegrating, the centre of gravity of the fighting had moved towards a line between Kursk and Voronezh, where there were no reserves and the poor state of the roads meant that, while some cavalry groups could be brought back from the Tsaritsyn line of attack, the vast majority was trapped out on the left flank, unable to help. The Politburo's response was to question the loyalty of the commander of the left flank attack and accuse Trotsky on 18 September of failing to subject him to sufficient political surveillance as instructed.[56]

Towards the end of September the situation on the ground forced the Politburo to adopt a stance closer to that of Trotsky. The Central Committee Plenum of 21–6 September accepted that the two flanks of the earlier attack were now entirely separate, necessitating the creation of both a Southern and a South-eastern Front. Because Denikin's advance in what was now the Southern Front was so alarming, this now had to become the major front, something agreed by the Republic's RVS on 27 September and implemented by Kamenev on the 30th. Trotsky could therefore "consign to the archives" the long memorandum he had planned to submit to the Politburo which went over once again the rationale behind his Donbas plan and the critical situation produced by its being ignored. The fall of Orel on 13 October finally convinced the Politburo to throw itself fully behind Trotsky once more. On 15 October he attended a Politburo meeting in person and insisted that, unless troops were moved from the South-east Front to the Southern Front, he would be forced to evacuate Tula; the Politburo agreed. Ten days later, while relations between Trotsky and Kamenev remained tense, Lenin was successfully mediating between them.[57]

In mid October Petrograd again came under attack from Yudenich. Lenin advised surrendering the city, given the desperate fighting at Orel, but Trotsky opposed him and on this, for the first time in many weeks, he had the full backing of the Politburo. Trotsky set off for Petrograd on 16 October and found when he arrived a scene of demoralisation and panic, for which he was quick to blame Zinoviev. Trotsky assessed the situation quickly and accurately in an order issued on 18 October. The Red Army outnumbered Yudenich's forces, but the enemy's British tanks made them highly mobile; the answer was to keep calm, avoid encirclement and at the right moment, advance and overwhelm the enemy. Trotsky experienced an example of the danger no sooner than he had issued his order. A rifle regiment based near his headquarters began to retreat in panic when a rumour spread that it was being outflanked. Trotsky later recalled the incident, the only time he led soldiers in battle:

I mounted the first horse I could lay my hands on and turned the lines back. For the first few minutes, there was nothing but confusion. Not all of them understood what was happening, and some of them continued to retreat. But I chased one soldier after another, on horseback and made them all turn back . . . After a mile and a half, the bullets began their sweetish, nauseating whistling, and the first wounded began to drop. The regimental commander changed beyond recognition. He appeared at the most dangerous points, and before the regiment had recovered the positions it had previously abandoned he was wounded in both legs . . . The impetus had been given, and with my whole being I felt that we would save Petrograd.[58]

He was right. Although Yudenich's men continued to advance, as far as Pulkovo Hill, the mood in the Red Army command was changed. On the 21st the line was held at Pulkovo and then the Red Army went on to the offensive. On the 23rd Tsarskoe Selo and Pavlovsk were retaken in bitter fighting and the danger was over. The situation had also been transformed at Orel: on 20 October the town was recaptured by the Red Army and four days later Voronezh fell to the Red Cavalry; this was ample justification for the policy of "Proletarians to horse!" because this cavalry force, led by Budyenny, had been fighting on the South-east Front and was believed to be too distant to take part in the assault. After a further three weeks of bitter fighting, Budyenny led the assault on the strategic railway junction at Kastornoe, capturing it on 15 November and opening up the railway to Kharkov, thus threatening Denikin's advance troops with encirclement. Quite suddenly Denikin's retreat quickly became a rout as he struggled to hold a defensive line on the river Don. The Civil War was over. Ironically Trotsky took little part in this triumph. On 14 November the Politburo resolved that he should resume diplomatic duties, leaving Stalin to finish off Denikin. Trotsky was sent to Dvinsk, near the border with Poland, where it was hoped secret talks could begin with the Poles about agreeing a common border. He arrived on 28 November, only to be told that the Poles had changed their minds.[59]

It had been a bruising time for Trotsky. He had been proved right, but in the process he had clashed bitterly with the Party conclaves in Moscow and their obsessive desire for Bolshevik organisational control over the army. Trotsky had evolved his own, rather different way, of operating. As he recalled in his memoirs:

After making the round of a division and ascertaining its needs on the spot, I would hold a conference in the staff-car or dining car, inviting as many representatives as possible, including those from the lower commanding forces and from the ranks, as well as from the local party organisations, the soviet administration and the trade unions. In this way I got a picture of the situation that was neither false nor highly coloured. These conferences always had immediate practical results.[60]

Observers noted that "he spent at least six hours every day presiding over conferences of commissars, railway officials, factory men and even doctors". This was not democracy, but neither was it the closet politics of administration.[61]

Notes

1 For the details of Muraviev's dilemma, see G. R. Swain "Russia's Garibaldi: the Revolutionary Life of M. A. Muraviev", *Revolutionary Russia*, No. 2, 1998.

2 Trotsky, *How the Revolution Armed* (New Park: New York, 1979), Vol. I, pp. 164–5.

3 Trotsky, *How*, p. 355.

4 For the Yaroslavl insurrection, see G. R. Swain, *The Origins of the Russian Civil War* (London, 1996), pp. 172–5.

5 For Muraviev's rebellion, see Swain, "Muraviev".

6 For the 4th Latvian Regiment, see G. R. Swain, "The Disillusioning of the Revolution's Praetorian Guard: the Latvian Riflemen, Summer–Autumn 1918", *Europe–Asia Studies*, No. 4, 1999; for Vācietis, see G. R. Swain, "Vācietis: The Enigma of the Red Army's First Commander", *Revolutionary Russia*, No. 1, 2003.

7 Swain, "Muraviev", p. 76; *The Military Papers of Leon Trotsky* (Microfilms from the Russian State Military Archive RGVA), *fond* 1, *opis* 1, *ed, khr.* 142 (hereafter RGVA 1.1.142), pp. 18–19, 23, 41, 50.

8 Trotsky, *My Life* (New York, 1970), pp. 414, 419; N. S. Tarkova, "Trotsky's Train: an Unknown Page in the History of the Civil War" in T. Brotherstone and P. Dukes (eds), *The Trotsky Reappraisal* (Edinburgh, 1992), pp. 27–8.

9 Trotsky, *My Life*, pp. 396–400; L. Reissner, "Sviyazhsk" in J. Hansen *et al.* (eds), *Leon Trotsky, the Man and his Work* (New York, 1969), p. 113; J. M. Meijer (ed.), *The Trotsky Papers*, Vol. I, pp. 69–71.

10 Trotsky, *My Life*, p. 401.

11 RGVA 1.1.147, pp. 1, 16, 126; 1.1.163, p. 75; 1.3.68, pp. 21, 37, 57.

12 Reissner, "Sviyazhsk", pp. 114–15.

13 Trotsky, *My Life*, p. 402; Meijer (ed.), *Trotsky Papers*, Vol. I, p. 81, Vol. II, p. 27; RGVA 1.1.68, p. 98.

14 Meijer (ed.), *Trotsky Papers*, Vol. I, pp. 69–71; RGVA 1.1.68, pp. 100–1.

15 RGVA 33987.2.18, p. 53.

16 Trotsky, *My Life*, p. 402; Trotsky also discusses the incident in his *Stalin* (London, 1969), Vol. II, p. 89.

17 Meijer (ed.), *Trotsky Papers*, Vol. I, p. 81; RGVA 1.3.68, p. 98.

18 Meijer (ed.), *Trotsky Papers*, Vol. I, p. 333.

19 Trotsky, *My Life*, p. 403; Reissner, "Sviyazhsk", pp. 116–17, *How*, Vol. I, p. 322; RGVA 4.3.200, p. 85.

20 RGVA 4.3.200, pp. 30, 39; Meijer (ed.), *Trotsky Papers*, Vol. I, p. 107.

21 Meijer (ed.), *Trotsky Papers*, Vol. I, pp. 99, 107.

22 Trotsky, *My Life*, pp. 405–8.

23 Reissner, "Sviyazhsk", p. 117; Trotsky, *Stalin*, Vol. II, p. 103; L. Trotsky, *Trotsky's Diary in Exile* (London, 1988), p. 83.

24 Trotsky, *Stalin*, Vol. II, p. 119; Trotsky, *My Life*, pp. 415–17.

25 *Bolshevistskoe rukovosdstvo: perepiska, 1912–27* (Moscow, 1996), p. 42; Stalin's activities in Tsaritsyn are dealt with by R. Argenbright, "Red Tsaritsyn: Precursor of Stalinist Terror", *Revolutionary Russia*, No. 2, 1991.

26 RGVA 1.1.142, p. 92.

27 Meijer (ed.), *Trotsky Papers*, Vol. I, pp. 135–7; the cancellation of Stalin's order is in Trotsky, *Stalin*, Vol. II, p. 75 and RGVA 33987.2.40, p. 30.

28 R. Service, *Stalin* (Basingstoke, 2004), p. 168.

29 *Rukovodstvo*, p. 54.

30 RGVA 4.14.4, p. 93.

31 Trotsky, *My Life*, pp. 441–2.

32 Meijer (ed.), *Trotsky Papers*, Vol. I, pp. 165, 167; RGVA 33987.2.40, p. 277.

33 Trotsky, *My Life*, p. 444.

34 Meijer (ed.), *Trotsky Papers*, Vol. I, pp. 247–57.

35 RGVA 1.1.42, pp. 87, 90; 33987.2.40, pp. 117, 147, 179, 182, 281, 283, 290, 291.

36 Meijer (ed.), *Trotsky Papers*, Vol. I, pp. 149, 155.

37 Meijer (ed.), *Trotsky Papers*, Vol. I, p. 155; RGVA 33987.2.40, p. 190.

38 Trotsky, *How*, Vol. I, pp. 183, 197, 199; Deutscher, *Armed*, pp. 425–7.

39 Trotsky, *My Life*, p. 447; Trotsky, *Stalin*, Vol. II, pp. 60–1.

40 Trotsky, *How*, Vol. II, pp. 125–6.

41 Meijer (ed.), *Trotsky Papers*, Vol. I, pp. 321, 328–30.

42 Trotsky, *How*, Vol. I, p. 84.

43 Trotsky, *How*, Vol. III, pp. 310, 314–17.

44 RGVA 4.3.202, p. 14; Meijer (ed.), *Trotsky Papers*, Vol. I, pp. 307, 309, 311.

45 Meijer (ed.), *Trotsky Papers*, Vol. I, pp. 323, 361, 367; Trotsky, *How*, Vol. II, p. 522.

46 V. Butt *et al.* (eds), *The Russian Civil War: Documents from the Soviet Archives* (Basingstoke, 1996), p. 81; the above summary is from G. R. Swain, *Russia's Civil War* (Stroud, 2000).

47 Meijer (ed.), *Trotsky Papers*, Vol. I, p. 391.

48 Meijer (ed.), *Trotsky Papers*, Vol. I, pp. 431, 459–61.

49 Trotsky, *How*, Vol. II, pp. 278–81, 294.

50 Meijer (ed.), *Trotsky Papers*, Vol. I, pp. 515–17.

51 Trotsky, *Stalin*, Vol. II, p. 101; Trotsky, *My Life*, p. 423; for the Petrograd campaign, see Swain, *Russia's Civil War*.

52 Meijer (ed.), *Trotsky Papers*, Vol. I, p. 595; Trotsky, *My Life*, p. 398; for the dismissal of Vācietis, see Swain, "Vācietis".

53 Trotsky, *How*, Vol. II, pp. 135, 337; Meijer (ed.), *Trotsky Papers*, Vol. I, p. 597.

54 Trotsky, *Stalin*, Vol. II, p. 111; Meijer (ed.), *Trotsky Papers*, Vol. I, pp. 605, 613–15, 619, 643–7; 651–5.

55 For Mironov, Trotsky, *How*, Vol. II, p. 423; Butt *et al.* (eds), *Civil War: Documents*, pp. 60–6; Trotsky, *Stalin*, Vol. II, p. 56.

56 Meijer (ed.), *Trotsky Papers*, Vol. I, pp. 667, 671.

57 Meijer (ed.), *Trotsky Papers*, Vol. I, pp. 682 (editorial note), 687; Trotsky, *How*, Vol. II, pp. 430–2 (this memo Trotsky consigned to the archives and then had published in Trotsky, *How*, is also reproduced in R. Pipes, *The Unknown Lenin* (New Haven, 1998), p. 70).

58 Trotsky, *My Life*, p. 429.

59 Meijer (ed.), *Trotsky Papers*, Vol. I, pp. 759, 765; for the rout of Denikin, see Swain, *Russia's Civil War*.

60 Trotsky, *My Life*, p. 416.

61 F. McCullagh, "Trotsky in Ekaterinburg", *Fortnightly Review*, Vol. 108, 1920, p. 541.

Chapter 5

Building a Workers' State

In 1919 Trotsky wrote about how the lessons of the Civil War could be applied to peaceful reconstruction.

When the Civil War is over, the dictatorship of the proletariat will disclose all its creative energy and will, in practice, show the most backward masses what it can give them: by means of a systematically applied universal labour service, and a centralised organisation of distribution, the whole population of the country will be drawn into the general soviet system of economic arrangement and self-government; the soviets themselves, at present the organs of government, will gradually melt into purely economic organisations.

Universal labour service and central planning were the key and, as he told the Seventh Congress of Soviets in early December 1919, this should be linked to the gradual adoption of a militia system for the Army. The Army would be transformed into an armed nation, bringing it close to the land and the factories, forming territorial districts for the regiments "so that every worker and peasant of the appropriate age-group belongs to a particular district and is consequently included beforehand in a particular regiment and can at once be called up and placed under arms". This was the militarisation of labour, a proposal which Lenin backed when the Central Committee met on 16 December 1919 to adopt Trotsky's proposals.[1]

Labour Armies

When Trotsky's proposals were published in *Pravda* there were widespread protests from the trade unions which, not surprisingly, had hoped that peace might bring an end to the restrictions on their activity. On 12 January 1920 both Lenin and Trotsky appeared jointly before the trade union leadership, but were unable to win them round. Salvation came not from workers declaring themselves willing to become soldiers, but from soldiers declaring themselves willing to become workers. Just before Trotsky and Lenin's bruising encounter with the trade union leaders, the commander of the Third Army operating in Siberia proposed on 10 January 1920 adopting a new name; his army would become the First Labour Army. Kolchak had been routed, he was captured and executed on 6 February, and economic recovery was clearly the order of the day, so the Siberian Red Army would become a Labour Army and restore the economy. Trotsky became the most enthusiastic advocate of the Labour Army idea. "Nothing could be simpler," Trotsky wrote, "than that the army, before releasing its men, should take a census of their productive skills, mark every soldier's trade in his service book, and then direct him straight from the demobilisation point to the working place where he was wanted."[2]

After a month of discussion, the Central Committee established its Main Committee on Universal Labour Conscription and at the same time brought the railways under military control, establishing a special shock group to carry out essential repairs. Trotsky, keen to see a Labour Army in practice, returned to his train and on 8 February set off for Ekaterinburg, the base of the First Labour Army, for a month-long visit. His journey showed how much still needed to be done. The train got stuck in a snowdrift and had to be dug out: this prompted a flurry of invective against sabotage by railway workers and the "kulak executive committees" of soviets which "loafed around" rather than keeping the tracks clear; the whole of the local soviet concerned was placed under arrest. On arrival he informed Lenin straight away that the militarisation of the railways should continue, since the centre had no control over railways in the provinces. He added that the coalmines of the Urals also had to be put under martial law: "on this question the opposition of local trade unionists, indeed those of the centre too, must be overcome". It was also essential to clarify the powers of the Labour Army when these came into conflict with the Commissariat of Supply; Trotsky urged Lenin to confirm that only the Labour Army had the power to reroute supplies. In a similar dispute he urged Lenin to reconsider a decree which excluded the rich mining district of Ishim from the territory controlled by the Labour Army.[3]

Trotsky's robust attitude towards labour was revealed in a speech he gave to the Ekaterinburg Party organisation on 25 February. He demanded:

An intensive struggle – ideological, organisational and by means of repressive measures – must be waged against manifestations of self-seeking among the working class: party elements in the trade unions must explain the radical differences between a trade union policy, which haggles and quarrels with the state, demanding concessions from it and eventually urging workers to go on strike, and a communist policy which proceeds from the fact that our state is a workers' state which knows no other interests than those of working people.

Exemplary treatment, he argued, should be handed out "to all scoundrels and traitors who take advantage of calamities and intensify these calamities through counter-revolutionary strikes and demonstrations". A week later the RVS of the First Labour Army agreed that desertion from the Labour Army would be treated in exactly the same way as desertion from the Red Army. Desertion was defined as:

(a) failure to appear for labour mobilisation;
(b) failure to appear for labour service;
(c) evading labour registration;
(d) absence from work without valid reason;
(e) wilfully leaving work;
(f) evading work by assuming fictitious duties, official missions, etc.;
(g) evading work by simulating illness; and
(h) intentional non-fulfilment of norms.[4]

Trotsky never saw discipline alone as the solution. Just as he had favoured the use of military specialists from the Old Army to win the Civil War, he favoured the recruitment of industrial specialists to bring about socialist reconstruction. This was nothing new. On the eve of his dramatic departure for Sviyazhsk in August 1918 he had made a speech speculating on the process of economic construction that he hoped the country was about to embark on even then. He talked of Soviet Russia entering "an original stage in its struggle finally to defeat capitalism", a stage that imposed certain distinct conditions. Among these was the need to gradually introduce a system of labour conscription, the need to increase labour productivity through the widespread adoption of Taylorism, and the need to make use of specialists: "without the leadership of specialists from various fields of knowledge and technology, the transition to socialism is impossible". He said the same to the Ekaterinburg Party organisations on 25 February 1919: "Extensive recruitment of specialists (engineers and technicians) is needed for the reorganisation of disordered industry; it must be explained to less conscious workers that, whereas in the past the specialists may have served capital, today they will serve the working class." For Trotsky it was less conscious workers who opposed his economic plans, just as it had been less conscious commissars who supported the Military Opposition.[5]

Trotsky had taken advantage of his journey from Moscow to Ekaterinburg to write an open letter in response to a private one he had received from a peasant, Ivan Sigunov. He urged Sigunov to be patient: the cities were starving, but if peasants sent workers food, the cities would revive and industrial goods would begin to flow into the villages. The Labour Army and universal labour service were the essential prerequisites for such a benign trade cycle. Perhaps because he felt this response offered the peasants very little, Trotsky spent some of his time in Ekaterinburg worrying about ways to improve the Bolshevik policy of grain requisitioning. It was quite obvious during Trotsky's time in the Urals that peasants were responding to the confiscation of their grain by reducing the area sown to that needed to satisfy their immediate family; they were also ruining the potential of Siberia's once flourishing dairy industry by slaughtering cows in response to a government decree confiscating all herds larger than two cows. A crisis had been averted so far, Trotsky argued, simply because victory in the Civil War had greatly increased the area from which grain could be confiscated, but was unavoidable in the longer term unless the policy was modified to create incentives.

Trotsky therefore proposed that, instead of the confiscation of grain, peasants should be encouraged to increase the acreage sown by being given the chance to pay a tax in kind, which would be graduated progressively to reward those who produced the most; the big producers would also be rewarded with the supply of fuel and industrial goods. Any force to be used, he argued, should no longer be applied at the point of harvest but to ensure sowing. As he explained in a letter to the Politburo, what he proposed "signified a certain slackening of pressure on the kulak; we shall contain him within certain limits but not reduce him to the level of a peasant producing only for subsistence". It was as a concession to the kulak that Trotsky's idea was rejected by the Politburo when he got back to Moscow in early March, even though other clauses of his paper spoke of the need to develop state farms and move towards collectivisation in certain areas.[6]

Trotsky returned to Moscow to attend the Ninth Party Congress which took place from 29 March to 4 April 1920. He was determined to push ahead with labour conscription, arguing in *Pravda* on 23 March that "since the Soviet state organises work in the interests of the workers themselves, compulsion is in no way opposed to the personal interests of the workers"; imitating the way he had tried to introduce incentives into peasant agriculture, he suggested that a sliding scale of rations could be established to encourage "a spirit of emulation". In his keynote speech on the economy Trotsky made very clear that the new communist society would remain highly regimented for many years to come. The organisation of labour, he believed, was the essence of organising a new society. "We are making the first attempt in world history to organise the labour of working people in the interests of the working majority: but that, of course, does not mean the destruction of the element of compulsion." Compulsion, he added, "is playing and will continue to play a great role for a considerable historical period". Trade unions had played a valuable role in a free-market economy but now "the workforce should be distributed according to an economic plan for the current state of our development; the working masses cannot be wandering around the Russian land, but must be collected together, ordered and commanded just like soldiers."

This required a change in the role of the trade unions. In his view trade unions would not be abolished as labour was militarised but would themselves become the agents of militarisation. The militarisation of society was "unthinkable without the militarisation of the trade unions". Trotsky was equally firm about the use of specialists. Echoing his experience of the Civil War, he called on the Congress to recognise that a single authority was needed to head industry, and if that meant "bourgeois specialists" then so be it. Trotsky saw few limitations to Russia's socialist development if his policies were followed, even if there was not a revolution in Germany as he, like all Bolsheviks, still hoped.

It is quite possible that we can go over to a more or less developed socialist economy in the course of the next three, four or five years . . . in the course of three or four years we can make gigantic steps forward and the remnants of class struggle here will be broken up and eliminated once and for all.[7]

Just before the opening of the Ninth Party Congress Trotsky had been appointed Commissar for Transport. The railways were the key to economic recovery, and the policy of Labour Armies made no sense without the railways standing at their core. As Commissar for Transport, Trotsky immediately merged the Rail and River Transport Administrations and set about undermining the influence of the Railway Workers' Union and the Marine Transport Workers' Union. During the Civil War the party had established its own arm within the Transport Commissariat, known as Glavpolitput, and soon Trotsky had plenipotentiaries from Glavpolitput travelling along the lines under military escort arresting local officials and issuing new instructions. By May 1920 the Party had endorsed Order 1042, effectively a five-year plan for railway construction and development. Such policies, and the hostility they provoked, were put on one side when, on 25 April, Poland attacked Soviet Russia.[8]

The Polish War

Initially Trotsky's tactics were identical to those employed during the Civil War. He left Moscow on 7 May and by the 9th was in Bryansk, from where he ordered the formation of "battle-police detachments" to stop further retreat and reissued the blood-curdling decree on desertion issued during the Civil War. However, by the time he got to Gomel on 10 May he had decided to introduce a radical change in command structure. Because "we have operating against us for the first time a regular army led by good technicians", he needed to have many more skilled officers operating at the most junior level. So in future those with the rank Army Commander would be put in charge of divisions as Divisional Commanders, with similar changes cascading down the hierarchy of command; all affected officers would retain their original rank and salary. By mid June the situation on the Western Front had stabilised and the Red Army had recaptured Kiev, lost in the first weeks of fighting.[9]

An early victory was prevented by the resumption of Russia's Civil War. After his forces had been beaten back to the Black Sea, Denikin had fled to the Crimea, which remained an isolated pocket of territory beyond Bolshevik control. There Denikin had been replaced as White commander by General Wrangel, who prepared to take advantage of the Polish War by breaking out of Crimea and advancing towards Moscow. Wrangel's ambitions caused renewed tension between Trotsky and Stalin. Trotsky had no problem with Stalin being sent to monitor Wrangel's activities, but he was furious when Stalin, learning from intelligence sources that Wrangel was about to attack, informed Lenin of this and asked him to inform Trotsky and Trotsky to inform the Red Army's Commander-in-Chief; as far as Trotsky was concerned, Stalin should have used the correct military channels to inform the Commander-in-Chief and not routed his message through the Party hierarchy. Even though Stalin's proposal that the Red Army launch a pre-emptive strike against Wrangel made military sense, Trotsky ordered him on 3 June not to do so, only to find that, as Stalin had predicted, Wrangel began his advance on 6 June.

A month later Trotsky clashed with Lenin. In July the British Foreign Minister, Lord Curzon, proposed a negotiated end to the war, which would establish a border for Poland that was roughly in accordance with the ethnic dividing line between Poles on the one hand and Ukrainians and Belorussians on the other. When the proposed Curzon Line was put to the Politburo on 13 July, Trotsky called for its acceptance while Lenin called for a continued advance towards Warsaw. Trotsky argued that, if the Red Army were not to appear in Poland as conquerors, the Bolsheviks had to exhaust all peace efforts before entering the country, otherwise they would simply play into the Poles' hands; in a memorandum to Lenin of 11 August Trotsky argued that the Poles were deliberately delaying the talks so that the Bolsheviks had time to capture Warsaw, something which would prompt France to intervene in the conflict. As Trotsky told the Moscow Soviet on 12 August, Wrangel was now the main danger to be faced and the Party should abandon the chimera of spreading revolution to Poland. When asked to tour the Warsaw Front as the Battle of the Vistula raged on 14–17 August, Trotsky refused; it was Lenin who insisted that Warsaw be taken and that the Red Army plan an advance on Danzig. Reality dawned on 19 August when the Politburo endorsed a paper making Wrangel the priority and instructing both Trotsky and Stalin to make suitable preparations. On 23 August, having refused to travel to Warsaw, Trotsky boarded his train and headed south.[10]

Trotsky recalled on his return from the Wrangel Front that he found Moscow favouring a second Polish offensive. "I declared that a repetition of the error already committed would cost us ten times as much, and that I would not submit to the decision that was being proposed, but would carry an appeal to the Party." Lenin still defended the continuation of the war, but without his former conviction. Trotsky then toured the Polish Front in September: "The two or three days that I spent at the Front were enough to confirm the conclusion I had brought with me from Moscow." On his return the Politburo almost unanimously resolved in favour of an immediate peace. When the armistice was signed on 12 October, its terms were such that the majority of the Politburo at first suggested a resumption of hostilities and were only brought to their senses by Trotsky's threat of resignation. At the end of October Trotsky set off for his final tour of the Front to oversee Wrangel's defeat, which was secured at the battle of the Sivash Sea on the Third Anniversary of the October insurrection.[11]

The Trade Union Debate

Throughout the Polish War Trotsky had continued to serve as Commissar of Transport. It had not been his top priority, but he had pushed ahead with his refurbishment programme and by the autumn Order 1042 had succeeded in nearly doubling the number of locomotives fit for use. For Trotsky running the railways was like a school of socialism. "All the fundamental questions of socialist organisation of economic life found their most concentrated expression in the sphere of transport: the great variety in the types of locomotives and cars complicated the work of the railways and repair shops; extensive preparatory work was set on foot to standardise the transport system." The key to success remained what Trotsky called "the organisation of labour", and on 3 September he established a new trade union for all transport workers, Tsektran, which was under central Party control and chaired by Trotsky himself. When the Polish War was over, Trotsky moved to take control of other trade unions.[12]

Before the outbreak of the Polish War, Trotsky had been able to rely on Lenin's support when it came to economic matters; after the war this was no longer the case. Lenin turned to Zinoviev who was asked "to re-establish proletarian democracy in the trade unions". The battle lines were drawn even before the war was over. When the Party held its Ninth Conference on 22–25 September, Trotsky was only allowed to speak on military matters; it was Zinoviev who made the keynote speech and who was responsible for passing a resolution which stressed that Tsektran and Glavpolitput, Trotsky's two agencies for militarisation, were temporary bodies which would disappear as soon as normal trade union life resumed; in the interim "petty interference" in trade union affairs would be kept to a minimum. By the time the Fifth Trade Union Conference gathered from 2 to 9 November, the Trotsky–Zinoviev clash was in the open. Trotsky made clear in his speech that labour conscription would continue and that in future other trade union leaders would be appointed rather than elected, as was the case with Tsektran. When on 8 November 1920 the Central Committee discussed the future of the trade unions, Lenin showed his hand. Trotsky proposed that in a future socialist society trade unions would cease to play the role they had traditionally played under capitalism and would become administrative organs of the state. This meant, he stressed, that the administrative controls over trade union activity seen in Tsektran should be extended to other trade unions. The Bolshevik trade union leader protested that the existing powers of Tsektran were bad enough, and to extend such powers was out of the question. Lenin submitted his own paper, distancing himself from Trotsky and suggesting that the trade unions should survive as independent, non-state organisations, but with a remit that was educational rather than managerial. In a clear warning to Trotsky, he stated that the era of the Labour Army was over.

The Central Committee backed Lenin, but since it had done so by just one vote it resolved to establish a commission chaired by Zinoviev to work towards consensus and report back to the Central Committee on

8 December. Until then, only Zinoviev was to be allowed to speak for the Party on trade union matters and he was permitted to tell the Fifth Trade Union Conference on 9 November that militarisation could lead to "petty officialdom and interference in trade union work". Trotsky perceived the powers given to Zinoviev by the Central Committee as an attempt to gag him and, although he was appointed to Zinoviev's Commission on the Trade Unions, he did not remain on it long; by early December he had resigned because the Commission refused to give him the same access to the press that it gave Zinoviev. In Trotsky's view "a reasonable" accommodation on the trade union question was impossible. When the Central Committee met on 8 December to hear Zinoviev's report, he called for the abolition of Tsektran and the dissolution of Glavpolitput; Trotsky fought a rearguard action and a compromise was agreed whereby Glavpolitput was abolished at once, but Tsektran was to continue operating until February 1921 when elections would be held for a new leadership. Trotsky was able to insist that those candidates for election should be selected "not only for their political reliability, but also for their industrial talents, their administrative experience, organisational ability, and practical proof of their interest in the material and spiritual welfare of the masses".[13]

Lenin's solution to this crisis was to continue the work for consensus and compromise. He asked the Zinoviev commission to resume its work. However, Trotsky continued his boycott and when it finally adopted trade union proposals known as the Platform of the Ten, Trotsky would not sign them. He did not want this issue resolved in the privacy of an internal Party commission but through broad Party debate. It was due to his persistence that the Central Committee agreed on 24 December that "a wide pre-Congress discussion" should be held within the Party as preparations began for the Tenth Party Congress in March. Trotsky launched his campaign with a speech to the Eighth Congress of Soviets on 30 December. Here he called for the sort of fusion between trade union activists and factory administrators that he had previously suggested in the Army. Just as he had once claimed that commissars and commanders were increasingly doing the same job and would not remain separate entities forever, so he now believed "it is essential to step firmly forward to the point that the separation into trade unionists and industrialists decreases . . . these two categories of work, these two streams need to get closer and become one; these two apparatuses should merge". As always he was keen to stress that the trade union question, the organisation of labour, was just one element, but a key element, in the question of how the economy would operate in a socialist society. In a pamphlet published for Congress delegates entitled *The Path to the United Economic Plan* Trotsky denied that statification of the trade unions meant that he was a super-centraliser: he insisted that he favoured a high degree of autonomy for economic enterprises, but an autonomy held in place by a firm economic plan; the operation of such a plan required "a small, carefully chosen and authoritative instructors' group" empowered to weed out duplication and purge those not up to the job.[14]

Zinoviev countered with organisational measures. On 3 January 1921 Zinoviev's Petrograd Party organisation called for elections to the Tenth Party Congress to take place on the basis of platforms and proposed as its platform Lenin's Platform of the Ten, which was published in *Petrograd Pravda* on 6 January. Trotsky objected and on 11 January persuaded the Moscow Party organisation to pass a resolution supporting his stance. On 12 January the Central Committee endorsed the idea of elections by platform and *Pravda* published both Lenin's Platform of the Ten and Trotsky's resolution. With the gloves now off, Zinoviev launched a bitter and effective campaign against Trotsky and the abuses perpetrated by Tsektran. As Trotsky noted ruefully: "Every village now knows what Tsektran is – it is a kind of animal which takes away the grain, it has a stick in its hand and does not allow workers to breathe freely; and then, when the worker is tired out, Tsektran offers him vinegar instead of the milk which Comrade Zinoviev has at his disposal."[15]

Trotsky returned to Ekaterinburg in February 1921 and it was while he was there that the disturbances which were to culminate in the Kronstadt mutiny began. For Trotsky the whole Kronstadt affair was a side issue in his clash with Zinoviev, which involved not only the future of the trade unions but also the question of who should control the Party organisations within the Baltic Fleet. The question of where Party cells in the Red Army should fit in the overall party hierarchy had exercised Bolshevik leaders on more than one occasion during the Civil War. Trotsky had won a blanket acceptance that such cells were not to be linked to the town or region in which troops were based, but that all army cells should be placed within a hierarchy of army committees which was subject to the Central Committee; otherwise the danger was that party commissars loyal to local political interest groups might hamper the implementation of national military strategy. However, the Baltic Fleet, no longer operating anywhere other than in the Gulf of Finland outside Petrograd, seemed an exception. It was essentially static, and Zinoviev had campaigned throughout 1920 that the Party organisations in the Baltic Fleet should be brought under the authority of the Petrograd Party organisation and not Trotsky and the Political Directorate of the

Baltic Fleet (known as Pubalt). As tension between Zinoviev and Trotsky increased over the issue of the trade unions, so the sailors were brought into the struggle; on 15 February the Party organisations within the Baltic Fleet condemned Trotsky's Pubalt and asked to be put under the authority of Zinoviev's Petrograd Committee.

Trotsky had travelled to Petrograd for this vote, and, no doubt because he was so roundly defeated, "the general spirit of the meeting made an extremely unfavourable impression on me: dandified and well-fed sailors, communists in name only, produced the impression of parasites in comparison to the workers and Red Army men at this time". He was glad to get away to the Urals, although Zinoviev's decision to accompany him could not have made for a pleasant journey. The Kronstadt mutiny began on 28 February when the crew of the battleship *Petropavlovsk* passed a resolution calling for the re-election of the soviets by secret ballot. When leading communists hurried to a mass meeting at Anchor Square on 1 March, they were shouted down and the sailors, including those "communists in name only" voted for the *Petropavlovsk* resolution. On 2 March the newly elected Provisional Revolutionary Committee arrested the remaining Bolshevik commissars.[16]

Zinoviev was informed of developments and hurried to leave the Urals. Trotsky took his time. He informed the Politburo that this was Zinoviev's problem and he should be the one to negotiate with the sailors, since he had won their confidence and Trotsky had not. Any action by Trotsky could appear as "revenge". When it was clear negotiations were impossible, Trotsky, as Commissar of War, was called on to issue a warning "to the garrison and population of Kronstadt and the rebellious forts" at 14.00 hours on 5 March 1921. All were ordered to hand over their arms immediately and release their captives: "only those who surrender unconditionally can count on the clemency of Soviet power"; the statement concluded that measures to retake the base were being prepared and there would be no further warnings. The military assault began on 7 March and was over by the 17th, but Trotsky took no part in it.

Thus when the Tenth Party Congress finally met from 8 to 16 March, it was against the backdrop of the Kronstadt events that the Trade Union Debate was finally concluded on 14 March. Zinoviev introduced the discussion and was greeted by applause. Trotsky's response was petulant. He took every opportunity to accuse Zinoviev of abusing Party rules to achieve his victory; he was particularly critical of Kamenev, who had originally sided with Trotsky and then changed his mind; and he condemned Lenin for appearing to stand above the fray when actually backing Zinoviev. Again he defended specialists: without his policies "the administration of the most important key factories could fall into the hands of incompetents who would wreck everything". "Worker democracy," he argued, "could only be understood from the viewpoint of the economic interests of the working class", and that meant clear limits on trade union power. The Party had the right "to assert its dictatorship even if that dictatorship temporarily clashed with the passing moods of the workers' democracy".

Lenin was furious with Trotsky's behaviour during the Trade Union Debate. In his view Trotsky had been wrong to wreck the work of the Zinoviev Commission by boycotting it. Lenin confided to some of his closest supporters during the Tenth Party Congress. "I have been accused: 'You are a son of a bitch for letting the discussion get out of hand'. Well, try to stop Trotsky! How many divisions does one have to send against him?" He went on to stress that he would come to terms with Trotsky, even though Trotsky, "a temperamental man", wanted to resign. Lenin's political solution to the crisis surrounding the Trade Union Debate was to make the Tenth Party Congress pass a resolution on party unity which would henceforth ban the sort of factional struggle within the Party seen between December 1920 and March 1921.[17]

Gosplan

The Kronstadt mutiny was only one of the many crises facing the Bolshevik Party during the Tenth Party Congress. Since autumn 1920 the peasants of Tambov province had been in open revolt and the situation was no better in Western Siberia. Lenin decided that a change of policy was essential. On 8 February he presented the Politburo with "Preliminary Rough Draft Theses Concerning the Peasants". These proposed that in the place of grain requisitioning, a tax in kind be set at a level lower than the previous year's procurement target, to be linked to a free trade in grain above that tax threshold. Lenin then organised a series of high-profile meetings with peasants from Tambov province, while the Politburo reflected on the issues concerned. By 24 February an agreed paper had been endorsed by the Central Committee to be presented to the Tenth Party Congress. With the Kronstadt crisis concentrating the minds of delegates, Lenin's New Economic Policy (NEP) was endorsed by the Congress on 15 March. Trotsky had absolutely no problem backing Lenin on this. As he pointedly reminded delegates, a year earlier he had suggested making concessions to the peasantry which were not so very different to those now being proposed.

After the Tenth Party Congress Trotsky took two months' leave, the first since returning to Russia. The statification of the trade unions had always been for him just part of the greater project of organising labour, which was, in turn, just a part of the need to introduce a proper economic plan. The introduction of NEP complicated the issue of planning. Agriculture now operated according to a free market and, in a series of moves introduced quickly after the Tenth Party Congress, large sectors of light industry geared to satisfying peasant demand were privatised as well; the state retained control of the banks, heavy industry and foreign trade, what the Bolsheviks called "the commanding heights". However, for Trotsky, introducing a market link between privately owned agriculture, with its associated enterprises, and state-controlled heavy industry might complicate the planning process, but it did not make it any less necessary.

On 7 August 1921 Trotsky presented a paper to a Central Committee Plenum suggesting that many of the economic changes agreed at the Tenth Party Congress were being implemented only erratically. He stated the problem thus.

The lack of a real economic centre to watch over economic activity, conduct experiments in that field, record and disseminate results and co-ordinate in practice all sides of economic activity and thus actually work at a co-ordinated economic plan – the absence of a real economic centre of this sort not only inflicts the severest of shocks on the economy, such as fuel and food crises, but also excludes the possibility of the planned and co-ordinated elaboration of new premises for economic policy.

The solution, he suggested was to reorganise the state planning body Gosplan. It had been agreed to set up Gosplan in February 1921 and, despite the onset of NEP, this had been done on 1 April, although the tasks of the new body were only vaguely defined. Not even Trotsky was clear how economic planning would work at this stage, but he stressed two things: first "an economic plan cannot be worked out theoretically", it had to be worked out through monitoring practice; and second, the plan had to be "put together around large-scale nationalised industry as a pivot". Trotsky was determined to refine his views on planning further and present them to the Eleventh Party Congress when it met on 27 March–2 April 1922.[18]

By then two concerns had come to the fore. First, Trotsky was keen to establish that, despite the privatisation of agriculture and large sectors of light industry, the economy remained socialist and therefore amenable to planning. For Trotsky, resorting to the market was just a way of introducing a more sophisticated mechanism for distribution than that offered by central direction and did not change the fundamentally socialist nature of the Soviet economy.[19] Trotsky's second point was that planning was not the same as Party interference in the management of the economy. The apparatus of the Party had grown enormously by the start of 1922: on 4 February he informed an astonished Lenin just how much of the state's budget was allocated to running the Communist Party. Two weeks before the opening of the Eleventh Party Congress Trotsky sent the Politburo a detailed memorandum insisting that excessive Party interference in economic affairs was wasteful; the economy did not need Party interference but the economic guidance of experts. "If NEP requires that the trade unions be trade unions," he wrote, "then this same policy requires that the Party be a party." In his view it was the duty of the Party "to govern only through the properly functioning state apparatus", not to interfere at every level; the Party should "send back ninety-nine per cent of the matters submitted to it for decision, on the grounds that they contain nothing of concern to the Party". Distancing the Party from the management of the economy was not a policy Lenin shared, writing on his copy of Trotsky's memorandum, "to the archives".[20]

Trotsky repeated his key themes in his speech to the Eleventh Party Congress. NEP was indeed socialist: if the revolution had taken place in Germany rather than Russia, Trotsky argued, it would have followed from the start policies similar to NEP; revolution in the West "would have been much more planned and much more cautious, we would only have confiscated those enterprises which were most essential to us, leaving moderate-sized enterprises in the hands of private capital". In Russia it had not been like that because in summer 1918 the Bolsheviks had had no choice but to nationalise everything; but with peace restored and recovery underway, the Party could now act more in that Western mode, using "capitalist methods of calculation" for several years to come. This, however, linked to his second theme. If "capitalist methods of calculation", and the market were going to be used to build socialism, the only way forward was to understand each economic sector in detail and devise a plan, and this had to be the task of specialists.

It is clear that the Party, even in the role of Party organisations, cannot decide all questions. Every economic question is complicated, yet round and about there are people who think that if this complicated question is put to the provincial Party committee or the Orgburo or the Politburo is will suddenly become a simple question.

As a result, the provincial Party committee, this "unspecialised apparatus, always in a hurry", contained the worst elements of bureaucratism, "that is addressing a problem without ever understanding the essence of that problem". For Trotsky "the ruling party does not at all mean the Party directly administering every detail of every affair". Zinoviev took the lead in challenging Trotsky, arguing that it was quite impossible to say "the Party will be a party and will only concern itself with agitation and propaganda". The Bolshevik Party "must direct economic life".[21]

After the Eleventh Party Congress, on 11 April 1922, Lenin tried to win Trotsky over by appointing him one of his three deputies. Trotsky explained at extraordinary length why he could not accept. Going paragraph by paragraph through the job specification, Trotsky stressed that role of the deputy was ill-conceived and therefore impossible to fulfil. The deputy had, in Trotsky's summary, "to ensure all is well in every field and in every connection". However, the Bolshevik Party had already established the Workers' and Peasants' Inspectorate (Rabkrin) to do just that; it was beside the point that Rabkrin was staffed by "useless has-beens intriguing against their former managers", the deputy was bound to find himself duplicating the work of Rabkrin and clashing with its leaders. A deputy could not be appointed as a jack of all trades, a deputy needed a specific brief, like chairing Gosplan. Thus Trotsky got back to the essence of the matter.

At the beginning of last year it was already plain that there was no organ for co-ordinating and actually controlling economic matters. The present organisation of Gosplan approximates *outwardly* to what I proposed last year, but only outwardly. In essence the parcelling out of responsibilities remains a fact, and it is absolutely unknown who in practice controls the indents for fuel, transport, raw materials or money . . . These questions are put before the Politburo and are solved by rule of thumb.[22]

Lenin may well have intended to make an immediate effort to persuade Trotsky to change his mind, but on 25 May he suffered a severe stroke from which he would never fully recover. This coincided with an injury Trotsky suffered while on a fishing trip on the Moscow river, which kept him out of action for much of the summer. When Lenin was well enough in mid July to return to the question of Trotsky's future, he was horrified to learn that Zinoviev, Kamenev and Stalin, rapidly emerging as the dominant triumvirate, had concluded that it was time to remove Trotsky from the leadership in view of his refusal to take on the post of deputy. Lenin responded: "Throwing Trotsky overboard is the height of stupidity. If you do not consider me already hopelessly foolish, how can you think of that?" So Trotsky was not sacked, but he still operated from the sidelines. On 23 August he again sent a memorandum to the Politburo: "It may be that the moment for serious discussion and settlement of the question of a planning organ is not yet", but with the changeover to NEP state funds had become a vital lever in the economic plan; their allocation should be predetermined by the plan, and yet Gosplan had no responsibility for these fundamental questions. "How can it have happened that when discussing the question of the allocation of funds and the volume of money in circulation, no one in the Politburo called Gosplan to mind?" Lenin's response was to try once again to persuade Trotsky to become a deputy. On 11 September he asked Stalin to organise a telephone vote of Politburo members; Trotsky replied, "categorically refuse".[23]

With Lenin

What brought Trotsky and Lenin together once again was the question of the state monopoly of foreign trade. In November 1922, with Lenin still ill and Trotsky out of the capital, the Central Committee decided to weaken the state's monopoly over foreign trade. For Trotsky this was an extraordinary proposal, since the state's control over foreign trade was in his terms one of the chief instruments of socialist construction. Lenin agreed and on 13 December wrote to Trotsky urging him to take on the defence of the foreign trade monopoly in his absence. In the event, this was a non-issue; when the Central Committee learned of Lenin's views it immediately backtracked and abandoned the proposals it had previously adopted. However, the incident brought Trotsky's views on Gosplan back to the forefront of Lenin's attention. Lenin was cautious. He wrote that he backed Trotsky's paper on the foreign trade monopoly "with the exception, perhaps, of the last lines about Gosplan". As subsequent correspondence made clear, Lenin could accept that Gosplan needed to have a role in regulating the export trade, but Trotsky had used the occasion to propose that Gosplan needed to have administrative rights. When on 23 December Lenin wrote a *Letter to the [Twelfth Party] Congress*, he said he backed Trotsky's idea that Gosplan resolutions should have legislative power "up to a certain point and under certain conditions".

Lenin was more emphatic in notes written between 27 and 29 December in which he called for a broadening of Gosplan's powers.

After a thorough examination of this question I have nevertheless come to the conclusion that it contains an essentially healthy idea, namely that Gosplan is somewhat divorced from our legislative institutions despite the fact that, being an assembly of competent individuals, experts and representatives of science and technology, it actually has the most data necessary to assess the situation.

Trotsky, therefore, "could be met halfway". Gosplan would have legislative powers, although Lenin suggested there needed to be a mechanism whereby these could be overruled on occasion; Trotsky's agreement could be sought on such a mechanism, but not on the person to head Gosplan. Lenin wanted a man with an academic background, not an administrator. That person also had to be politically reliable: "the overwhelming majority of academics, of which Gosplan is naturally made up, is heavily burdened with bourgeois views and prejudices"; it would therefore also be necessary to form a Gosplan Presidium "which must consist of communists and keep watch day in and day out on the degree of devotion of the bourgeois scholars and on their renunciation of bourgeois prejudices and likewise on their gradual transition to the point of view of socialism". The caution he had once shown towards military specialists had not left him.[24]

With Lenin showing open support for Trotsky, the question of Trotsky's position inevitably came back onto the agenda. On 6 January 1923 Stalin again proposed to the Politburo that Trotsky should be appointed a deputy, but this time with a specific brief to preside over the Council of Labour and Defence. This proposal was part and parcel of Stalin's own attempt to rationalise the competing organisations responsible for running the economy by increasing the powers of the three deputies and establishing them as a formal Collegium of the Council of People's Commissars, while leaving Gosplan untouched. On 15 January the Politburo received another of Trotsky's lengthy and closely argued memoranda. Trotsky saw Stalin's proposal as a criticism of his own. First, he was uncertain as to whether it would correct "the multiplicity of directing establishments with undefined mutual relationships and fragmented responsibilities which generated chaos from the top down", but second it gave primacy to the question of finance. This was a new strand to Trotsky's argument; short-term financial considerations were hampering long-term planning. "I judged the mistake in our economic policy of the most recent period to be the primacy accorded to financial questions, a galloping rouble cannot be the regulator of the economy", but Stalin's planned reorganisation would mean that the only commissariat still fully represented in economic discussions would be the Commissariat of Finance, not Gosplan, "thus the mistaken inter-relationship between finance and industry receives in Comrade Stalin's project new organisational expression". He ended his memorandum with this telling analogy for Gosplan's role in the economy: "I would say that Gosplan would discharge the role of Staff HQ and the Council of Labour and Defence that of the RVS."

Stalin responded two days later by suggesting that Trotsky could, if he wanted, combine the role of deputy with that of heading Gosplan, surely a way of ensuring the correct relationship between the two. Trotsky replied with another memorandum on 20 January which made clear that Stalin's concession did not change the fundamental problem which was that creating a special collegium of deputies was not the solution to the economic crisis, for all members of such a body would be "responsible for everything and for nothing". What Stalin was doing was to ensure that all leading Bolsheviks were dealing with several jobs, while the self-same job was being assigned to several people. For Trotsky the real issue was this, "the Politburo sought to settle ten or twelve practical economic questions of vast importance in a single session, without the slightest preparation, after ten minutes discussion beforehand"; that was not planning.

As this row developed, it became personal: Stalin could not help mentioning that Trotsky had been invited to be a deputy before, but had declined; Trotsky responded that this had never been brought to the Politburo, was confidential, and Stalin had no right to mention it; Stalin produced evidence of the September telephone discussion and Trotsky had to back down. Stalin suggested Trotsky tended to exaggerate and panic, making such claims that unless something were done "the cock would crow" over Soviet power; Trotsky responded that the cock would indeed crow over Soviet power unless the question of Gosplan and its future were seriously addressed. Zinoviev also became involved: in February Trotsky put to the Politburo some ideas on how the Party's central institutions, the Central Committee and the Central Control Commission (CCC), might improve their work; Zinoviev denounced the ideas as "likely to lead to a split", although, after Trotsky's protests, it was agreed to amend the Politburo minutes to remove Zinoviev's assertion that Trotsky's proposals would create a "dual authority".[25]

Yet for all this dissension, Trotsky's campaign that the issue of planning should be taken seriously was making progress. On 13 February the Politburo backed Trotsky rather than the Commissariat of Finance on the issue of enterprises having the right to use their turnover capital to provide credit and on 20 February it was agreed that Trotsky's theses on organising industry would be the basis for discussion at the Central Committee Plenum on 22–23 February. That plenum resolved to accept Trotsky's theses as a basis for debate at the Twelfth Party Congress and established a commission to take things further; that commission agreed a text on 6 March, which was then subject to amendment on the 8th. And in all this Trotsky was backed by Stalin, who even proposed that, in Lenin's absence, it should be Trotsky who delivered the main Congress report. When Trotsky declined, insisting that he could only report on his own area of concern, i.e. industry, he added "besides, there are differences between us and I am in the minority". Stalin responded, "I do not see any differences", implying that he, despite their tetchy relationship, was ready for far-reaching changes in economic policy.[26]

It was because Trotsky felt he was making progress on his campaign to introduce a genuine system of economic planning through Gosplan that he behaved so cautiously when approached by Lenin to confront Stalin over what had become known as the Georgian Affair. One of the main political events of 1922 had been to transform Soviet Russia, Soviet Ukraine and other Soviet Republics formed within the former Russian Empire into a newly constituted Soviet Union. In this process Lenin and Stalin had disagreed about the degree of autonomy the constituent republics of the Soviet Union should have. However, it was not so much Stalin's disagreement on points of principle which infuriated Lenin, for Stalin was always ready to compromise on these, but the brutal way Stalin had forced his opponents into submission, in the case of Georgia by condoning physical assaults on those communists who disagreed with him. Behind the Georgian Affair stood a purely personal matter. Stalin, as Party General Secretary, was responsible for ensuring Lenin followed the health routine imposed by the Politburo. But Lenin was not just a party symbol, but a person with human relationships, and his wife Nadezhda Krupskaya understandably felt she had a role in caring for Lenin's welfare. This tension caused a number of minor incidents, and finally exploded when Stalin lost his temper with Krupskaya and swore at her. It was these incidents which prompted Lenin to draft a Testament to be read out at the Party Congress following his death which was critical of Stalin, the power he accumulated, and the way he used that power, and which concluded by calling for Stalin to be removed from the post of Party Secretary.

On 5 March 1923 Lenin sent his secretary to Trotsky's apartment, where he was ill, suffering from lumbago, to ask if he would take up the Georgian Affair at the Twelfth Party Congress. Trotsky gave the impression that he accepted, and sent the secretary back to Lenin to find out if he could discuss the matter with Kamenev, who was deputising for Lenin as the Head of Government and was anyway about to attend a Party conference in Georgia. Back came the secretary to say Kamenev should be kept out of the business because he "will immediately show everything to Stalin, and Stalin will make a rotten compromise and then deceive us". However, an hour later, Lenin, fearing he was about to die, changed his mind and informed Kamenev as well as Trotsky. When Trotsky and Kamenev met to decide what to do, Kamenev had just come from a meeting with Krupskaya, who had told him that Lenin had just dictated a letter to Stalin breaking off all relations with him. Despite all this Trotsky did not take up the fight against Stalin, saying to Kamenev:

Remember, and tell others, that the last thing I want is to start a fight at the Congress for any changes in organisation. I am for preserving the status quo. If Lenin gets on his feet before the Congress, of which there is unfortunately little chance, he and I will discuss the matter together anew. I am against removing Stalin.[27]

Nevertheless, Trotsky's relations with Stalin remained tense. On 16 April Lenin's secretary, who had been on leave for three weeks, informed Trotsky, Kamenev and Stalin that Lenin had wanted the article he had written on the Georgian Affair published before the Twelfth Party Congress, due to open the next day. The article had been among the papers given to Trotsky on 5 March, and Trotsky, lacking clear instructions as to what to do with it, had returned it to Lenin's office while keeping a copy for himself. Stalin accused Trotsky in writing of behaving improperly, but then apologised and agreed to issue a written statement to this effect. When on the 18th Stalin's written apology was still not in circulation, Trotsky threatened to take the issue to the Party's conflict commission. However, despite the intensity of this row, Trotsky opposed Kamenev's view that Lenin's article be published and endorsed Stalin's proposal that only leading provincial delegates to the Congress be given a summary of Lenin's views at a special private meeting.[28]

In his speech to the Twelfth Party Congress, held from 17 to 25 April, Trotsky made clear that he was not giving a report on the current state of the economy, but an overview of how economic policy should develop. His vision was simple. Under NEP the key task was to increase production and at the same time to ensure that the benefits of any increased production flowed to the socialist sector of the economy. The economy was a little richer, but, he asked, had the socialist sector benefited or the capitalist? The picture was not good: trade between the country and town was still essentially only in consumer goods, yet economic recovery demanded that industrial goods find a market. At this point in his speech Trotsky produced what would become a famous graph, depicting the gap between industrial prices and agricultural prices in the form of a pair of open scissors; the only way to close the scissors and bring prices back into alignment, he explained, was to lower industrial costs. Trotsky's message was Thatcherite. It would not be enough for industrial trusts as a whole to be profitable, but within trusts every factory had to be profitable, even if that meant redundancies. Profits accumulated by the state as a result of this rigor would be diverted into state investments.

For this to happen it was essential to plan, and organising a proper system of centralised planning was the key task the Twelfth Party Congress had to address. "Comrades, I insist on this especially because the question of planning is essentially a question of leadership; we speak in far too general terms about leadership in the economy, but surely leadership in the economy is planning more than anything else." Trotsky then went on to sing the praises of Gosplan and to repeat his view that Gosplan should be the Staff HQ of the Council of Labour and Defence. Zinoviev was quick to contradict this Civil War analogy, pointing out, "It is impossible to say that the time has come when the Party should refuse to lead the economy; the very opposite, the organised and planned interference of the Party will alone lead to that aim which stands before us."[29]

The German October

By summer 1923 the political crisis that had arisen in Germany aroused hopes among the entire Bolshevik leadership that the Soviet Union's isolation as the only socialist state in the world would end. When the German government declared early in 1923 that it was incapable of paying the reparations owed to the wartime Allies, French troops occupied the Ruhr. The resulting economic chaos caused hyperinflation and widespread labour unrest which culminated in a general strike early in August forcing the resignation of the government. In this atmosphere the German Communist Party made rapid progress, especially in its campaign to wrest control of the trade union movement by building up communist-dominated factory committees. In July more than half the votes in the Metalworkers' Union went to communists and between July and October the number of Communist Party cells in the trade unions rose from 4,000 to 6,000; by late summer half the labour force supported the communists.

On 23 August the Politburo held a special session to discuss the situation in Germany. Trotsky was both enthused and alarmed. He felt a revolution was imminent, but was convinced that revolution in Germany would prompt capitalist Europe to intervene, sucking the Soviet Union into a war fought not only in defence of socialist Germany but also for the Soviet Union's own survival. Both Zinoviev and Stalin argued that Trotsky was exaggerating, and that there was plenty of time to prepare, since the revolution would mature only in the autumn at the earliest and possibly not until spring the following year. A four-member commission was delegated for insurrectionary work within Germany: this, like all the other Politburo resolutions on Germany, was agreed unanimously.[30]

Over the summer Trotsky's relations with Stalin were no longer strained. A witness to the Politburo meeting of 8 August noted how Zinoviev and Trotsky studiously ignored each other, while Kamenev and Trotsky exchanged only a cursory nod; Stalin on the other hand "greeted Trotsky in a most friendly manner and vigorously shook hands with him across the table". Stalin was well aware that during summer 1923 Zinoviev was working on a scheme to limit Stalin's control over the Party Secretariat, a scheme in which Trotsky had shown no interest. Thus Trotsky and Stalin were basically agreed on policy towards Germany. Trotsky was worried by what he called "the temporising policy with regard to the armed insurrection" on the part of the German Communist leadership, but his colleagues had no problem with him writing in *Pravda* on 23 September about the need for a clear timetable for revolution. In October 1917, although there had been "a deliberate postponement of ten days", the Bolsheviks had set themselves a clear timetable, he argued, and in Germany the communists should do the same and "fix a time in the immediate future, a time in the course of which the favourable revolutionary situation cannot abruptly react against us, and then concentrate every effort on preparing the blow".[31]

In this *Pravda* article Trotsky assumed that in setting a date for insurrection "the toiling masses were in constant ferment and the Party obviously supported by an unquestionable majority of toilers"; it was precisely because this was not the case that the German Communist Party leadership was so "temporising". It recognised that, at best, the communists were supported by half the organised working class, a long way short of "an unquestionable majority of toilers". Nevertheless, when the Politburo again debated Germany at the end of September, all doubts were put aside. Optimistic reports had been received from the commission working underground and a quantity of arms had been accumulated. As in October 1917, it was a question of making an essentially offensive action seem defensive, but the Politburo's plan was that the communists would organise mass demonstrations on 7 November, the anniversary of the October Revolution; this would provoke counter-measures by the authorities; then, the communists could respond with renewed and "justified" demonstrations culminating with a seizure of power on 9 November, the fifth anniversary of the overthrow of the Kaiser. The German Communist leader, Heinrich Brandler, refused point-blank to accept this timetable, and in the end it was agreed that the timing of the uprising would be left to German communists.

In the German states of Saxony and Thuringia the communists had, since 1922, been supporting minority governments of left-wing Social Democrats. Brandler favoured a tactic of forcing the left-wing Social Democrats to include the communists in the Saxon and Thuringian government as a way of precipitating a broad political crisis. Once this tactic had been agreed in principle, Moscow insisted on determining its timing, informing Brandler on 1 October that he should act at once. Brandler returned to Germany from Moscow on 8 October and by the 12th the communists had, as planned, joined the Saxon Government. Once in power, the communists began openly arming the Red Hundred Militia it had been forming for some time; the consequent stand-off with Berlin was therefore planned and deliberate. It came on 20 October when Berlin ordered that the Red Hundreds be disbanded. The communists refused and summoned a conference of factory councils at Chemnitz to organise a general strike and other actions to resist Berlin's intervention. However, the conference of factory councils, the voice of "the majority of toilers", rejected the communist proposal for a general strike or any other kind of resistance and Brandler concluded he had no choice but to call off the insurrection.[32]

The political impact of the failed German October would not have been so dispiriting if it had not coincided with a new domestic crisis in Russia. Provoked largely by lay-offs in the state industrial sector and delays of several months in the payment of wages, policies which followed on logically from Trotsky's insistence that state enterprises run at a profit, a rash of strikes broke out in September and continued into October. Some of these strikes involved dissident communists who branded NEP "New Exploitation of the Proletariat" and called for a renewal of soviet democracy. The Politburo responded on 18 September by establishing a commission under Felix Dzerzhinskii, head of the security police (*cheka*), which reported two days later and then presented its conclusions to a Central Committee plenum on 23 September. One of its decisions was that it was the duty of Party members not only to inform the Central Committee and the CCC about factional activity but the *cheka* as well.[33]

Showdown

Zinoviev and Stalin were agreed on the need to strengthen Party control over non-party specialists. By talking about the danger of war if the revolution in Germany succeeded, Trotsky revived issues that had been rumbling under the surface since the Civil War had ended. Suddenly the Red Army needed to be put on alert, after two years when it had successfully adjusted to a peace footing. Trotsky had been so busy on economic matters that the Red Army and the RVS had been left to run themselves, and the RVS was still dominated by non-party military specialists, not perhaps the best people to command when a revolutionary war in Europe was in prospect. Trotsky returned from his annual holiday to discover that Party "interference" in the economic commissariats had been extended to his own commissariat. At the Politburo meeting of 23 September it was proposed to radically revise the composition of the RVS. Trotsky was incandescent with rage. This was the day *Pravda* had published his article calling for the German communists to adopt a time-table for insurrection, and he announced grandiloquently that he would resign all his Russian posts and move to Germany to help the revolution there. Zinoviev promptly declared that if anyone were needed in Germany it was not Trotsky but Zinoviev himself. It was therefore left to Stalin to try and cool tempers by insisting that two such revolutionary leaders as Zinoviev and Trotsky were both needed at home in Russia. Stalin's attempt at reconciliation might have worked if one of Zinoviev's supporters had not accused Trotsky of "putting on airs"; Trotsky stormed out.

After Trotsky had left the meeting, V. Kuibyshev, the chairman of the Central Control Commission, was sent to see him to ask if he could be persuaded to return; he categorically refused. When the Central Committee resumed discussion of the RVS on 25 September it hoped to broker a compromise by deciding to delay implementing its full list of proposals. Trotsky explained his walk-out in a letter to the Central Committee on 4 October. He gave two reasons. First, he had not been consulted on the RVS proposal which, given the situation in Germany, could have dramatic consequences; capitalist Europe could well interpret the expansion of the RVS as an aggressive move on the Soviet Union's behalf. Second, the Party leadership had dressed up as a routine reorganisation a move which was actually part of a political struggle directed against him. He adduced as evidence something Kuibyshev had said to him when sent to persuade him to return to the plenum. Trotsky heard him say, "We cannot denounce you as an enemy, but we think that it is in the Party interest to struggle against you." Kuibyshev insisted his actual words were rather different: "It is not enmity that makes us vote against you . . . [but] your temperament often leads you far astray."[34]

Faced with a real or imagined assault on his position, Trotsky determined to counter-attack. At the first Politburo meeting held after the September Central Committee Plenum it had been agreed that a private conference of the Politburo should be held to try and resolve matters. Delays in arranging this persuaded Trotsky it was not happening and prompted him to write another letter to the Central Committee on 8 October to outline his case. The crux of his discontent was this: at the Twelfth Party Congress he had insisted that his resolution on the economy be adopted in practice, not just as a piece of propaganda rhetoric. He had warned what would happen if the planned economy and strict reduction of overheads in industry were not addressed, but despite what the Congress decided about strengthening Gosplan, in practice it had been relegated in importance, doing useful work but not introducing the planned regulation of the economy. As a result, "To an even greater extent than before the Congress, the most important economic issues are being solved in a hurry, without due preparation, regardless of their impact on planning." The situation could be summed up like this: "There is no management of the economy; chaos begins at the top."

Looking for the reason for this, Trotsky turned to Stalin and his work in the Secretariat and Orgburo. Conceding that the Twelfth Party Congress had resolved, as Zinoviev insisted it should, to increase Party control over economic management, the Party, under Stalin's guidance, had gone about this in the most inappropriate way. Instead of "a thorough selection of managerial personnel" the Orgburo had developed its own criteria: "in the last eighteen months a specific secretary's psychology has been formed", secretaries were chosen for their political loyalty and the net result was "an unprecedented bureaucratisation of the Party apparatus". Given the take over of the Party's official channels by those sharing the "secretary's psychology", it was scarcely surprising that "the most acute and pressing problems were being discussed outside the official Party apparatus, thus creating the conditions for illegal factions inside the Party". And yet, instead of addressing the interests of industry, the September Plenum decided to extend the tentacles of that "secretary's psychology" into the RVS.[35]

Whether this had been his intention or not, Trotsky's letter quickly began to circulate more widely than within the Central Committee. When the Politburo's private conference finally met on 11 October it endorsed a resolution calling for a turn "towards Party Democracy". However, this did not prevent the CCC taking measures on 13 October to prevent any further discussion of Trotsky's letter, and indeed Trotsky wrote on 15 October that he had played no part in distributing his letter more widely. It was too late. That same day 46 prominent Party leaders, some of them long associates of Trotsky and others the sort of economic leaders instinctively hostile to the hierarchy of secretaries, signed a common platform which echoed Trotsky's demands. On 19 October the Politburo responded to Trotsky's attack of ten days earlier. His letter was in fact "a letter-platform" and he had tried to incite factionalism. The Politburo was implementing the programme adopted at the Twelfth Party Congress, ignoring only what was "artificial and far-fetched". Trotsky's repeated talk of planning never addressed practicalities. Of course industrial prices had to come down, but if that meant closing the loss-making Putilov plant in Petrograd then the Politburo would not do it. As to the question of personnel and the appointment of secretaries, Trotsky's attitude was "nothing else but preparation of the ground for separating the Soviet apparatus from the Party". The Politburo suggested that Trotsky's true agenda here was his own ambition. His attitude, it resolved, was this: "Either the Party confers on him practically dictatorial powers in the sphere of economics and the armed forces, or he actually refuses to do any work in the fields of economics or industry."[36]

Trotsky replied to the Politburo statement on 23 October. In his view it was not "factional" to point out irregularities in the way the Central Committee worked. It was quite illogical for the Politburo to resolve on 11 October that a turn towards democracy was needed, while at the same time stating that the situation in the Party was "normal". He then reminded the Politburo of his main concern, that the poor regulation of the economy was the root cause of the economic crisis, and that Lenin had agreed that Gosplan should have legislative powers; on 2 June 1923 Krupskaya had sent all Politburo members a copy of Lenin's note of 27 December 1922 agreeing to this. He did not want to separate state and Party, he just wanted "real, true Party leadership in solving all major problems, not simple occasional interference". As to Gosplan, the Twelfth Party Congress had decided that no economic decisions could be implemented "without the knowledge of Gosplan" but this had not happened. He ended this letter with a pointed aside for the future: "in October 1917 some important executives deserted their posts".[37]

Work towards a resolution of this crisis began at a joint plenum of the Central Committee and the CCC held on 25–7 October. Although by now Trotsky talked of "the other Politburo within the Politburo and the other Central Committee within the Central Committee", and accused the Secretariat of "turning the CCC into the Secretariat's weapon in this inner Party contest", he still kept coming back to the question of planning and the economy. There had to be some way in which economic matters were properly discussed before they came to the Politburo: "I cannot vote at the Politburo if experienced people, who know the matter inside out, have not worked on these questions: if I were discharged of some work and were appointed to Gosplan, I would not oppose; I confirm that all our crises are 50 or 75 or 100% aggravated by the extemporising approach." Stalin's response was bewilderment.

Is anybody against improving Gosplan? Trotsky often has to abstain in Politburo because the question is not elaborated enough. And what if we also abstained? What would happen? Abstention cannot become a theory. It is ridiculous to form a platform on the need to improve Gosplan.

The problem, Stalin stressed, was that Trotsky and the 46 had gone over the heads of the Central Committee, thus repeating what had happened during the Trade Union Debate when Trotsky had "refused to carry out Lenin's recommendation for settling the matter within the trade union commission of the congress". The Joint Plenum resolved to forbid factional discussion on the basis of platforms and to endorse the Politburo's course towards internal Party democracy.[38]

The course towards internal democracy was mapped out at a Politburo meeting on 5 November with the adoption of a resolution "On Building the Party". On 7 November Zinoviev announced that the pages of *Pravda* would be used for an open discussion of how to link the Party and the masses. Trotsky's participation in this was severely hampered by influenza which developed during a hunting trip at the end of October; he was bedridden for much of the last two months of 1923 and the first of 1924, with several Politburo meetings being held in his flat to enable him to participate. Trotsky's problem was that the open discussion unleashed a lot of anger at the way the Party operated, but little support for his technocratic vision of planning. Despite everything, Stalin was keen to mend fences; as Trotsky recalled, at this time Stalin "displayed an utterly unexpected interest in my health".[39]

Compromise was the obvious solution and Trotsky was willing to respond. The September Plenum had established a Commission on Internal Party Democracy, chaired by Molotov. It reported on 29 November, resulting in a further commission being formed to draft the final text of the resolution "On Building the Party", with a sub-committee comprising Kamenev, Stalin and Trotsky to dot the i's and cross the t's. On 5 December the subcommittee met at Trotsky's flat. As the record of that meeting made clear:

Trotsky considered it necessary to adopt a far more decisive and explicit formulation of those steps needed to remove any doubt about the Central Committee's intention to act as agreed. With particular persistence Trotsky underlined his fears that collective statements of disciplined workers to the Central Committee would be considered factional . . . [and that] the habit of using bureaucratic methods of administration in the Party would become a serious obstacle to implementing the new course.

Kamenev and Stalin assured him that such fears were groundless and the resolution was adopted unanimously.[40]

Trotsky agreed to sign the resolution "On Building the Party" on condition that the Central Committee recorded, but did not publish, his reservations. He was worried that the resolution of the October Plenum against factionalism could condemn action that the new resolution "On Building the Party" actually sought to encourage. He also disliked the way the Politburo dismissed as "a storm in a teacup" his deeply felt concerns about Gosplan. Nevertheless he accepted Kamenev and Stalin's repeated assurances that the Politburo would implement its new course. It seems there was another element to settling this dispute. Documents from the January 1924 Central Committee Plenum make clear that at this time Stalin proposed that Trotsky "take charge of industry" and that at two meetings in Trotsky's flat Stalin and Trotsky "talked about Gosplan". Trotsky's offer to run Gosplan was being taken seriously, despite Lenin's earlier statement that this would be a mistake; after all, Stalin had already proposed once before that Trotsky could run Gosplan.[41]

Notes

1 L. Trotsky, *Terrorism and Communism* (Ann Arbor, 1961), p. 47; *How*, Vol. III, p. 23.

2 I. Deutscher, *The Prophet Armed, Trotsky: 1879–1921* (Oxford, 1970), pp. 493–6.

3 Trotsky, *How*, Vol. III, pp. 75–6; F. McCullagh, "Trotsky in Ekaterinburg", *Fortnightly Review*, p. 546; J. M. Meijer (ed.), *The Trotsky Papers*, Vol. II, pp. 47, 57, 75.

4 Trotsky, *How*, Vol. III, pp. 83, 89.

5 RGVA 4.14.4, p. 15 *et seq.* (the numbering sequence breaks down in this file and it is clear that this speech on economic questions dated approximately July 1918 has found its way by mistake into the "Protocols of the Republican Revvoensovet"); Trotsky, *How*, Vol. III, p. 83.

6 RGVA 4.14.4, p. 76; J. Channon "Trotsky, the Peasants and Economic Policy: a Comment", *Economy and Society*, Vol. 14, 1985, No. 4, pp. 513–20.

7 Trotsky, *How*, Vol. III, pp. 95–6; *Devyatyi s"ezd RKP: stenograficheskii otchet* (Moscow, 1920), pp. 79–97, 163, 171, 360.

8 W. G. Rosenberg, "The Social Background to Tsektran" in D. Koenker *et al.* (eds), *Party, State and Society in the Russian Civil War* (Indiana, 1989), p. 352; A. J. Heywood, *Modernising Lenin's Russia* (Cambridge, 1999), p. 136; A. J. Heywood, "A Tale of Two Policies. Trotsky, Foreign Trade and the Plight of the Soviet Railway System, December 1919–March 1921". Unpublished paper kindly made available by the author.

9 Meijer (ed.), *Trotsky Papers*, Vol. II, p. 175.

10 Meijer (ed.), *Trotsky Papers*, Vol. II, pp. 209, 215, 229, 241, 257; *How*, Vol. III, pp. 224, 253.

11 L. Trotsky, *My Life* (New York, 1970), pp. 457–9.

12 Heywood, "A Tale"; Trotsky, *My Life*, p. 465.

13 L. Schapiro, *The Origin of the Communist Autocracy* (Cambridge, Mass., 1977), pp. 273–84.

14 RGVA 4.14.4, pp. 190, 208. (The drafts of all Trotsky's writings while he was Commissar of War are kept in the Military Archives and are therefore reproduced in the microfilm of this collection. It proved easier for this author to consult these drafts than the incomplete edition of Trotsky's *Collected Works* held in the British Library.)

15 Schapiro, *Origin*, p. 289.

16 Schapiro, *Origin*, pp. 258–9, 3–4–05; L. Trotsky, *The Writings of Leon Trotsky: 1937–8* (New York, 1975), pp. 376–8.

17 *Stenograficheskii otchet X s"ezda RKP* (Petrograd, 1921), p. 147; Deutscher, *Armed*, p. 509; R. Pipes, *The Unknown Lenin* (New Haven, 1998), p. 124.

18 Meijer (ed.), *Trotsky Papers*, Vol. II, pp. 579–81.

19 Meijer (ed.), *Trotsky Papers*, Vol. II, p. 661.

20 Pipes, *Unknown*, pp. 142, 148.

21 *Odinatsatyi s"ezd RKP (b): stenograficheskii otchet* (Moscow 1961), pp. 132–4, 270–2, 387–9; Trotsky, *Writings 1936–7*, p. 42.

22 Meijer (ed.), *Trotsky Papers*, Vol. II, pp. 731–3.

23 Pipes, *Unknown*, pp. 166, 171; Meijer (ed.), *Trotsky Papers*, Vol. II, pp. 745–7.

24 Deutscher, *The Prophet Unarmed, Trotsky: 1921–1929* (Oxford, 1978), p. 67; Meijer (ed.), *Trotsky Papers*, Vol. II, pp. 775, 789–801.

25 Meijer (ed.), *Trotsky Papers*, Vol. II, pp. 817–33; for Zinoviev's intervention, see *Arkhiv Trotskogo* (Moscow, 1990), Vol. I, pp. 29, 32. This affair is thoroughly discussed in Erik van Ree "'Lenin's Last Struggle' Revisited", *Revolutionary Russia*, No. 2, 2001, pp. 85–122.

26 Trotsky, *My Life*, p. 179; L. Trotsky, *Stalin* (London, 1968), Vol. II, p. 179; *Arkhiv Trotskogo*, Vol. I, pp. 33, 35, 40.

27 Trotsky, *My Life*, pp. 483–6.

28 *Arkhiv Trotskogo*, Vol. I, p. 65; R. Service, *Lenin: a Political Life* (Basingstoke, 1995), Vol. III, pp. 312–14.

29 *Dvenatsatyi s"ezd RKP (b): stenograficheskii otchet* (Moscow, 1923), pp. 46; 282–313.

30 B. Bazhanov, *Bazhanov and the Damnation of Stalin* (Ohio, 1990), pp. 46–8; for the situation in Germany, see G. R. Swain, "Was the Profintern Really Necessary?", *European History Quarterly*, No. 1, 1987, pp. 57–77. For Trotsky and "temporising", see V. Vilkova, *The Struggle for Power in Russia in 1923* (New York, 1996), p. 157.

31 Bazhanov, *Bazhanov*, p. 44; J. V. Stalin, *Collected Works* (Moscow, 1953), Vol. VII, p. 362; L. Trotsky, *The First Five Years of the Communist International* (London, 1974), Vol. II, pp. 349–50.

32 Bazhanov, *Bazhanov*, pp. 46–8; E. H. Carr, *The Interregnum, 1923–4* (London, 1969), pp. 209–31.

33 Vilkova, *Struggle*, pp. 46, 58.

34 Bazhanov, *Bazhanov*, p. 50; Vilkova, *Struggle*, pp. 37, 41, 43, 45.

35 Vilkova, *Struggle*, pp. 46–55.

36 Deutscher, *Unarmed*, pp. 14–15; Vilkova, *Struggle*, pp. 27, 75, 80, 102–21, 141.

37 Vilkova, *Struggle*, pp. 139–64.

38 Vilkova, *Struggle*, pp. 37, 173–6.

39 Deutscher, *Unarmed*, p. 118; Bazhanov, *Bazhanov*, pp. 54–6; D. Hincks, "Support for the Opposition in Moscow: the Party Discussion of 1923–4", *Soviet Studies*, No. 1, 1992, pp. 147, 149–50; L. Trotsky, *Stalin* (London, 1968), Vol. II, pp. 207–9.

40 Vilkova, *Struggle*, pp. 205–6.

41 Vilkova, *Struggle*, pp. 229–30, 322, 334, 350.

Chapter 6

Combating Thermidor

Only three days after Trotsky had signed his joint agreement with Kamenev and Stalin that would have made him head of Gosplan, he reneged on it. In the programmatic essay *The New Course*, written on 8 December and published after some haggling in *Pravda* on 11 December 1923, Trotsky denounced the increasingly bureaucratic leadership of the Party, asserting that the old, established leadership was in conflict with a younger generation. In one of those exaggerated parallels he loved, he compared the situation among the Bolshevik leaders with the time in the history of the German Social Democratic Party when the once radical allies of Marx and Engels slipped almost imperceptibly into a new role as the fathers of reformism. It was a nice image, but Kamenev, Stalin and Zinoviev were hardly going to relish the implication that only Trotsky was the true revolutionary and that they were mere reformists.

In writing *The New Course*, Trotsky not only insulted his Politburo colleagues but, in Bolshevik terms, he gave them the moral high ground. He had reached an agreement and then broken it. He had done the same with Lenin at the height of the Brest Litovsk crisis. During the Trade Union Debate he had joined the Zinoviev Commission only to declare he would take no part in its work. The resolution against factionalism adopted at the Tenth Party Congress had been aimed specifically at preventing this sort of behaviour. Whether or not Trotsky's behaviour had verged on factionalism in autumn 1923 could be open to interpretation, but *The New Course* was factionalist beyond doubt. He had signed up to a compromise, and then broken with it, challenging the revolutionary credentials of his Politburo comrades in the process.

A Petit Bourgeois Deviation

Why did Trotsky break the agreement so recently entered into? First he was infuriated by the growing evidence that *Pravda* was not giving fair coverage to the debate taking place within the Party. At the Politburo meeting on 29 November Stalin had proposed that all the material for the "Party Life" section of *Pravda* should be sent to the Party Secretariat, not the paper's editorial offices. When key journalists resigned in protest, two commissars were sent in to replace them, one a supporter of Zinoviev, the other a supporter of Stalin. *Pravda*'s coverage changed immediately, becoming the mouthpiece of the leadership. Trotsky's supporters charged, with justification, that the paper doctored the results of votes at rank and file meetings. When on 5 December Trotsky had insisted on lodging his reservations about the agreement he had just entered into, he added: "I consider it to be my duty to point out with all my energy that any attempt to use the unanimous adoption of this resolution in order to pro vide unanimity in the Party by means of bureaucratic measures would lead to results directly opposite to those we are all striving for."[1]

Between them Stalin and Zinoviev were "fixing" the outcome of the Party discussion. For those who had "fixed" the proceedings of the Prague Conference in 1912, this was nothing new and nothing to be ashamed of. For Trotsky it was an unpleasant example of how the Bolshevik Party was reverting to type; it was the sort of thing his comrades in the Inter-district Group had always warned against. It might seem strange that what had begun as an argument about planning had ended up focusing on the Party's bureaucratic methods, but for Trotsky these were intimately linked: Gosplan was not "a storm in a teacup"; the Party's failure to engage with Gosplan reflected its failure to produce economic managers of the right calibre, and that resulted from the Party Secretariat and its obsession with producing secretaries all of a type, loyal but incapable of running the economy. For Trotsky "building the party" meant learning to operate as he had done in the Red Army, by calling conferences of experts and consulting widely. That is why *The New Course* stressed that "a renewal of Party staff must be carried out in order to replace old bureaucrats with fresh ones"; the actions of the Secretariat in "fixing" press coverage of the Party discussion did not suggest that a purge of provincial Party secretaries was imminent, quite the reverse.

There was a second reason for Trotsky's decision to break the 5 December agreement. By December 1923 Trotsky had begun to worry about the danger of a Thermidor reaction, although it would be a while before he adopted this term borrowed from the French Revolution. For Trotsky, three class elements operated in the Soviet Union: the workers, the peasants and the new bourgeoisie linked to the intelligentsia. Most of the time the proletariat kept the new bourgeoisie firmly in its place, but that did not mean that if private capital expanded more quickly than state capital and it was private capital that satisfied the peasant market, then private capital might become strong enough to position itself between the workers' state and the peasantry and gain enormous economic and political influence, possibly sufficient to bring about a counter-revolution. In *Results and Prospects* Trotsky had envisaged the inevitable post-revolutionary clash between workers and peasants as an open struggle: but what if this were a more gradual process, what if the counter-revolution took the form of a gradual restructuring of the state apparatus in a bourgeois direction? The solution was to use Gosplan to correct the imbalance between industry and agriculture: but what if the quiet counter-revolution had already penetrated the bureaucracy, changing its nature, opposing Gosplan and opening up a gap between the Party and the workers? Bureaucratism was itself then an expression of negative features which could, if left to fester, lead to counter-revolution. If the country faced a quiet counter-revolution through bureaucratism, the crisis could not be solved by the Secretariat resorting to bureaucratic methods.[2]

Trotsky's *New Course* prompted an immediate response. He was criticised in *Pravda* on both 13 and 14 December. The line was clear, Trotsky had broken a unanimous agreement and had written an essay appealing over the heads of the Central Committee to the rank and file, seeking to turn them, especially the Party youth, against the Party's central institutions. As such Trotsky's views "clearly deviate from the organisational principles on which our Party had been built for many years and undoubtedly includes elements which we are accustomed to see on the pages of newspapers which for a number of years systematically criticised 'Bolshevik centralism', 'Bolshevik committee men' and 'Bolshevik bureaucracy'." With this none too subtle allusion to Trotsky's long association with the Mensheviks and the Interdistrict Group, the Bolshevik leadership revealed how it planned to cope with the Trotsky problem; they would remind the Party that Trotsky's Bolshevism was at best skin deep. Zinoviev began the process the following day, reminding *Pravda* readers that "before entering our Party" Trotsky had wanted the Party to be "a conglomeration of tendencies"; this was wrong then and was wrong now. Trotsky's "greatest error" was to attack the Party apparatus which, far from being a source of danger was "the right hand of our Party".[3]

Trotsky responded with an essay submitted to *Pravda* on 23 December but published only on the 28th. Here he came close to repeating some of his concerns of 1904 about the danger of substitutionism in the Bolshevik Party. The ban on factions was being used to ban debate: "If factions are not wanted, there must not be any permanent groupings;

if permanent groupings are not wanted, temporary groupings must be avoided; finally, in order that there should be no temporary groupings, there must be no differences of opinion, for wherever there are two opinions, people inevitably group together." Yet how, he asked, in a party of half a million members, was it possible to avoid differences of opinion? The resolution of the Tenth Party Congress could help struggle against factionalism, which was indeed a danger, but "it is criminal to shut your eyes to the danger represented by conservative bureaucratic factionalism". Here was a statement his opponents, and most true Bolsheviks, could never accept: that the Party apparatus could itself be a faction and not "the right hand of our Party" was beyond Bolshevik comprehension.[4]

The Politburo hit back in *Pravda* on 31 December. Trotsky's article of the 28th was "a direct confession that he had set up a faction" and reminded Bolsheviks "of the fierce factional battles within the united Russian Social Democratic Labour Party Central Committee"; "to set the Party off against its apparatus means precisely to deviate from Leninism", the Politburo stressed. The article then pointed out that although Lenin had come round to supporting Trotsky's views on Gosplan, he was absolutely adamant that Trotsky was not the right man to be its president. Thus although the Politburo resolved to intensify planning and "strengthen Gosplan, increasing its role in relation to financial and credit policy", two of Trotsky's most insistent demands, Trotsky would not be the beneficiary. The Central Committee Plenum on 14–15 January 1924 was dominated by the Trotsky affair. Trotsky's behaviour was condemned and ominously the Plenum agreed to establish a Military Commission to review the work of the Commissariat for War. These moves were then endorsed by the Thirteenth Party Conference, held on 16–18 January 1924, at which Trotsky and those who had signed the Platform of 46 were accused of "a petit bourgeois deviation from Leninism".[5]

Trotsky left Moscow on 18 January for a rest cure in the Caucasus. He was thus in Tbilisi when news came of Lenin's death on 21 January. Stalin advised that it would be difficult for him to get back for the funeral and so he should proceed to Sukhumi and look after his health. Trotsky's journey to Tbilisi had taken three days, so he could have been back in Moscow by the 24th or 25th, in ample time to attend the funeral first planned for the 26th but then postponed until the 27th; for whatever reason he chose not to attend. While he was at Sukhumi the Central Committee's Military Commission visited him and proposed changes to the personnel of the RVS, most notably the dismissal of his deputy throughout the Civil War, E. Sklyanskii. In February the Central

Committee accepted the Military Commission's report and in March a Central Committee Plenum confirmed Sklyanskii's dismissal. Trotsky did not return from the Caucasus until the eve of the Thirteenth Party Congress, 22–31 May 1924.[6]

The Congress was preceded by a Central Committee Plenum at which Lenin's Testament, with all its criticisms of Stalin, was read out. A year earlier Trotsky had made it clear that he was opposed to Stalin's dismissal and he had not changed his opinion. At the Congress Zinoviev called on Trotsky to recant his "petit bourgeois deviation". Trotsky refused. Trotsky's view was that everything he had done since 8 December 1923 had been in line with the 5 December resolution "On Building the Party" and that the Party leadership, not he, Trotsky, had deliberately misinterpreted that resolution. Since the Party had subsequently adopted views on Gosplan similar to his own he did not understand how he could represent "a petit bourgeois deviation". He accepted that some of his statements had been exaggerated, but stressed that he had made them in view of his Party duty to draw attention to dangers and errors. Paraphrasing the British view "my country right or wrong", Trotsky declared that he believed in "my Party right or wrong" and would accept any discipline the Party administered. Kamenev put the official view. Trotsky had broken the agreement of 5 December: "Instead of reform, he attempted to carry out a revolution in the Party; that is the basis of his sin." The congress endorsed the Thirteenth Party Conference verdict that Trotsky had engaged in "a petit bourgeois deviation".[7]

The Lessons of October

Trotsky ruminated for a long time over how best to respond to his humiliation. Before leaving the Caucasus for the Thirteenth Party Congress he had made a speech to the Tbilisi Soviet on 11 April in which he discussed the reasons for the failure of the German October Revolution. Although he was still honest enough to concede that "fairly broad masses were still marking time in the ranks of the German Social Democrats", he nevertheless concluded that the German communists had "let the revolution slip through their fingers" since "Germany did not have a Bolshevik Party nor a leader such as we had in October". He returned to the theme of Germany in a Moscow speech of 21 June: by now he had convinced himself that "one could not imagine better prepared and more mature conditions for the seizure of power" than October 1923 in Germany. Asking himself the question, "Did the communists have the majority of the working masses behind them?" he answered, "This is a question which cannot be answered with statistics but is decided by the dynamic of the revolution – the masses were moving steadily to the communists." Trotsky now believed any discussions about the mood of the masses merely reflected a lack of confidence among the leaders of the Party itself; "assertions that no aggressive fighting mood was to be observed among the masses were made more than once here, too, on the eve of October". Thus the actual failure of the German Revolution was linked to the near betrayal of the October Revolution by Zinoviev and Kamenev, something he had already alluded to in his letter to the Politburo of 23 October 1923.[8]

In autumn 1924 these ideas were fully developed in *Lessons of October*, an essay published as the preface to that volume of his collected writings dealing with 1917. His target was Zinoviev and Kamenev, not Stalin who he still felt, on issues other than the operation of the Party Secretariat, held views closer to his own. Trotsky's argument was that the disagreements of October 1917 about whether or not to seize power were profound and "by no means accidental". They reflected a persistent right-wing strand in Bolshevism, associated with Kamenev, which ran from April 1917 right through to October; this was not "a mere episodic difference of opinion but [represented] two tendencies of the utmost principled significance". Trotsky now went further than he had gone before in drawing an analogy between the events in Russia in October 1917 and events in Germany in October 1923: "we witnessed in Germany a classic demonstration of how it is possible to miss a perfectly exceptional revolutionary situation of world-historic importance" because the German communists were led by the heirs of this right-wing tendency within Bolshevism.[9] Here, as in Odessa prison and during the Brest Litovsk crisis, Trotsky was wilfully seeing what he wanted to see, blinded by the passion of the debate.

Trotsky's book was announced in *Pravda* in October and finally published on 6 November, the eve of the anniversary of the Bolshevik insurrection. A Central Committee Plenum held on 25–7 October decided to reply to Trotsky by means of a literary debate. This focused first on Trotsky's attitude to Party organisation, and second on his disdain for the peasantry. Throughout November members of the Politburo outlined their responses. Bukharin seized on the moment Trotsky had joined the Party in summer 1917: Trotsky had still then talked of "Bolshevik sectarianism", but this sectarianism was actually "the organisational principle of Bolshevism". Zinoviev pointed out that if Trotsky had had his way the Party "would have been excluded from the immediate leadership of economic and state organs". For Kamenev, Trotsky still believed that his "estimate of the driving forces of the revolution was right"; Trotsky still believed in *Results and Prospects* which "is built entirely on an underestimation of the peasantry". Stalin did not take part in the literary debate, but organised the series of Party cell meetings called to condemn Trotsky.[10]

Trotsky always denied he had written *Lessons of October* for the purpose of factional struggle, but it is hard to see what purpose it had other than to denounce those who had dared to brand him "petit bourgeois"; his own suggestion that he had simply penned a preface to a volume of his collected writings belied the fact that he had spoken on the theme repeatedly during the spring and summer. As Stalin commented, the essence of *Lessons of October* was this: "the main core of the Party is no good and must be changed". On any analysis the pamphlet misrepresented both the Russian and the failed German Octobers in order to discredit his Party opponents. As Grigorii Sokolnikov, a Politburo member not touched by association with Zinoviev and Kamenev in 1917, stated, there was no continuity between Kamenev's actions in April 1917 and his actions in October 1917; in April the danger to the Party came from the Bagdatiev Left not the Right. As to Germany, there simply had never been a real prospect of revolution; Bukharin made the most telling point, stating that "an analogy with the Russian October is quite out of place here, since in Germany there were no armed soldiers who favoured revolution".[11]

The consequences for Trotsky were immediate. A national conference of Red Army commissars demanded that Trotsky be sacked as Commissar of War. Shortly afterwards this demand was repeated by the communist cell of the RVS. His case was to be discussed at a joint plenum of the Central Committee and CCC on 19–20 January, but Trotsky felt too ill to attend; to pre-empt its decision he resigned on 15 January. Trotsky's resignation letter stressed that he had stuck by the decisions of the Thirteenth Party Congress and had not used the *Lessons of October* to revive the earlier factional debates; he was therefore ready to take on any new tasks assigned by the Central Committee. When the Committee met on 25 January it accepted Trotsky's resignation, but Stalin refused to back Zinoviev and Kamenev in their call for Trotsky's expulsion from the Politburo and Central Committee; he was issued with a final warning and left for the Caucasus to nurse his health. There, in March and April 1925 he wrote *Whither England?*, a pamphlet outlining the prospects for revolution in Britain in the aftermath of the collapse of the first Labour Government.[12]

The Dnieper Dam

Trotsky returned to Moscow in May 1925. He thus arrived in the capital just as Stalin made one of his most controversial speeches ever. Addressing a conference of the Moscow Party Organisation on 9 May Stalin raised the possibility of building "socialism in one country". Stalin took as his text the following passage from an article Lenin had written in 1915:

Uneven economic and political development is an absolute law of capitalism. Hence, the victory of socialism is possible, first in several or even one capitalist country taken separately. The victorious proletariat of that country, having expropriated the capitalists and organised its own socialist production, would stand up *against* the rest of the world, the capitalist world, attracting to its cause the oppressed classes of other countries, raising revolts in those countries against the capitalists, and in the event of necessity, coming out even with armed force against the exploiting classes and their states.

Stalin asserted that this prediction by Lenin accurately described the policy the Soviet Union was following, both internally and externally.[13]

Trotsky had never opposed the idea of "socialism in one country" if the correct economic policy were followed. He had said as much at the Ninth Party Congress and had always argued that, despite NEP, the Soviet Union was building socialism. He was therefore happy to join the Presidium of the Supreme Council of the National Economy and take up three posts within it: he would chair the Concessions Committee, the Electro-Technical Board and the Scientific-Technical Board. Within the Concessions Committee he was soon deeply involved in studying the terms of trade between the Soviet Union and the rest of the world. Trotsky was convinced that the Soviet Union could only survive if it took an active part in world trade, on terms favourable to its economic development and therefore "advanced the project of developing a system of comparative indices of the Soviet and world economy". As to the two economic committees, he was especially interested in the institutes of technical science and assiduously visited many laboratories, even studying textbooks on chemistry and hydrodynamics: "Not for nothing had I planned in my youth to take university courses in physics and mathematics."[14]

Happy to associate himself with the task of building socialism in one country, Trotsky published in *Pravda* that autumn the essay *Towards Capitalism or Socialism*. This made very clear that the Soviet Union was on its way to socialism. There had always been a danger under NEP that state industry would develop more slowly than private agriculture, with the threat that capitalism might be restored. However, that was now unlikely since private capital's share of commerce had recently fallen by half and over 60 per cent of industrial product came from the state sector. This steady advance of socialist industry could not continue indefinitely, he warned. Industry stood in 1925 at 71 per cent of the 1913 production levels; but what would happen as it grew nearer to 100 per cent? With no new factories being brought into production the old problems of NEP could reassert themselves, if the relative weight of socialist industry began to wane and the relative weight of private trade began to increase. The logic of *Towards Capitalism or Socialism* was clear. Socialism in one country could work if the correct economic policy was followed and state industrial investment gradually accelerated.[15]

Trotsky's greatest interest at this time was in the Dnieper Dam Project, a massive state investment in hydroelectricity. On 15 July 30,000 roubles had been released to start work on the technical and financial plan for this immense project. More than this, the decree announcing the project had made clear the following:

Owing to the very close connection between the proposed hydroelectric construction project on the Dnieper and the proposals for restructuring the whole economy of the southern region, it is necessary to have an overall plan for technical and economic measures in this region and a financial plan for their implementation both during construction and after the station is opened for use. The drafting of these plans is assigned to Comrade L. D. Trostky, member of the Presidium of the Supreme Council for the National Economy. Comrade Trotsky is assigned to organise an appropriate interdepartmental conference to allow the plan to be co-ordinated with the requests and needs of the Commissariat of Transport, the Commissariat of Agriculture and other offices, and to draft this overall economic, technical and financial plan.

Trotsky was not head of Gosplan, but he was Economic Plenipotentiary of the South, virtual dictator of his native region. Outline plans were to be ready by mid October, so that the loans and other funds needed could be incorporated into the 1925–6 budget.[16]

Over summer 1925 there was a further move by Zinoviev and Kamenev to have Trotsky removed from the Central Committee. Trotsky had a long-standing association with the American journalist Max Eastman, who had written a short account of Trotsky's youth. In response to the Politburo's assault on Trotsky during the Thirteenth Party Congress and the *Lessons of October* controversy, Eastman had published a book in the United States entitled *Since Lenin Died* which gave a sympathetic account of Trotsky's behaviour and laid all the blame on the Politburo, accusing it among other things of deliberately suppressing Lenin's Testament. As early as May Trotsky had written to Stalin explaining that he had had no recent contact with Eastman and that it was impossible that the documents Eastman claimed to have seen had come from him. However, when the British Communist Party asked for guidance as to how it should respond to members' queries, Stalin insisted on 18 June that Trotsky would have to write a fuller explanation. Trotsky's initial draft was rejected, but on 1 July a text was finally agreed. As Stalin confided to Molotov: "Kamenev and Zinoviev want to establish the preconditions for making Trotsky's removal from the Central Committee necessary, but they will not succeed in this because they do not have supporting facts; in his answer to Eastman's book, Trotsky determined his fate, that is he saved himself."[17]

If Stalin had saved Trotsky, that is not how Trotsky saw it. At this time Trotsky met his old deputy Sklyanskii who was about to set off to America on a trade mission. During their heart-to-heart, Sklyanskii asked at one point: "What is Stalin"? Trotsky responded: "Stalin is the outstanding mediocrity of the Party." Then, "in that conversation I realised with absolute clarity the problem of Thermidor". Trotsky was returning to the danger of a quiet counter-revolution sketched out 18 months earlier: "A victorious counter-revolution may develop its great men; but its first stage, the Thermidor, demands mediocrities who cannot see farther than their noses – their strength lies in their political blindness, like the mill horse who thinks that he is moving up when he is only pushing down the belt wheel." And, from Trotsky's view point, Stalin was soon behaving like a mill horse: only five days after the funds for the Dnieper Dam Project had been agreed on 15 July, Stalin told Molotov: "I do not think we can afford to take on the Dnieper Project either this year or next year, given our financial situation . . . We face the danger of squandering some of the kopecks we have managed to accumulate." Three weeks later he let Bukharin know that the project needed to be prevented "even if Trotsky will be somewhat offended". Such concern was not unreasonable, Trotsky had himself suggested an emergency meeting of industrialists to check that there was sufficient financial underpinning for economic spending already agreed.[18]

Trotsky ran the Dnieper Dam Project in the same way that he planned the Civil War campaigns, through consultation and consensus. He accepted that the Project could not be hurried and agreed that the feasibility study be extended by an extra year. "The best personnel, nationally and internationally," he recalled, "were brought in to check the estimates for the project." Stalin became alarmed that such work methods were beginning to change the Party's relationship to the economy. He told Molotov that planners were allocating funds "while the Politburo is changing from a directing body into a court of appeals"; it was often "Gosplan specialists who are in charge". As a move to recover some of the power the Politburo seemed to have lost over the economy, it was agreed on 15 October that the Politburo would establish a special commission to co-ordinate economic work and that the Politburo would devote at least two sessions a month to the economy. The revival of Politburo "interference" in the economy at the end of 1925 and beginning of 1926 was something Trotsky found difficult to bear. Those who worked with him noticed that he would frequently rant and rave against "ignoramuses", "know-alls" and "technical incompetents" when referring to representatives of the Politburo. And yet he stuck to his post, convinced that if schemes like the Dnieper Dam Project came off, the socialist sector would triumph.[19]

Zinoviev, Kamenev and the Kulak Danger

Trotsky missed the Fourteenth Party Conference in April 1925 and thus did not notice the first signs that the Zinoviev–Kamenev–Stalin triumvirate was disintegrating. Throughout April the Politburo had been discussing the related issues of the level of the agrarian tax and the regulations concerning the hiring and firing of rural labour. As part of these discussions Bukharin told a mass meeting in the Bolshoi Theatre in Moscow on 17 April that the government's policy towards peasants could be summed up in these words: "Enrich yourselves!" When the Fourteenth Party Conference opened ten days later the phrase was condemned, but the practical results of the Conference were to reduce the tax burden, make it easier to hire rural labour, and make it easier for peasants to lease unexploited land. For Zinoviev these were mistaken concessions: in May he insisted on being allowed to refer to them as a "retreat", and in June he declared that moves supposed to help poor peasants were actually helping kulaks. In September Kamenev made a speech attacking those Party members who tried to gloss over the fact that kulaks now felt powerful enough to frustrate the harvest and delay making deliveries. After some protests, and in Stalin's absence from Moscow, Zinoviev wrote in *Pravda* on 19–20 September that "the development of NEP together with the delay in world revolution is really pregnant with the danger of degeneration".

When the Central Committee held a Plenum in October hard bargaining succeeded in papering over the cracks, but this did not hold. A week after the Plenum Kamenev spoke to the Moscow Party Organisation of a "pro-kulak" deviation and by mid November Zinoviev's *Leningradskaya*

Pravda was carrying bitter attacks on the Politburo's policy. The Leningrad Provincial Party Conference, 30 November–10 December, was the occasion for a sustained assault on the Politburo; the Moscow Provincial Party Conference, 5–13 December, saw the Politburo counter-attack. At another Central Committee Plenum on 15 December a compromise was proposed which would have given the Leningrad Party Organisation representation on the Secretariat, but it was rejected by the Leningraders. At the Fourteenth Party Congress, 18–23 December, the Party was more divided than ever before and in an unheard-of break with tradition, Zinoviev was allowed to make a counter-report. He believed that, while the numerical strength of the kulaks was insignificant, their economic power was far greater and "the kulak has his complement in the city, in the new bourgeoisie and among some of the specialists"; it was essential, therefore to isolate the rich peasant, "the political character of the rich peasant" could not be ignored. In Bukharin's view, Zinoviev was interpreting NEP as a retreat, when in fact for Lenin it had been "a strategic manoeuvre", and part of that manoeuvre was to make concessions not to the kulak as Zinoviev believed, but to the middle peasantry.[20]

Just before the Congress, Trotsky jotted down some notes about the possibility of forming a bloc with Zinoviev, but rejected the idea. He could see no issues of principle in what was essentially "a ferocious apparatus struggle", although he was prepared to concede that behind the bluster from Leningrad there was, "bureaucratically distorted", some genuine working class concern at "the failure of industry to keep up with the demands of the market". The solution to this, however, was planning and investments like the Dnieper Dam Project. The problem was, Trotsky noted a few days later, that Zinoviev still did not recognise the leading role of industry; in his scheme "the planning principle is almost entirely pushed aside by credit and finance regulation". "One must state firmly and distinctly," he concluded, "that the essence of the question lies not in the present level of differentiation in the countryside, nor even in the rate of differentiation, but in the rate of industrial development." Trotsky had very clear reasons why he did not side with Zinoviev and Kamenev at the Fourteenth Party Congress.[21] Despite all the frustrations of Politburo "interference", he felt progress was being made and he was prepared to work with Stalin to see it through. Indeed, at this time rumours were rife that Trotsky and Stalin had come to an understanding to revive the proposal that Trotsky should be put in charge of the economy, this time by making him Chairman of the Supreme Council of the National Economy. In the first three months of 1926 Trotsky was under pressure from advisers to pursue just such a strategy.[22]

Trotsky was a member of the key Politburo commission planning the budget for the coming year. Indeed, his presence seemed to be being felt, for the Central Committee Plenum on 25 February passed a resolution calling for a strengthening of socialist elements of the economy. Things began to unravel only in the middle of March 1926 with the proposal that a loan of 300 million roubles should be used to stimulate industry. The Commissariat for Finances protested and proposed reducing the loan to 225 million; the industrialisers fought back and eventually it was agreed on 25 March that the figure should be 240 million. Even so, some planned expenditure was going to have to be cut and Stalin insisted the axe fall on the Dnieper Dam Project.[23] When Trotsky drafted his speech for the Central Committee Plenum of 6–9 April his target was still Kamenev; however, once it became clear that the Dnieper Dam Project was to be scrapped, Trotsky lost patience. He explained that it was not the cuts themselves so much as they way the decision had been reached that upset him: he had helped draft the proposed resolution on the economy three months earlier; it had then disappeared into a commission for redrafting, from which it emerged just days before the Plenum opened. He had already stated at the February Plenum that it was intolerable for Politburo members to be presented with resolutions prepared behind their backs, and now it had happened again; this was symptomatic of the "apparatus regime". Trotsky backed 90 per cent of the new proposal, but wanted to go just that bit further and increase the budget allocation for industry in 1926–7 by 20 per cent, financing this by additional savings from unproductive spending. The apparatus had stifled this necessary debate.[24]

The United Opposition

During the April Central Committee session Trotsky voted for a resolution proposed by Kamenev and by the end of the session Trotsky, Zinoviev and Kamenev had their first meeting as organisers of a new United Opposition. Zinoviev and Kamenev were optimistic that, with Trotsky on their side, they had gained the organisational power to confront the Stalinist apparatus. As part of the necessary political choreography for their new alliance, Zinoviev and Kamenev made a public statement to the effect that Trotsky had been right all along to warn of the dangers of the bureaucracy, while Trotsky pointed out that he should have made clear that when criticising the bureaucracy he had meant only Stalin and not Zinoviev and Kamenev. This agreement left completely unconsidered the long-standing dispute between Trotsky and Zinoviev over the use of specialists, and yet this was still on his mind; on 2 May Trotsky wrote that one of the greatest failings of the April Plenum was the way it had ignored "the link between the economy and the Party regime". Economic activists felt themselves to be responsible only to the Secretariat when "the choice of economic workers must be dictated by business capability", he stressed once again.[25]

Immediately after the April Plenum Trotsky resigned his posts linked to the Dnieper Dam Project, retaining only his job on the Concessions Committee. He then left for Germany to consult with doctors and stayed there for much of May. It was therefore from Berlin that he observed the British General Strike. Trotsky was appalled by the coverage given to the strike by *Pravda* and put this down to the malign influence of the Anglo-Russian Joint Advisory Council (ARJAC).[26] Although in his spring 1925 pamphlet *Whither England?* Trotsky had made no criticisms of this organisation, he now felt it to be the prime illustration of the way Stalin's methods for building socialism in one country could push the Soviet Union from the revolutionary path. With the formation of Britain's first Labour Government in January 1924 the new Trade Union Congress chairman became Albert Purcell, a Left-winger who had visited Soviet Russia in 1920. Purcell invited the Soviet trade union leader Tomsky to visit the Hull Trade Union Congress in September 1924 and then attended the Soviet Trade Union Congress in Moscow in November. ARJAC, set up as a result of these visits, was originally supposed to work for the integration of the Soviet trade unions into the International Federation of Trade Unions, and when no progress was made on this, its precise purpose was unclear. However, it did give the Soviet trade unions an outlet to the West and so it continued, but its existence became questionable when the Trade Union Congress "betrayed" the British "Revolution" and called off the May General Strike.

On his return to Moscow Trotsky persuaded Zinoviev to join him and on 3 June raised in the Politburo the question of ending the work of ARJAC. The resolution was rejected, but Trotsky followed it up three days later with a warning that if the problem of bureaucracy were not seriously addressed, then the Party would find itself under the rule of an autocrat. Trotsky and Zinoviev then decided to take their struggle to the rank and file. On 6 June about 70 communists from the Krasnaya Presnya District in Moscow took the local railway line to a dacha outside the city where they were addressed by M. M. Lashevich, the Deputy Commissar for War and a long-term supporter of Zinoviev. One of those present at the meeting informed the Krasnaya Presnya District Secretary, M. N. Ryutin, who dutifully informed the Moscow Party Secretary. Within days the CCC had issued its penalties, Lashevich was given a strict reprimand and informed that his case would be taken up at the next Central Committee Plenum with the recommendation that he be expelled.[27]

For Stalin the Lashevich affair had enormous significance. It showed how much stronger Zinoviev's opposition was than any of the other groups the leadership had faced so far, largely because "it is better acquainted with our methods". Zinoviev therefore had to be challenged when the Joint Plenum of the Central Committee and the CCC met on 14–23 July. Stalin expressed the hope that, if Zinoviev could be struck down hard enough "Trotsky and others will once again become loyal". Therefore the Joint Plenum would propose removing Zinoviev from the Politburo and leaving Trotsky as a member, "although there are no less profound disagreements with Trotsky". Trotsky and Zinoviev prepared for the Joint Plenum with similar care. They read out a joint statement, the "Declaration of 13", which stressed the need to restore Party democracy; to end the tyranny of the apparatus; and to change economic policy in order to raise industrial wages, increase taxes on kulaks, and introduce "a real five-year plan"; on the international plane the statement criticised the work of ARJAC and condemned the Politburo for not having broken with the TUC at the height of the General Strike.[28]

The joint statement raised an issue that was of enormous importance for Trotsky, but less important for Zinoviev and Kamenev. The statement insisted that there was only one cause of bureaucratism and that was "the divergence between the direction of economic policy and the direction of the feelings and thoughts of the proletarian vanguard"; any other explanation was "secondary and did not encompass the essence of the question". While Zinoviev and Kamenev put much of the bureaucratisation of the Party down to Stalin and his personality, Trotsky did not – how else could he have continued to work with Stalin all these months? The emergence of Stalin was a symptom of bureaucratisation, which was in turn the product of objective circumstances, and only when those circumstances changed would the Stalin problem disappear. For workers to become active participants in the Party once again they needed a decent salary, a higher standard of living and a decent cultural environment, and all of that depended on planning. Bureaucracy thrived because it was the kulaks rather than the workers who benefited from current policies. The problem of bureaucracy was rooted in economic backwardness. "The lag of industry behind the economic development of the country as a whole," the statement argued, "signifies, in spite of the growth in the number of workers, a lowering of the specific gravity of the proletariat in society." The result was that "under the guise of a union of the poor peasants with the middle peasants, we observe steadily and regularly the political subordination of the poor peasants to the middle peasants and through them to the kulaks." It was then "entirely obvious that the state apparatus, in its composition and level of life, was to an overwhelming degree bourgeois and petit bourgeois . . . and favoured the land-leaser, merchant, kulak, the new bourgeoisie."[29]

When the Joint Plenum ended, Zinoviev was expelled from the Politburo and Lashevich from the Central Committee and from his post as Deputy Commissar of War. Not everything worked out as Stalin had hoped. Trotsky did not break with Zinoviev, despite the fact that Stalin was careful to ensure that the final resolution made no mention of Trotsky, leaving Zinoviev and Lashevich to take the blame for the organisation of illegal meetings and the sending of agents with "tendentiously collected secret Party documents" to towns throughout the Soviet Union. When Trotsky returned from his summer break in September determined to continue his alliance with Zinoviev, Stalin commented in a letter to Molotov: "If Trotsky 'is in a rage' and thinks of 'openly going for broke', that is all the worse for him. It is quite possible that he'll be bounced out of the Politburo now – that depends on his behaviour. The issue is as follows: either they must submit to the Party or the Party must submit to them."[30]

The Party statutes allowed members of the Central Committee to address any Party organisation. So, at the end of September Zinoviev, Trotsky and other Opposition leaders began a series of meetings with rank and file workers; on 30 September Trotsky addressed the workers of the Ryazan–Uralsk Railway and on 1 October the workers of the Aviopribor aircraft manufacturing works in Moscow's Krasnaya Presnya District. This second meeting was attended by the local district secretary Riutin and the Moscow Party Secretary Uglanov, who ensured that, despite the applause with which Trotsky was greeted, the Opposition was voted down 78 votes to 27. Outside the capital, the interventions of the Party apparatus were less civilised, and organised groups of "loyal Party supporters" would shout down or even rough up speakers supporting the Opposition.

Incidents such as these meant that among rank and file Oppositionists there were increasing demands for the formation of a new party. That was not what either Trotsky or Zinoviev wanted, and so they looked to agree a compromise with the leadership, a compromise hammered out at a meeting of the CCC on 11 October and formalised in a statement of 16 October. Essentially this meant an end to appeals to the rank and file. Trotsky and Zinoviev accepted that such behaviour had been factional and declared their willingness to demobilise the Opposition as a faction and dissociate themselves from advocates of a new party; however, they would continue to stand by their principles and advance their criticisms of the leadership within the Central Committee.[31] In December 1923 Trotsky signed a compromise agreement and then broke it; this time it was Stalin's turn. On 18 October 1926 Max Eastman published a version of Lenin's Testament in *The New York Times*; meetings organised by the United Opposition constantly demanded the publication of the Testament. At the same time the *cheka* discovered that Opposition leaflets were still circulating in Odessa despite the compromise. When the Central Committee and CCC held a Joint Plenum on 23–26 October, Stalin called for a report on the Opposition's continued activities. Trotsky exploded, accusing Stalin of bad faith; pointing at him he declared, "the First Secretary poses his candidature to the post of gravedigger of the revolution". Stalin turned pale, rose, and rushed from the hall, slamming the door behind him. After the meeting, Trotsky's ally Yurii Pyatakov returned to Trotsky's flat shaken and at a loss for words. Trotsky's wife recalled the scene:

He poured a glass of water, gulped it down and said: "You know I have smelt gunpowder, but I have never seen anything like this! This was worse than anything! And why, why did Lev Davidovich say this? Stalin will never forgive him until the third and fourth generation!" Pyatakov was so upset that he was unable to relate clearly what had happened. When Lev Davidovich at last entered the dining-room, Pyatakov rushed at him asking: "But why, why have you said this?" With a wave of his hand Lev Davidovich brushed the question aside. He was exhausted but calm.

The next day Trotsky was expelled from the Politburo.[32]

When the Fifteenth Party Conference opened on 26 October 1926 the Opposition was able to put its case. Kamenev was the most emollient: the Opposition believed the Soviet Union was a proletarian state in a country with a peasant majority, meaning that at ground level some power was inevitably in the hands of the peasantry; this meant that the Soviet Union faced not only external danger but an internal danger as well. That danger was currently manifested thus: "the bureaucratic deformations of the state apparatus are an expression of class"; non-proletarian elements were getting an increasing grip on the administration of the state, diluting worker representation and strengthening the bureaucratic voice. "This is a tendency in the state apparatus, promoted by the dominant petit bourgeois atmosphere and must be combated by the increased participation of workers in running the state." The Opposition had violated Party discipline to make its case, "but you must not deny that this violation of discipline has arisen from no other causes than the anxiety to correct

Party policy". He concluded: "Can the existing differences be settled within the boundaries of joint work, yes, this can and must be done."

Trotsky took the same line. Common work was possible. If the Opposition were not convinced that victory would come, it would have broken with the communists and founded another party.

He who believes that our state is a proletarian state, with bureaucratic deformations stemming from petty bourgeois pressure ... [which] do not allow the necessary allocation of national resources, then that person must struggle, by Party methods and along the Party's path, against that which is false.[33]

Stalin was not impressed and warned delegates that the Opposition would not be satisfied: "If they do not renounce their fundamental views, if they have decided to adhere to their old opinions, it means that they will temporise and wait for 'better times'." All three leading Oppositionists refused to recant their views, but the Conference concluded they had eaten enough humble pie. The expulsion of Zinoviev and Trotsky from the Politburo was confirmed, along with that of Kamenev, but they remained on the Central Committee.[34]

After the Fifteenth Party Conference, Trotsky used his private diary to raise again the issue of a Thermidor counter-revolution. On 26 November he noted that the path towards Thermidor now seemed clear as Party policy drifted to the Right. "The official adoption of the theory of socialism in one country gives sanction at the theoretical level for these moves to the Right which have already taken place and signifies the first open break with Marxism." And yet, despite these fears, he concluded, "to speak of Thermidor as an accomplished fact would be a crude distortion of reality", although "the possibility of Thermidor" was clearly there. This put an enormous responsibility on the Opposition. Despite its defeat, the struggle needed to go on even if only "Liebknecht's fate" awaited it. Liebknecht, Trotsky's old acquaintance from the Vienna days, had led the German communist insurrection of January 1919 and died at the hands of the counter-revolutionary *Freikorps*. It was a chilling analogy; clearly, Trotsky's outburst about Stalin as the gravedigger of the revolution was not an aberration.[35]

China

The thrust of the statements made at the Fifteenth Party Conference was that the Party could work through its differences. For a while this did seem to be the case and Trotsky confined his activity in winter and spring 1927 to writing letters of protest to the Politburo about what he saw as intolerable aspects of the inner Party regime. Then, in April 1927 Trotsky became obsessed with the way events were unfolding in China and resolved to launch a new assault on the Stalin and Bukharin leadership. For several years the Soviet Government had been involved in the politics of nationalist China, sending both political advisers to the nationalist party the Kuomintang (KMT) and Chinese Communist Party (CCP) and military advisors to the nationalist generals. The political advisers had come up with an unusual solution to how the KMT and CCP should relate to each other; because socialist revolution was only conceivable after a national revolution had driven the occupying imperial powers from China, the CCP should be an affiliate member of the KMT and remain within the ranks of the KMT, even when from late 1925, and more obviously throughout 1926, Right-wing forces managed to gain the upper hand in the KMT leadership.

Initially China was not an issue for the Opposition. On 20 March 1926 Chiang Kai-shek established himself as virtual dictator within the KMT leadership; Trotsky, still then loyal to the leadership, suggested at a Politburo meeting that the CCP should leave the KMT. In April Zinoviev put the same proposal to the Politburo on behalf of the Opposition while Trotsky was absent in Germany, but then withdrew it when he met with overwhelming criticism. Over the summer Chiang Kai-shek began a dramatic military advance, hugely expanding the territory under his control; as he did so he established a regime which took a very negative attitude to the labour movement, particularly on the question of strikes. At the end of September Trotsky wrote an article, which he never sent for publication, suggesting once again that the CCP should break with the KMT; keeping the CCP within the KMT was the same sort of mistake as telling British communists they had to work with ARJAC. Trotsky had wanted to raise the issue of China during the Fifteenth Party Conference, but Zinoviev would not agree.

By autumn 1926 it seemed that the situation in China was improving. In November 1926 the KMT administration carried out a reshuffle and gave two cabinet posts to communists. On 30 November when Stalin addressed the Comintern Executive on the question of China, he was upbeat and urged the Chinese communists to take advantage of these favourable new circumstances to use strike action to improve the lot of workers; the time had come for a cautious revolutionary advance. To help that advance, Stalin arranged in February 1927 for one of the Left KMT leaders, then in emigration in France, to be transferred to China via Moscow. On 19 February the workers of Shanghai declared a strike, calling it off after a week when they felt their demands had been met. In this newly radicalised climate the Left was able to remove some of the KMT Rightists from the leadership and at the KMT Congress on 10–17 March limitations were put on Chiang Kai-shek's authority. On 21 March a second Shanghai strike overthrew the local warlord and the Nationalist Army entered the city.[36]

Trotsky returned to the question of China early in March 1927, but his fellow Oppositionists would not support another a resolution calling for the CCP to leave the KMT. Trotsky wrote on 22 March: "I confess that at the present time the situation in China arouses in me far greater concern than does any other problem … the more the KMT takes on the character of a governing party, the more it becomes bourgeois". On 31 March he wrote to the Politburo stating that while he accepted the issue of the CCP remaining in the KMT had been settled, it was surely time to think about forming soviets in big cities like Shanghai, "not as an instrument of proletarian dictatorship, but one of revolutionary national liberation and democratic liberation". Certainly the situation in Shanghai seemed to be reaching a climax, with frequent clashes between Chiang's military authorities and the communist organisers of the insurrection. Stalin was optimistic that, if the right tactics were followed, Chiang could be removed from the scene: on 5 April he called a meeting of activists involved in Chinese matters and told them, "I know Chiang Kai-shek is playing a cunning game with us, but it is he that will be crushed; we will squeeze him like a lemon and then be rid of him".[37] On 12 April Chiang Kai-shek began a massacre of the Shanghai insurgents. As reports of the deaths of thousands of communists came in, a Central Committee Plenum was being held in Moscow on 13–16 April. At it Stalin and Trotsky clashed. Stalin insisted that soviets, whatever they might have been in the past, were organs for "ushering in the proletarian dictatorship, a Chinese October": Trotsky conceded that socialist revolution was not on the agenda, but stressed that soviets had existed in Russia in 1905 long before the victory of the socialist revolution; "whoever opposes the formation of the soviets must say 'all power to the KMT'".[38]

The debate continued in the press. Stalin wrote two articles on China, one calling for the strengthening of mass organisations "as prepar-atory elements for future soviets" and accepting that the CCP needed to "preserve its independence" within the KMT, and the other reminding communists that in summer 1906 Khrustalev-Nosar had tried, and failed, to re-form the St Petersburg Soviet; soviets were only appropriate when the revolutionary tide was advancing, not receding. Trotsky responded with an article, *The Chinese Revolution and the Theses of Comrade Stalin*, the thrust of which was that it was stupid to talk of "substitutes for soviets instead of soviets themselves"; *Pravda* would not publish it. Trotsky complained to the CCC about this decision, and sent the article to the Secretariat for distribution to all Central Committee members. Supported by Zinoviev, Trotsky asked the Central Committee to hold a closed session on the China crisis at which no stenographic record need be kept, but the Politburo, meeting jointly with the CCC Presidium, rejected the idea. Trotsky's response lambasted Stalin.

The Politburo resolution states that we want to force the Party into a discussion. If by a discussion what is meant is the roar of the apparatus, the shouts and whistling of claques that have been organised in advance, the packing of cells with goons trained to use violence against the Opposition, the overwhelming of workers cells with threats and cries about a split – then, of course, we do not want such "discussion"! . . . It is possible to mechanistically suppress anything for a short period of time . . . but Lenin called such methods rude and disloyal.[39]

As part of his co-ordinated campaign against the Opposition, Stalin persuaded Lenin's widow to write to Zinoviev. Krupskaya had supported the Opposition until the start of 1927, but now she expressed her astonishment that Zinoviev supported those who "banged on" about China. Zinoviev left it to Trotsky to respond. Although Trotsky referred to the defeat of the prospective revolutions in Germany in 1923, in Britain in 1926 and now China in 1927, and spoke of Stalin and Bukharin as "betraying Bolshevism at its very core, its proletarian internationalism", he did not focus his attention on the tactical issues of these failed insurrections. He concentrated on the point that, by stressing the notion of socialism in one country, Stalin and Bukharin had weakened the "international revolutionary mood of our proletariat". This was a point he had also made in his unpublished *Pravda* article; surveys of worker opinion revealed that many workers saw no reason "to interfere" in the affairs of Britain or China. Stalin and Bukharin had created a climate in which workers thought in purely national terms. And this was because, rather than being strong, in fact Stalin's position was weak. Not, of course in terms of his power within the apparatus, but because he and Bukharin were under "pressure from the growing Right-wing".[40]

It is impossible to separate Trotsky's impassioned response to the Shanghai massacre in China from his growing fear of Thermidor. Chiang Kai-shek's actions were a metaphor for the dangers facing the Russian Revolution. Trotsky had long accepted that, if the correct economic policy were not followed, then the sort of kulak counter-revolution envisaged in *Results and Prospects* could occur; since December 1923 he had felt that this might not be an overt clash but could take the form of a creeping counter-revolution, as the political influence of the kulaks gradually penetrated the state bureaucracy; by April 1926, after Stalin thwarted the Dnieper Dam Project, he was openly calling this process Thermidor. Stalin and Bukharin were not "betraying Bolshevism at its very core" because they were traitors, but because they had failed to stand up to growing class pressures from the Right. And had the same not happened in China? The CCP, the party of Chinese workers and peasants, in a temporary NEP-style coalition with the Chinese bourgeoisie, had allowed Right-wing forces to emerge to the point where first Chiang Kai-shek emerged as a "Bonaparte" and then carried out his Thermidor. Trotsky wrote of Stalin's weakness in May 1927 because he felt he would soon be replaced by a Russian Chiang Kai-shek. And yet Stalin's weakness might just provide Trotsky with the opportunity to intervene, stop the drift to the Right and save the day. Victory was not certain, but it had to be tried. As he later recalled: "We went to meet the inevitable debacle, confident that we were paving the way for the triumph of our ideas in a more distant future . . . when the struggle is one of great principles, the revolutionary can follow one rule: *Fais ce que dois, advienne que pourra* [Do what must be done whatever should happen]."[41]

Trotsky was still a member of the Comintern Executive, which met on 18–30 May. He sent a written statement to the meeting about the alarming drift to the Right in the Bolshevik Party since the end of 1923: "The attempt to represent the struggle against the Opposition as a struggle against Trotskyism is a woeful, cowardly way of masking the Right deviation in the Party," he asserted. When he addressed the meeting on 23 May and again on 24 May he not only repeated the points made in his unpublished *Pravda* article but noted that the demand that the Opposition be expelled from the Party came not only from the current leadership, but also from the former liberal politician N. V. Ustryalov, now an emigré in Harbin, who wrote openly of the need for other former liberals to collaborate with the more sensible and nationally minded Bolsheviks. Stalin addressed the meeting shortly after Trotsky had made his speech of the 24th: he summarised the content of his published *Pravda* articles on China and then stated that Trotsky had clearly violated the terms of the 16 October truce and embarked on a new factional struggle.[42]

Expulsion

Stalin was absolutely right. On 25 May Trotsky and his supporters published their Declaration of 83 which was circulated to Comintern delegates the next day. Repeating the established criticisms of Stalin's policy in China, the declaration stressed that he had acted "so as not to drive away" the bourgeoisie and "not to frighten" the petit bourgeoisie; things were not so different in the Soviet Union where the theory of socialism in one country, "a crude retreat from Marxism", made it difficult for the Party to understand "the *class content* of the economic processes which are going on". In early June Zinoviev wrote *The Declaration of the 83 and Our Tasks* in which he asserted that the Opposition was now so strong that "even if Stalin succeeded in cutting of its head", it would survive: the disagreements with the leadership were now so deep that the declaration had to be taken to the rank and file; with thousands of signatures it would ensure that there was proper open debate in the run-up to the Fifteenth Party Congress.[43]

Trotsky was called before the CCC on 24 June. After repeating his views on events in China, he outlined more fully what he meant by the Thermidor danger. "Every specialist, every civil servant, every 'lady', whether soviet or half-soviet, knows that the workers' temperament is 'no longer that of 1918'; you hear it at the stalls, on the street and in the tram." Quietly a bourgeois ideology was seeping in, and kulaks, traders and specialists felt safe enough to build themselves ostentatious houses. A blow from the Right was imminent: "but it would not come from the Right-wing of the Party, for that was only the transmission mechanism, the real danger, the core danger came from the bourgeois classes which were raising their heads." In the French Revolution those who carried out Thermidor believed that they were just changing a few key personnel, not changing the class nature of the regime, but they had changed the class nature of the revolution in France; the logic was clear, the removal of Trotsky and Zinoviev from the Bolshevik Central Committee would change the class nature of the Soviet regime. In such circumstances, Trotsky concluded, it was the duty of the CCC not to expel people, but to "create a more healthy and flexible regime in the Party".[44]

The speech had its impact. To Stalin's fury the CCC made some key concessions. It confirmed that, as a Central Committee member, Trotsky did have the right to attend any Party cell at any time; the CCC also accepted that drafting the Declaration of 83 was not a breach of discipline. When, on 27 June, Trotsky made a second appearance before the CCC its chairman, now Sergo Ordzhonikidze, urged Trotsky to talk less of Thermidor and stand by the Party in a joint struggle against bureaucratism; in a conciliatory gesture he ruled out of order those commission members who tried to raise the irrelevant issue of whether or not, during the Civil War, Trotsky had ordered communists to be shot. But Trotsky was not interested in conciliation. Despite opposition from Zinoviev, he issued a further declaration on 28 June which, after the routine attacks on Purcell and Chiang Kai-shek, turned to Stalin's domestic policies: Stalin, Trotsky said, was getting closer and closer to the petit bourgeois and bureaucratic "bigwigs", linking himself directly with their specialists; Stalin welcomed the praise heaped on him by such specialists, his road was "the road from the dictatorship of the proletariat to that of compromise with petit bourgeois bigwigs, who offered a bridge to the big bourgeoisie".[45]

In spring 1927 not only had the Soviet Union's China policy ended in disaster, but the British had broken off diplomatic relations after raiding the offices of the Anglo-Russian Co-operative Society. With the danger of war with Britain on everyone's minds over the summer of 1927, it was easy for Stalin to encourage press speculation about an unholy alliance between Chamberlain and Trotsky. At the CCC Orzhonikidze had criticised one such *Pravda* article, and perhaps for that reason Trotsky thought he would get a sympathetic hearing when he wrote to Ordzhonikidze on 11 July complaining that on 27 June the Central Committee, which had had not attended because that was the day he had addressed the CCC, had described his actions as defeatist. In this letter Trotsky shot himself in the foot. He stated that, if war broke out, the Opposition would behave like Clemenceau had in France during the First World War, i.e. support the war but criticise its management; at one point in the letter Trotsky wrote "if someone says that the political line of ignorant and dishonest copycats must be swept away like garbage precisely in the interests of the workers' state, that does not make him a defeatist". Most Bolsheviks, unlike Trotsky, had not been in Paris during the First World War and it was easy for Stalin's supporters to suggest that what Trotsky meant was that he would not support Stalin in the event of war, but work towards his overthrow.[46]

A Joint Plenum of the Central Committee and CCC was held on 29 July–9 August to resolve what to do about the Opposition. Stalin responded to Trotsky's reference to "garbage" in his letter to Ordzhonikidze: "will it be surprising if the Party turns the broom the other way and uses it against the Opposition", adding "the Opposition must emphatically and irrevocably abandon its Thermidor twaddle and its foolish slogan of a Clemenceau experiment". Trotsky still linked the two. Bukharin and Stalin's policy could not survive a war, for a war would bring out the underlying class contradictions forcing "a turn either towards Thermidor or towards the Opposition", for he doubted "to the highest degree" Stalin's capacity to follow the correct line in the defence of the "socialist fatherland".[47] As the Plenum proceeded, Trotsky agreed to moderate his stance, at Zinoviev's suggestion. Trotsky made clear that the Opposition were not "conditional defencists" and did not believe that the era of Thermidor had already arrived: "We are ready to meet any suggestion which might improve inner Party relations [and] create conditions guaranteeing a thorough examination of our real disagreements." Thus on 8 August the Opposition issued a statement to declare they would defend the Soviet Union unconditionally, and that, although the Thermidorian danger existed, the Party itself was still not infected. Stalin commented as he closed the Plenum that the Opposition had offered not peace, but a temporary armistice.[48]

In the negotiations which led to this armistice, Trotsky had proposed a separate section which noted his "deeply held conviction" that the situation in the Party would only improve if there were a change in the press coverage given to the Opposition and if the Fifteenth Party Congress were prepared for "as under Lenin", with documents circulated in advance. On 9 August, Trotsky was forced to accept, albeit under protest, Ordzhonikidze's ruling that the matters raised in this section should not be publicised since they were not formally part of the agreement. It was not therefore surprising that the truce barely lasted a month. The key work of the Opposition was first to draft a 70-page Platform, which it hoped would be discussed at the Fifteenth Party Congress, and then to popularise it among the rank and file. The Platform was duly sent to the Politburo on 3 September, but on the 8th Stalin advised that it could not be circulated to the wider party since it was a factional document. Trotsky and Zinoviev responded by deciding to circulate the Platform themselves, but on the night of 12–13 September their printing press was seized by the *cheka*. Trotsky was summoned to the Comintern Presidium on 27 September to explain the printing press affair in Stalin's presence. He declared:

Stalin's personal misfortune, which is fast becoming the Party's misfortune, is the colossal disparity between his intellectual resources and the power the state and Party machine have concentrated in his hands; [his] bureaucratic regime will lead irreversibly to one-man rule.

Stalin responded simply that "the present regime in the Party is an exact expression of the regime that was established in the Party in Lenin's time".[49]

Deprived of the written word, the Opposition had no choice but to organise public meetings once again. In late October and early November an estimated 20,000 people attended meetings organised by the Opposition, usually in groups of 100 to 200, held in people's flats; thus in Moscow Trotsky spoke at two workers' meetings in Krasnaya Presnya

District, one of them attended by 150 people with Trotsky standing in the door connecting the two rooms. However, occasionally they were bigger affairs. On one occasion over 300 workers from Moscow's Hammer and Sickle Factory heard an Opposition supporter read out Lenin's Testament, and on 4 November the Opposition took over the lecture theatre of the Polytechnical Institute in Moscow's Bauman District and a crowd of 2,000 gathered; when the electricity was cut off the meeting continued by candlelight. The highpoint of this activity would come on 7 November with the celebrations to mark the tenth anniversary of the October Revolution. Members of the Opposition were called on to take part in the official demonstrations, but march separately under their own banners with such slogans as "Down with the Kulak, the Nepman and the Bureaucrat" and "Carry Out Lenin's Testament"; such demonstrators found themselves being roughed up by the security services.[50]

The Opposition campaign prompted a Joint Plenum of the Central Committee and CCC on 23–26 October to resolve that Trotsky and Zinoviev should be expelled from the Party at the Fifteenth Party Congress. At this meeting Trotsky denounced Stalin once more, to the accompaniment of jeers, catcalls and even missiles thrown by loyal Stalinists.

The rudeness and disloyalty, which Lenin wrote about, is no longer just a personal quality; these have become the qualities of the ruling faction, its policies, its regime . . . But the Party regime does not live for itself. In the Party regime we find an expression of all the policies of the Party leadership. This policy has, during the last years, moved its class element firmly from left to right: from the proletariat to the petit bourgeois, from the Party to the specialist, from the rank and file to the apparatus, from the landless and poor to the kulak, from Shanghai workers to Chiang Kai-shek . . . from the English proletariat to Purcell . . . that is the very essence of Stalinism.

Stalin, he said, was "carrying out the social order of Ustryalov", in other words, the order of the bourgeoisie, while his call for the expulsion of the Opposition was "the very voice of Thermidor". Stalin responded that he was rude, but only "to those who grossly and perfidiously wreck and split the Party"; the resolution to expel Trotsky and Zinoviev was passed.[51]

Although Trotsky wanted to continue the struggle, Zinoviev had had enough. He had made clear to Trotsky at the outset that he would never let things get to the point of expulsion from the Party. The Central Committee and CCC held another Joint Plenum on 12–14 November and Zinoviev insisted the Opposition should declare on 14 November that there would be no more public meetings; the declaration, however, did not prevent the Central Committee and CCC deciding the same day to endorse the decision to expel Trotsky and Zinoviev from the Party. The issue then was how to get back into the Party. At meetings held between 20 and 27 November Zinoviev, Kamenev and Trotsky tried to thrash out an agreed policy. A joint statement noted that "the task of the Opposition is to carry out propaganda in the Party, not to brawl with specially trained units" and that "the Party will not allow itself to split, nor will the Opposition allow itself to break away". All three leaders therefore accepted the need to capitulate and cease factional activity for the sake of unity, and initially all three were united in accepting Trotsky's view that, as he had insisted in 1924 to the Thirteenth Party Congress, it was impossible for the Opposition leaders to retract their views.[52]

That was how things stood when the Fifteenth Party Congress, 7–19 December 1927, opened. By the end of the Congress, however, Zinoviev and Kamenev, who had called on Trotsky to recant at the Thirteenth Party Congress, were ready to state that their views were "wrong and anti-Leninist", in return for which they were put on Party probation for six months, opening the way for a return to the Party. Trotsky would not recant. At their last meeting Zinoviev reminded Trotsky that Lenin had warned in his Testament about the Trotsky–Stalin conflict risking a split in the Party: "Think of the responsibility you bear!" Zinoviev said. Trotsky responded: "Lenin also wrote in his Testament that if the divergence of views inside the Party coincided with class differences, nothing would save us from a split." For Trotsky Thermidor had advanced to the point where the Party itself was infected. By expelling the Opposition Stalin was acting as an agent of Thermidor, and a split in the Party was therefore inevitable. Zinoviev and Kamenev could not accept that the Party had degenerated so much and still saw the Party bureaucracy as recoverable, if the malign influence of Stalin could be removed.[53]

Trotsky summed up best what he meant by Thermidor in a letter he wrote to an old ally on 12 August 1927.

You ask yourself: why is the regime so bad? Is it the nasty character of Stalin? No, the Party regime is a function of the political line. Namely because Stalin relies on Chiang Kai-shek, Purcell, the civil servant, the village high-ups etc., he is forced to follow a policy not relying on the consciousness and will of the proletarian vanguard but squeezing him under the apparatus, from above, and thus reflecting and mastering the pressure of other classes on the proletariat . . . This is the road to Thermidor.

For Stalin, Thermidor was "twaddle". Trotsky was not splitting the Party to save it but just rejecting Lenin's theory of Party organisation and proving that he was still a Menshevik. Addressing the October Central Committee and CCC Plenum, the last occasion on which the two men met, Stalin concluded his speech by turning to Trotsky's 1904 pamphlet *Our Political Tasks*, which Trotsky had dedicated to the Menshevik leader Akselrod: "From Lenin to Akselrod – such is the organisational path that our Opposition has travelled . . . Well, good riddance! Go to your 'dear teacher Pavel Borisovich Akselrod'."[54]

At the end of December Trotsky was informed that he had been instructed to accept a post in Astrakhan; he replied to the Politburo that his recurrent malaria made this impossible on health grounds because of the humid climate on the Caspian Sea. A week later, on 3 January 1928, he was summoned to a meeting with the *cheka*. He refused to attend. Then on 12 January he was informed that he was being deported under article 58 of the criminal code to the dry climate of Alma Ata; the deportation took place by force on 17 January. Trotsky was not downcast. It was for him just a stage in the struggle against Thermidor. He told Natasha as they tried to sleep on the hard bunks of the train taking them east: "I did not want to die in my bed in the Kremlin."[55]

Notes

1 V. Vilkova (ed.), *The Struggle for Power in Russia in 1923: from the Secret Archives of the Former Soviet Union* (New York, 1996), pp. 229–30, 268–76, 307, 311.

2 N. Allen (ed.), *Leon Trotsky: the Challenge of the Left Opposition (1923–25)* (New York, 1975), pp. 87–92.

3 Vilkova, *Struggle*, pp. 242–5; R. Wade (ed.), *Documents in Soviet History* (New York, 1995), Vol. III, pp. 96–100.

4 Allen, *Challenge*, pp. 79–84.

5 Vilkova, *Struggle*, pp. 311–28, 336; Wade, *Documents*, p. 115; B. Bazhanov, *Bazhanov and the Damnation of Stalin* (Ohio, 1990), p. 62; I. Deutscher, *The Prophet Unarmed, Trotsky: 1921–1929* (Oxford, 1978), pp. 132–4.

6 L. Trotsky, *My Life* (New York, 1970), pp. 511–2; Bazhanov, *Bazhanov*, p. 65. Stalin told Trotsky both the day originally planned for the funeral and "that he could not get back in time", Trotsky, *My Life*, p. 508. Why Trotsky accepted this when it was patently difficult yet possible to return is unclear.

7 *Trinadtsatyi s"ezd RKP (b): stenograficheskii otchet* (Moscow 1924), pp. 163–8, 211.

8 Allen, *Challenge*, pp. 165–6, 168–9.

9 Allen, *Challenge*, pp. 200–1.

10 Wade, *Documents*, pp. 222–31; *Inprecor* 15.12.1924, 23.1.1925.

11 J. V. Stalin, *Collected Works* (Moscow, 1953), Vol. VII, pp. 7–9; *Inprecor* 11.12.24; Wade, *Documents*, p. 231.

12 Wade, *Documents*, pp. 291–6 (also reproduced in Allen, *Challenge*); Deutscher, *Unarmed*, p. 163.

13 Stalin, *Works*, Vol. VII, p. 115.

14 Trotsky, *My Life*, pp. 518–19.

15 Allen, *Challenge*, pp. 322–74.

16 L. T. Lih *et al.* (eds), *Stalin's Letters to Molotov* (New Haven, 1995), pp. 86, 87 n.1.

17 Lih *et al.* (eds), *Stalin's Letters*, pp. 69–84, 94.

18 Trotsky, *My Life*, pp. 512–3; Lih *et al.* (eds), *Letters*, pp. 86–7, 92.

19 Allen, *Challenge*, pp. 228–9; Lih *et al.* (eds), *Letters*, p. 89; N. Valentinov, "Dopolnenie k 'Dnevniku' L. Trotskogo", *Sotsialisticheskii vestnik*, No. 2–3, 1959, p. 50.

20 E. H. Carr, *Socialism in One Country* (Basingstoke, 1958), Vol. I, pp. 274–336; Wade, *Documents*, pp. 343–9.

21 Allen, *Challenge*, pp. 384–9, 391–2.

22 V. Serge, *Memoirs of a Revolutionary* (Oxford, 1963), p. 210; B. Souvarine, "Pis'mo v redaktsiyu", *Sotsialisticheskii vestnik*, No. 4, 1960; L. Trotsky, *The Writings of Leon Trotsky 1936–7* (New York, 1975), p. 119.

23 A. Cummins (ed.), *Documents of Soviet History* (New York, 1998), Vol. IV, p. 11; Carr, *Socialism in One Country*, p. 354. Trotsky stated in July 1926 (*Arkhiv Trotskogo*, Vol. II, p. 23) that Stalin began to manoeuvre against him "two and a half months after the Fourteenth Party Congress", or mid March. Letters to colleagues (*Arkhiv Trotskogo*, Vol. I, pp. 187–8) show what for Trotsky was an incomprehensible row with Stalin at the very end of March.

24 *Arkhiv Trotskogo*, Vol. I, pp. 207, 209–19.

25 Deutscher, *Unarmed*, pp. 262–5; *Arkhiv Trotskogo*, Vol. I, p. 227.

26 Trotsky, *My Life*, p. 528.

27 Lih *et al.* (eds), *Letters*, pp. 100, 106, 108, 112.

28 Cummins (ed.), *Documents*, p. 48; Deutscher, *Unarmed*, pp. 271–9.

29 Cummins (ed.), *Documents*, pp. 50–51.

30 Cummins (ed.), *Documents*, p. 63; Lih *et al.* (eds), *Letters*, p. 129.

31 P. Broué, *Trotsky* (Paris, 1988), pp. 491–5; Deutscher, *Unarmed*, 293–4; Stalin, *Works*, Vol. VIII, p. 223.

32 Deutscher, *Unarmed*, pp. 296–7; *Arkhiv Trotskogo*, Vol. II, p. 188.

33 Cummins (ed.), *Documents*, pp. 100–17; *Pyatnadtsataya konferentsiya Vsesoyuznoi KP (b)* (Moscow, 1927), p. 534.

34 Lih *et al.* (eds), *Letters*, p. 69; Stalin, *Works*, Vol. VIII, p. 256.

35 D. Law, "Trotsky and Thermidor", in F. Gori, *Pensiero e Azione Politica di Lev Trockij* (Florence, 1982), p. 443; Deutscher, *Unarmed*, p. 309.

36 For China, see A. Pantsov, *The Bolsheviks and the Chinese Revolution* (London, 2000), pp. 84–124; Trotsky's letter of September 1926 is in L. Evans and R. Block (eds), *Leon Trotsky on China* (New York, 1976), pp. 113–9; Stalin's speech is in *Works*, Vol. VII, p. 389.

37 Evans and Block (eds), *Trotsky on China*, pp. 125, 130, 133; Serge, *Memoirs*, p. 217.

38 Evans and Block (eds), *Trotsky on China*, pp. 149–57.

39 Stalin, *Works*, Vol. IX, pp. 230, 239; Evans and Block (eds), *Trotsky on China*, pp. 210–12.

40 *Arkhiv Trotskogo*, Vol. III, pp. 57–9.

41 Trotsky, *My Life*, pp. 530–1.

42 Evans and Block (eds), *Trotsky on China*, pp. 216–38; Stalin, *Works*, Vol. IX, pp. 288–311.

43 R. Daniels, *A Documentary History of Communism* (London, 1985), Vol. II, p. 79; *Arkhiv Trotskogo*, Vol. III, p. 382–6.

44 *Arkhiv Trotskogo*, Vol. III, pp. 87–112.

45 For Stalin on Trotsky's first appearance at the CCC, see Lih *et al.* (eds), *Letters*, p. 135; *Arkhiv Trotskogo*, Vol. III, pp. 115–26, 211–18.

46 Deutscher, *Unarmed*, pp. 349–56; Stalin, *Works*, Vol. X, p. 56.

47 Stalin, *Works*, Vol. X, pp. 52, 87; *Arkhiv Trotskogo*, Vol. IV, pp. 32–45.

48 *Arkhiv Trotskogo*, Vol. IV, pp. 67–8; Stalin, *Works*, Vol. X, p. 91.

49 *Arkhiv Trotskogo*, Vol. IV, pp. 68–70; Broué, *Trotsky*, pp. 521–2; D. Volkogonov, *Trotsky: the Eternal Revolutionary* (London, 1997), p. 291; Stalin, *Works*, Vol. X, p. 166.

50 Trotsky, *My Life*, pp. 531–2; Broué, *Trotsky*, pp. 525–8; Volkogonov, *Trotsky*, pp. 300–11.

51 *Arkhiv Trotskogo*, Vol. IV, pp. 218–24; Stalin, *Works*, Vol. X, p. 180.

52 I. Thatcher, *Trotsky* (London, 2003), p. 151; Trotsky, *Writings 1932*, pp. 246–7; *Arkhiv Trotskogo*, Vol. IV, pp. 266, 267–9.

53 Trotsky, *Writings 1936–7*, p. 66.

54 *Arkhiv Trotskogo*, Vol. IV, pp. 73–4; Stalin, *Works*, Vol. X, p. 211.

55 V. Serge and N. Sedova Trotsky, *The Life and Death of Leon Trotsky* (New York, 1973), p. 157.

Chapter 7

Exile and Internationalism

Just ten days before Trotsky was deported to Alma Ata, Stalin set off on a tour of Siberia to identify just why it was that, despite a decent harvest, grain was not arriving at state depots. His conclusion was that kulaks were hoarding grain to try and force up the price, and his response was to resort to force, thus violating the underlying principle of the free market in grain established by Lenin at the Tenth Party Congress. Writing in summer 1927 Stalin mused on the question of timing in politics. Poring over the events of 1917, as was so often the case during the conflict with Trotsky, he asked himself: "Why, then, did Lenin brand as adventurers the group of Petrograd Bolsheviks headed by Bagdatiev in April 1917, when that group put forward the slogan 'Down with the Provisional Government, All Power to the Soviets'. How could the slogan 'All Power to the Soviets' be correct in September 1917 but wrong in April 1917." "The Opposition does not understand," he decided, "that the point is not to be 'first' in saying a thing, running too far ahead and disorganising the cause of the revolution, but to say it at the right time, and to say it in such a way that it will be taken up by the masses and put into practice."[1] Having criticised as premature the Opposition's call for an assault on the kulak and industrialisation, Stalin now resolved to implement the policy himself. His actions set in train the events that would see him emerge as Party and state dictator, pursuing the policies of industrialisation and collectivisation against which history would judge him.

Although in April 1928 the Central Committee condemned some of the excesses committed by Stalin during his tour of the Urals, he was determined to push ahead with his plans. Things came to a head at the July Central Committee Plenum where Stalin secured a slim majority for his policies. Throughout autumn 1928 Bukharin was optimistic that Stalin's policies could be reversed, but in the event the November Central Committee Plenum endorsed them and in December Stalin called for the Five Year Plan to be fulfilled within four years. In January 1929

Bukharin, Stalin's ally in the struggle against the United Opposition, was condemned at a Joint Plenum of the Central Committee and CCC for heading a "Right deviation". Summer 1929 saw the first tentative move to collectivise agriculture, followed by the decision in November to embark on a full-scale collectivisation campaign; in December 1929 Stalin called for the elimination of the kulaks as a class, prompting five weeks of terror when one million households were reduced to the state of outcasts and deported.

On 2 March 1930 Stalin signalled a retreat, writing an article in *Pravda* entitled *Dizzy with Success*, which blamed the chaos of the collectivisation campaign on overzealous officials. Stalin's speech to the Sixteenth Party Congress in July 1930 made clear that he feared that his opponents might make political capital from this temporary retreat, and that is precisely what happened. Stalin's supporters were dividing into the fully committed and the pragmatists, and the pragmatists like Sergei Syrtsov and Beso Lominadze demanded in autumn 1930 that collectivisation be put on hold and the tempo of the Five Year Plan reduced. It was the end of 1930 before this opposition had been defeated. His position reinforced, Stalin made his famous speech of 4 February 1931 in which he called for the fulfilment of the Five Year Plan in three years on the grounds that "We are fifty or a hundred years behind the advanced countries: we must make good this distance in ten years; either we do it, or we shall go under." But the cost was enormous. Collectivisation continued during the winters of 1930–31 and 1931–2, and by autumn 1932 there was famine.

In March 1932 the former Krasnaya Presnya District Party Secretary Ryutin wrote a 200-page programme detailing the failings of Stalin's policies, which soon circulated widely, especially to delegates to the September Central Committee Plenum, and became the accepted programme of those opposing Stalin. The problem for Stalin was that, even in his own terms, his policies seemed to have failed. Catching up with the advanced countries was all about strengthening Soviet defence capabilities, yet when in September 1931 Japan invaded Manchuria and for the next 18 months the threat of war in the Far East seemed real indeed, the famine meant that the Red Army's food reserve had been used up for relief measures. Even loyal supporters distanced themselves from Stalin at this time. Ordzhonikidze, the Commissar for Heavy Industry, criticised Stalin's spokesman Molotov when it came to drafting the Second Five Year Plan; there could be no more great leaps forward, according to Ordzhonikidze, the Second Five Year Plan had to be about consolidation and a recovery in the standard of living. Similarly Sergei Kirov, who had replaced Zinoviev as the Party chief in Leningrad, came out strongly in the Politburo against Stalin's demand that Ryutin be executed. Only the dramatic recovery in the Soviet economy in the second half of 1933 drew the teeth of such criticism.[2]

Stalin's Zigzag

Trotsky's ability to influence these events was limited not only by his exile, but by his insistent belief that Stalin, as a Thermidorean prisoner of the Right, was not serious about industrialisation. It took Trotsky a while to settle in Alma Ata. Compared to Moscow it was extremely backward, with few paved streets and fewer houses with running water and electricity. Trotsky, his wife Natasha and younger son Lev were allocated the comparative luxury of a whole house with electricity to themselves. In summer they were allowed to visit a dacha in the mountains, a holiday marred by the news that Trotsky's younger daughter Nina had died on 9 June. They were, of course, constantly under surveillance by the *cheka*. Their house was situated conveniently close to police headquarters and the *cheka* accompanied them even on hunting trips, with good reason, as it turned out, because Trotsky toyed with the idea of fleeing across the border to China. Despite this close surveillance, with the help of Lev, Trotsky soon established clandestine contacts with supporters in Moscow and further afield. Between April and October 1928 Trotsky sent out 800 letters and 550 telegrams, and received over 1,000 letters and 700 telegrams.[3]

Many of his correspondents, notably Christian Rakovskii, who would stay at Trotsky's side longer than most, wondered if the Opposition should not back Stalin as he confronted Bukharin over the assault on the kulaks. Trotsky dismissed this out of hand and saw confirmation in the decision of the Central Committee in April 1928 to criticise Stalin's excesses. However, the issue would not go away. In summer 1928 the Sixth Congress of the Comintern was due to take place, and the Opposition wanted to try to present an appeal to that body protesting at their expulsion at the Fifteenth Party Congress. Karl Radek, one of those who in 1926 had suggested that Trotsky form an alliance with Stalin rather than Zinoviev, sent a round robin to fellow Oppositionists in June 1928 arguing that any appeal to the Comintern would be greatly strengthened if the Opposition allied itself with Stalin in his growing critique of Bukharin; the Opposition could ask to be allowed back into the Party to support what was clearly Stalin's new course. Trotsky would not agree: the change in

Party policy was not serious, just a zigzag; for it to be serious the nature of the Party regime should change and that meant changing the leadership. There was, however, a hint of compromise in the final text of this declaration which stated: "With Stalin against Bukharin maybe, but with Bukharin against Stalin never."[4]

Not long before the July Plenum opened, Trotsky picked up rumours that Stalin had approached Zinoviev and Kamenev, offering them a deal, but then rejecting their insistence that Trotsky and other Opposition exiles be allowed to return. Imagining that this put Stalin in a relatively weak position, he misjudged developments at the Plenum itself. When Trotsky obtained a copy of the stenographic record of the July Central Committee Plenum, he convinced himself that it was Bukharin not Stalin who had emerged victorious. So, on learning shortly afterwards that at the end of the Plenum Bukharin had organised a secret meeting with Kamenev at which the latter urged all former Oppositionists, including Trotsky, to rally against Stalin, Trotsky organised the remnants of his underground organisation in Moscow to publish a leaflet denouncing Bukharin and detailing his conversation with Kamenev. This was indeed "with Stalin against Bukharin".[5]

Kamenev was convinced that the crisis in the Party leadership offered Trotsky a way back into the leadership and in September contacted those close to him in Moscow to urge Trotsky to make a direct appeal to the October Central Committee Plenum. In a circular letter of 21 October Trotsky responded to this suggestion with disdain. He ridiculed the alleged comment by Zinoviev that Stalin had triumphed in July. "From the political point of view this is absurd," he wrote, for in his view Stalin was still at the Centre, veering first to the Right and then to the Left; he could well "steer a course to the Left by giving Zinoviev and Kamenev a little longer leash", but the crux of the matter was that he would quickly veer to the Right for "the conditions necessary for Thermidor to materialise can develop in a comparatively short time". Thermidor was still the danger, he argued, and there was even a candidate for Bonaparte; Klim Voroshilov, he alleged, had hinted in June that the military might act in support of the Right. Trotsky insisted that any declaration he made to the October Plenum "would not alter the legal position of the Opposition" and concluded "we must strike twice as hard, three times, ten times as hard against capitulators" like Kamenev.[6]

Thus, whereas Radek took up Kamenev's proposal and wrote to the Central Committee in October suggesting that it made no sense to keep in exile politicians who favoured the industrialisation campaign, Trotsky would have none of it. In Trotsky's view "only an absolutely thoughtless person could regard a return of Centrism [Stalin] to the road of the Right as impossible." His supporters therefore could not form alliances but should become independent participants in any moves to push the Centre to the Left, "without ceasing for a single instant to criticise and unmask Centrism as the fundamental obstacle in the way of awakening the activism of the proletarian core of the Party". What Stalin was engaged in was "a Left zigzag", not a "genuine Left course". However, many rank and file Trotskyists supported Radek in this disagreement. On 2 December Trotsky received a letter from two activists stating that they now saw it as their duty to back Stalin; in their view what was happening was not simply "a Stalinist adventure".[7]

At about this time Trotsky was approached himself by an intermediary sent by Stalin to see if there was any basis for an agreement. According to Trotsky's own account, "I answered him to the effect that at the moment there could be no question of reconciliation, not because I did not want it, but because Stalin could not make his peace with me; he was forced to pursue to the end the course set him by the bureaucracy." For Trotsky, the power of Thermidor was such that, even if Stalin had personally wanted an agreement, he would not have been in a position to grant it. At the end of 1928 Stalin nevertheless contacted the leader of the Trotskyist underground in Moscow, who had recently been arrested, and asked whether he and his followers would be prepared to return to the Party; the response was that this could happen only if Trotsky and other exiles were allowed to return and hold their own conference to agree tactics. Not surprisingly Stalin concluded from these approaches that the Opposition would resume its factional campaign as soon as it could and that Trotsky was irreconcilable.[8]

On 16 December 1928 Trotsky was visited by the *cheka* and asked to make a categorical promise that he would cease all contact with his supporters, or face more isolated exile. In a letter to the Central Committee he refused point blank "to abstain from political activity . . . only completely corrupted bureaucrats could demand such a renunciation from revolutionaries". The Politburo's verdict came a month later. On 20 January 1929 the same *cheka* officer returned to inform Trotsky that he was being exiled abroad. Three weeks later he stood on the quayside of his favourite city, Odessa, and bade farewell to his son Sergei, predicting mistakenly, "we'll be back". As the ship taking him to exile in Turkey entered the Bosphorous on 12 February one of the *cheka* agents accompanying him handed over the sum of $1,500, a grant from the Soviet Government to enable its former Commissar of War to settle abroad.[9]

For the first three weeks Trotsky was a rather embarrassing house guest at the Soviet Consulate in Constantinople. However, when it was clear that he was intent on continuing his campaign against Stalin in the foreign "capitalist" press, Trotsky was found a villa to rent on the island of Prinkipo, where he was to spend the next four years. Apart from the grant he had received from the Soviet Government, Trotsky was able to survive on the money earned from his writings. He had started work on *My Life* while still in Alma Ata, and royalties from that and his *History of the Russian Revolution* became his main source of income, supplemented by occasional commissioned articles. On this modest income his family both lived and subsidised the *Bulletin of the Opposition*. In all, 65 issues of this newspaper were produced: from July 1929 to March 1931 in Paris; then in Berlin; then, after Hitler came to power, back to Paris; then in Zurich for 1934 and back to Paris from 1935–9; the last four issues came out in New York. It has been estimated that two-thirds of the *Bulletin of the Opposition* was written by Trotsky himself, although its production was always the work of Lev.[10]

In one of his last letters from Alma Ata, Trotsky had expressed alarm at the way his supporters seemed increasingly willing to support Stalin and "the Centre": "You say that by attacking the Centrists 'we are helping the Right' . . . with our relentless criticism we are helping the working class core of the Party free itself from the half-heartedness and falsity of Centrism, thereby creating a real proletarian bulwark against the Right danger." While still living in the Soviet Consulate he wrote that "for Stalin the main enemy remains, as before, the Left; this no longer needs to be proved". From Prinkipo he stressed in March that Stalin's talk of industrialisation meant that "only outwardly" he seemed closer to the Opposition. The crux of the matter was Thermidor, as he repeated in April.

The problem of Thermidor and Bonapartism is at bottom the problem of the kulak. Those who shy away from this problem, those who minimise its importance and distract attention to questions of the Party regime, to bureaucratism, to unfair political methods and other superficial manifestations and expressions of the pressure of kulak elements upon the dictatorship of the proletariat resemble a physician who chases after symptoms while ignoring functional and organic disturbances.[11]

Fewer and fewer of Trotsky's supporters in the Soviet Union still saw things in this way. At the Sixteenth Party Conference in April 1929 some 38 second level Oppositionists issued a joint statement and capitulated, and they were quickly followed by such leading Oppositionists as Radek and Preobrazhenskii; on 13 July *Pravda* published a statement by ten prominent Oppositionists. Putting a brave face on it, Trotsky responded by slipping into the realm of self-delusion, reinforced by his growing distance from Soviet politics. He asserted that "Stalinist cadres, gritting their teeth, are carrying out a zigzag further to the Left than they would wish"; this had confused some comrades, but inevitably there would be "an immediate swerving of the Stalinists to the Right". What those comrades thinking of capitulation needed to ask themselves was this: "What has produced the Left twitch of the apparatus – our attack, our irreconcilability, the growth of our influence, the courage of our cadres." Stalin had moved over to the Left "only under our whip".[12]

Rhetoric of this kind did not stem the flow of Oppositionists returning to the Party. Even Christian Rakovskii, who headed those Oppositionists not ready to capitulate, wanted to return to the Party. He drafted a statement issued on 22 August 1929 which argued that it had been wrong to exclude the Opposition from the Party as its analysis had been proved right by events. Stalin's new course marked a clear improvement, but for it to be accepted as secure the Opposition, including Trotsky, had to be allowed to return to the Party. To ease that return, the Opposition would again renounce all factional activity and rely simply on "those rights guaranteed to all Party members". Trotsky signed Rakovskii's document, but with little enthusiasm. It was "as far as anyone could go on the road to concessions to the apparatus", and it was only possible to sign it because Thermidor was not yet an established fact. Stalin could safely ignore Rakovskii's proposal, since Oppositionists were lining up to capitulate without imposing conditions; on 3 November *Pravda* printed the statements from more of Trotsky's erstwhile supporters.[13]

It was to try and stem the tide of capitulations that Trotsky decided, after some hesitation, to seek the help of Jacob Blumkin. Blumkin had been the Left SR who on 6 July 1918 assassinated the German ambassador; he had subsequently joined the Bolshevik Party and become a *cheka* officer, working on clandestine operations abroad. He had identified with the Opposition, and returning from a mission in India over summer 1929, stopped off in Constantinople. Initially Trotsky refused to see him, but then gave him a message for his supporters which called for a purge of capitulators and a strengthening of cadres in preparation for a crisis that he predicted Stalin would face in the autumn. Blumkin returned to Russia, but before he could contact anyone he realised he was under surveillance. Fearing imminent arrest, he went to see Radek, who got him to hand over Trotsky's letters to his superiors and organised a meeting with Ordzhonikidze as CCC Chairman. It did no good; Blumkin was arrested, charged with treason and executed.[14]

By autumn 1929 Trotsky had turned to analysing how growing economic problems would yet force Stalin to turn to the Right. Proper planning, drafted well in advance after due consultation with experts, would link economic growth to improvements in the standard of living: Stalin's planning seemed to be the very opposite of this, taking place in a complete absence of detailed information; "politics is being carried on with the lights out". Trotsky warned in December 1929 of imminent economic crisis: "any capitalist crisis would be child's play in comparison", he argued. These views were taken further in February 1930 when he highlighted the growing disproportions in the First Five Year Plan and the increasing danger of inflation as the government tried to plug supply gaps by spending beyond the agreed limits. He predicted a panicky retreat: "For how many months will the present leadership drive the Party along the road of Ultra-Leftism; not for very many."[15]

Thus Stalin's *Dizzy with Success* speech seemed to Trotsky to be the long-delayed zigzag to the Right he had always predicted. The moderation of policy associated with the speech coincided with some leaders of the "Right deviation" recognising their errors and capitulating. Trotsky was worried that this might signify the first stage in a resumption of a Right-Centre bloc; indeed he still considered it likely that Voroshilov would impose a military dictatorship in the manner of Chiang Kai-shek: "Klim's military dictatorship, coupled with certain surviving elements of the Soviet system would indeed be our own, native born, form of Bonapartism in its first stage." However, from within the Soviet Union Rakovskii put a very different gloss on the return of the Right; he argued that the time had come for the formation of an emergency or "Coalition Central Committee" of Left, Centre and Right. Trotsky was not sure. At first, writing in October 1930, he thought the idea could attract much support "as the only means of saving the Party from complete collapse", but a month later he had doubts; whatever Bukharin and his supporters might say, theirs was "the policy of Thermidor". Thus in his view a Coalition Central Committee, if formed, "could in itself solve nothing, but it could make it easier for the Party to solve the tasks before it", in other words, defeating Thermidor.[16]

A Coalition Central Committee

The relative ease with which Stalin dealt with the opposition from Syrtsov and Lominadze forced Trotsky to reassess his attitude to the Party bureaucracy. Before his exile, it had been very simple: the bureaucracy was inherently a creature of the Right and Thermidor, a reflection of capitalist forces. Since then, things had changed for, however chaotically, the bureaucracy had turned itself into the driving force of industrialisation. Back in November 1927 he had noted that "although the Stalin apparatus completely serves the political pressure to the Right, organisationally it retains its independence". In April 1930 he conceded that, "in certain very broad limits", the bureaucracy could play an independent role, developing its own self-serving and privileged interests whilst also serving the Party regime; the danger, as ever, was that a Bonaparte could as easily grasp control of this bureaucratic machine as anybody else. By April 1931 this analysis had advanced further, the apparatus "without having absolute independence nevertheless enjoys a great relative independence: the bureaucracy is in direct possession of state power; it raises itself above the classes and puts a powerful stamp upon their development." However, the class concerned still reflected his obsession with the Right danger. Trotsky now accepted that "the crushing of the Right-wing of the Party and its renunciation of its platform diminished the chances of the first, step by step, veiled, that is Thermidorean form of overthrow" which he had been concerned about since December 1923. However, "the plebiscitary degeneration of the Party apparatus [as he now referred to it] undoubtedly increases the chances of the Bonapartist form." Finally dropping Voroshilov as a candidate for military dictator, he now suggested three other generals for the post, "Tukhachevskii, Blücher or Budyennyi".[17]

While Bonapartist Thermidor, rather than creeping Thermidor, was still the danger, Trotsky did not see its triumph as inevitable, as he explained in September 1931. He was still convinced that the way the bureaucracy was undertaking the industrialisation campaign would lead to a crisis, the ruling apparatus would begin to collapse and the Party fall apart; at that point it would be a choice between a Bonapartist intervention and the formation of a Coalition Central Committee, a body that would be "in essence an organising commission for the reconstruction of the Party". His interest in the notion of a Coalition Central Committee was greatly reinforced when contact was re-established in summer 1931 with one of his oldest supporters, I. N. Smirnov. Smirnov had capitulated in July 1929 when Stalin put him in charge of establishing a new motor industry in Nizhnyi Novgorod; it was in relation to the needs of that industry that Smirnov visited Berlin in July 1931. There, by chance, he met Trotsky's son Lev. Smirnov promised to keep in touch.[18]

Moves to encourage the formation of a Coalition Central Committee were then put in jeopardy by another intemperate outburst from Trotsky.

At the end of 1931 a German Communist paper published a story about how White Guard groups were about to assassinate Trotsky, whose villa was to all intents and purposes unprotected. Trotsky interpreted this article as Stalin organising an alibi for himself in advance of the Soviet authorities trying to kill him, so he wrote to the Politburo on 4 January 1932 detailing how Zinoviev and Kamenev had warned him in 1926 that Stalin could even then be planning an attempt on his life. Predicting that Stalin's "political crash will be one of the most terrible in history" he piled insult on insult: Stalin was "his Bonapartist Almightiness", "corrupter of the Party" and "gravedigger of the Chinese Revolution". Stalin forced Zinoviev and Kamenev to reply ridiculing Trotsky's allegation and on 20 February 1932 Trotsky and all members of his family living abroad were deprived of their Soviet citizenship.[19]

Despite this vicious exchange, Trotsky adopted a much more measured tone when he wrote an Open Letter to the Soviet Presidium on 1 March 1932. Although this was in part protest at his loss of citizenship, it was devoid of polemic and was soon circulating among Soviet leaders. The Stalinist regime, he said, was approaching a decisive crisis as workers were becoming impatient with low living standards and managers more questioning of Stalin's leadership. "The two processes are interconnected," Trotsky said. "Can there be," he asked, "anything more malignant, more degenerate and more shameful than the introduction of super-monarchical authority into the Party of the proletariat?" Stalin's strength lay in the Party machine, divorce him from that machine and he would be nothing: "It is time to carry out Lenin's final and insistent advice – remove Stalin." In a similar vein Trotsky wrote in an article published in June 1932: "Today, as on the day we first raised our voice of warning . . . we are ready to place ourselves at the disposal of the Communist International and Soviet state [with] only one condition, we must have the right to defend our ideas."[20]

In September E. S. Goltsman arrived in Berlin entrusted with a packet of materials sent by Smirnov, details of which were quickly published in the *Bulletin of the Opposition*. These documents concentrated on the grave disproportions in industry and described "the growing conviction about the need to change the Party leadership". In particular Smirnov raised the need for a broad bloc of former Left Oppositionists and Rightists. When Goltsman arrived, the Rightists had still not agreed to take part in such a bloc, but while he was in Berlin news came that a comprehensive Opposition bloc had been formed, all of whom supported the platform drafted earlier in the year by Ryutin. In reality Stalin was one step ahead of the game. In September one of Smirnov's associates was taken into custody, and Goltsman was arrested as he returned to the Soviet Union. Then on 9 October Zinoviev and Kamenev were expelled from the Party for attempting to revive their faction.[21]

The extent of the opposition to Stalin at this time was clearly wide-spread. When Stalin got his revenge at the staged show trials of 1936, 1937 and 1938, the threads of the conspiracies in which his enemies were allegedly involved always led back to the summer and autumn of 1932. Stalin's version of events thus went something like this: Smirnov approached various former Trotskyists and persuaded them to throw in their lot with a conspiracy that was well underway by September and October 1932. That conspiracy centred around Zinoviev and Kamenev, but its unprincipled nature was reinforced by the way in which all elements to it were prepared to adopt the programme drawn up by the Right-winger Ryutin. For Stalin the Coalition Central Committee was nothing other than "the case of the anti-soviet bloc of Rights and Trotskyists", the title he gave to the last of the purge trials.[22] Yet, if Stalin thought Trotsky's adhesion to this new opposition was clear-cut, the reality was rather different. Far from embracing this news of widespread opposition within the higher echelons of the Stalinist apparatus, Trotsky was over-come by uncertainty. He was worried that so many of those involved in these moves against Stalin were Rightists. In his view "Party democracy is not an abstract ideal, least of all is it designed to serve as a screen for Thermidorean tendencies"; he would not democratise the Party if it benefited the Right, for Ryutin and his friends "represented the most thoroughgoing Thermidorean wing in the camp of the Right". And yet at this time in terms of practical politics his stance and that of the Right were identical – he called for the Second Five Year Plan to be delayed, which was precisely the demand of the Right.[23]

At the end of 1932 he explained in an unpublished note the tortuous reasoning behind his decision not to support the slogan "Down with Stalin!" For supporters of Thermidor this would mean the overthrow not only of Stalin but the bureaucracy and the whole apparatus of com-munist rule; "Down with Stalin!" could mean "Down with Bolshevism!" In his view it was still quite possible, despite everything, that in the struggle against Thermidor "we will find ourselves in a united front with the Stalinists". Under a slogan like "Down with Stalin!" the Left risked "dissolving into the general dissatisfaction with Stalin, something we cannot, we will not, we must not do". Against all the evidence, he detected in one of Stalin's speeches of January 1933 signs of concessions to the kulaks. The kulaks as a class might have been deported to Siberia, but kulak ideology and kulak psychology continued; the Soviet peasant could still become "a force for Thermidor". With this Rightist danger ever-present, he explained both at the end of 1932 and again in March 1933, the Trotskyists could not support the slogan "Down with Stalin!", the slogan of those wanting to replace Stalin with a Coalition Central Committee.[24] Instead Trotsky resolved on one final effort at reconciliation. On 15 March 1933 he wrote a letter to the Politburo making clear that the only way to avoid disaster was to revive the Party and "the Left Opposition was willing to offer the Central Committee full co-operation in returning the Party to the track of normal existence". A preliminary agreement could and should be reached; "no matter how tense the atmosphere, its explosiveness can be removed through several successive stages, provided there is goodwill on both sides". To facilitate this he was ready "to enter into preliminary talks without any publicity". Rumours that Trotsky was in secret contact with Moscow began to circle in the West; the only Soviet comment was that there was no truth to the story that Trotsky was to return to the Soviet Union.[25]

Reviving the International

In July 1933 Trotsky was given permission to settle in France by the Radical Prime Minister Edouard Daladier. He sailed from Prinkipo on the 17th and arrived in Marseilles a week later. He hoped that by leaving the isolation of Turkey he would be able to play a fuller part in the political life of Europe; this hope turned out to be quite unjustified. At one level he was sad to be leaving Prinkipo, as these lyrical lines bear witness.

Prinkipo is an island of peace and forgetfulness. The life of the world reaches here after long delays and hushed down . . . Prinkipo is a fine place to work with a pen, particularly during the autumn and winter when the island becomes completely deserted and woodcock appear in the park. Not only are there no theatres here, but no movies. Automobiles are forbidden. Are there many such places in the world? In our house we have no telephone. The braying of the donkey acts soothingly on the nerves . . . The sea is under the window, there is no hiding from the sea.

And his first weeks in France were anything but calm. Trotsky and Natasha were to settle at St Palais near Royan on the Atlantic coast, but as they arrived their new home caught fire. For a healthy man escaping from a fire ignited by dry leaves would have been no problem, but Trotsky was flat on his back with lumbago, and the incident sparked off a series of high temperatures and fevers which forced him to take to his bed until the end of September. When he had recovered enough to move, he took refuge in the Pyrenees for three weeks in October, before resettling on 1 November at Barbizon, on the edge of the Fountainbleau Forest near Paris.[26]

Trotsky moved to Paris because he wanted to be near those of his supporters in the West who had established "a firm nucleus for a new International". On his arrival in Prinkipo he had called on all his supporters within the communist parties of other countries to remain within those parties and declare their loyalty to the Communist International. By 1933 he had changed his mind and his supporters organised a conference in Paris in August 1933 to establish something more organised, in line with Trotsky's statement issued as he arrived in France that: "we cease to be a faction; we are no longer the Left Opposition; we become embryos of new parties". He had come to this conclusion for two reasons. The first of these he also announced on his arrival in France: "A current towards the Left is forming in the socialist parties and we should orient ourselves towards these currents." However, it was not simply that the heyday of the Right-wing control of socialist and social democratic parties seemed to be passing.[27]

Trotsky was keen to leave Prinkipo and involve himself in the politics of Europe because he had finally concluded that Thermidor was a mirage. The explanation for this dramatic change of track emerged only in October when his health had recovered sufficiently for him to write again. Suddenly Trotsky made no mention of Thermidor. Instead he recognised that the Stalinist bureaucracy, far from being the creature of Thermidor, was "the gatekeeper of the social conquests of the proletarian revolution". Trotsky's analysis of the emergence of the Stalin bureaucracy had changed completely. Initially he saw Stalin and the Centrists as a hapless group, being manipulated, often unconsciously, by Thermidorean forces. Then he began to notice that the bureaucracy could play a limited role and act apparently independently, influencing the class struggles that had produced it. Now he went even further: the bureaucracy was in control, and its intervention in the class struggles had been to defend the workers' state, while carving out for itself a privileged position of power; the Soviet Union was a degenerate workers' state. The bureaucracy, once the weapon of the Right, was now the prop of the Left.

Some of Trotsky's supporters abroad had undertaken a similar analysis and concluded that the Stalinist bureaucracy was a new class. Trotsky was adamant that this was not the case. "In so far as the bureaucracy robs the people, we have to deal not with class exploitation but social parasitism," Trotsky stressed. Although it "squandered unproductively a tremendous portion of the national income, the Soviet bureaucracy was interested at the same time, by its very function, in the economic and cultural growth of the country". If the economy ever collapsed completely, Trotsky predicted, then "in place of the workers' state would come not 'social bureaucratic' but capitalist relations". Using one of the medical analogies he loved he insisted "a tumour can grow to tremendous size and even strangle the living organism, but a tumour can never become an independent organism". In these circumstances, he suggested, Soviet workers understood that they must hold back from a final clash with Stalin: "The workers fear that they will clear the field for the class enemy if they overthrow the bureaucracy . . . they would have settled accounts with the despotism of the apparatus had the western horizon flamed not with the brown colour of fascism but with the red of revolution." Therefore what was needed was the formation of a genuine revolutionary International to ensure "the inevitable crisis of the Stalinist regime would open the possibility of revival in the USSR".[28]

Ever since writing *Results and Prospects* Trotsky had juggled to balance the two elements of his vision, the kulak danger and the need for a European revolution. After a decade thinking about little else than the danger posed by a kulak Thermidor, he had returned to the question of Europe. There was a clear logic to Trotsky's new perspective. The formation of Left-wing governments elsewhere in Europe could conceivably have produced a more relaxed climate in Russia, making it possible to criticise Stalin's leadership and call for more modest and rational economic planning without running the risk of being branded a traitor. The problem for Trotsky was that while he understood the big picture, he had absolutely no understanding of European politics nor the limited horizons of most of those European politicians who had rallied to his side.

When Trotsky was sent into foreign exile he had to establish his authority. He therefore used his autobiography *My Life* to establish the myth that his confrontations with Stalin had continued non-stop since the end of 1922 and had begun then on the express orders of Lenin who, fearing for the future of the Party if Stalin remained in charge, appointed Trotsky his true successor. This myth was successful to the extent that Trotsky rapidly became the hero of all dissident communists, but it was possible only by Trotsky claiming to be, what Lenin had indeed once called him, the best of Bolsheviks. As the best of Bolsheviks he had to deny the two things that had motivated his political career since his 1903, that he differed from Lenin on the issues of Party organisation and the peasantry. He was forced to appear as a second-rate Lenin, and when it came to organising his followers he denied himself any of the organisational flexibility he had shown before the revolution.

More than once the squabbling among his French supporters had driven Trotsky to the point of distraction; in summer 1930 he had summoned them all to Prinkipo in the vain hope that they might be persuaded to agree. However the start of 1934 brought renewed optimism that French Trotskysists might be able to bring real influence to bear on the politics of their country. On 6 February 1934 the authoritarian Right in France staged a massive demonstration in Paris aimed at preventing Daladier from forming his second administration. To all on the Left, this was a clear attempt by "fascists" to seize power, and the French trade unions organised a massive counter-demonstration, supported not only by the socialists but the communists as well. Suddenly, the Left in France had been reinvigorated and Trotsky called on his supporters to enter the French socialist party and help move it further to the Left. He was understandably delighted at these spontaneous moves towards a united front, and quite correct in calling for moves of this kind to be organisationally strengthened – but his slogan showed how out of touch he was. He called for the formation of soviets as the natural "revolutionary apparatus of the united front". It was true, as he said, that in 1905 the soviets had played such a role, but the reality in Europe was that they were everywhere associated with insurrection and any call for their formation would be universally understood as a call for immediate insurrection, no matter how often Trotsky explained he was just making a historical analogy with 1905. In the terms of his historical analogy he was calling for the formation of united front committees, which was precisely what the socialists and communists were calling for.[29]

Ironically, Trotsky's new tactic was almost crowned with immediate success: the revival of working class unrest in the West coincided with signs of political evolution in the USSR. The year 1934 was the year of reconciliation, a path clearly marked out at the Seventeenth Party Congress, a path resented by Stalin and encouraged by Sergei Kirov, the human face of Stalinism. Bukharin and other Right leaders were reincorporated into important positions and early in 1934 the Soviet bureaucracy made a final effort to appeal to the Left Opposition. The greatest success of this operation was to persuade Rakovsky, Trotsky's most loyal ally and close friend – one of the handful of people with whom he used the initimate *ty* – to capitulate. Rakovsky's argument was that "the victorious offensive of fascism requires the unity of all forces in the defence of Soviet power". At the same time the secret police briefed Party activists that Trotsky was about to seek permission to return to the Soviet Union, and indeed reports soon circulated in Paris that a member of the Central Committee had made an unsuccessful attempt to contact Trotsky directly.[30]

Although the events of 6 February 1934 ushered in a revival of the Left in France, something which would culminate in the formation first of a united front in July 1934 and then a popular front in July 1935, in the immediate term they resulted in the formation of a Right-wing government which was embarrassed by Trotsky's presence in France. He had been living incognito, but in April 1934 his whereabouts were discovered and the government decided he should leave the country. Since no state would accept him, this order could not be implemented at once and so Trotsky had to flee, pursued by the press, until he found sanctuary near Grenoble, where he lived in complete isolation for the next 11 months.

Although Trotsky had ceased to talk about Thermidor since his arrival in France, he had not yet officially announced the demise of the concept. And, occasionally, it could resurface even now; early in 1935 he noted in his diary that moves to strengthen the rights of collective farmers represented "a further concession to the petit bourgeois tendencies of the peasants" and could herald a move to the Right and a retreat from industrialisation. However, for the most part he stuck to his belief that "the main key to the internal position of the Soviet Union today is outside the Soviet Union; should the western proletariat surrender the European continent to fascism, the isolated and profoundly degenerated workers' state will not maintain itself for long." The death knell for Thermidor was sounded in February 1935 when Trotsky announced that the term "Thermidor" had become worn out with overuse; "it has lost its concrete content and is obviously inadequate for the task of characterising either that stage through which the Stalinist bureaucracy is passing or the catastrophe it is preparing". Aware that an awful lot of ideological baggage was being shed by this final act, Trotsky described his change of mind as a moment of "self-criticism" and "a partial correction", for "our tendency never made claims to infallibility".[31]

Although the assassination of Kirov in December 1934 gave Stalin the opportunity to reassert his authority, it was not immediately obvious that the prospects for the progressive evolution of the Soviet Union were over. And in spring 1935 the growing campaign for Left unity in France seemed to be bearing real fruit. At the start of June 1935 Trotsky noted with satisfaction that "the correctness of our entry into the French socialist party is now proved by objective facts". To influence events he needed to escape his virtual house arrest in Grenoble and the election of a Labour Government in Norway offered a way forward. Trotsky arrived in Norway on 18 June 1935 where he and his family lived for the next

18 months with the Left-wing editor and member of parliament, Konrad Knudsen. Here, although Trotsky found time to reformulate his ideas on the post-Thermidorean Soviet Union in the treatise *The Revolution Betrayed*, his move to Norway actually decreased rather than increased his influence on European politics. In France his fractious followers soon rejected the policy of "entering" the socialist party and working within it, the policy Trotsky had so recently praised, and returned to the policy of forming ideologically pure but politically ineffective sects. This blow badly affected his health, and he was bedridden at home or in hospital for the last three months of the year. On 27 December 1935 he was so exhausted by the infighting of his European collaborators that he asked for a months' leave of absence: "These disgusting trivia not only rob me of my ability to cope with more serious affairs, but give me insomnia, fever, etc." His disciples were proving quite incapable of turning the reviving European labour movement to his advantage. It was at this time that he turned to Natasha on one of their winter walks and said despairingly: "I am tired of it all, all of it – you understand."[32]

Although Trotsky repeatedly condemned the sectarianism of his followers, and clearly despaired that his international strategy was disintegrating before his very eyes, his false position as a second Lenin meant that he was equally guilty himself of fostering sectarianism. In spring 1936 two of his once ardent supporters were released from Stalin's prison camps and returned to Europe. Ante Ciliga, a member of the Yugoslav Communist Party, was a Croat by ethnicity but had been born an Italian citizen; lobbying by prominent figures in the West and the Italian Government secured his release. The case of Victor Serge was similar. He was born in Belgium and lived much of his life in France: an international campaign secured his release also. When Ciliga arrived Trotsky was at first delighted to publish his accounts of the horrors of life in Stalin's camps. However, Ciliga's experience had persuaded him that all forms of sectarian politics were wrong and that communist and socialists should resist Stalinism together. This prompted Trotsky to issue a statement: "Comrade Ciliga considers it possible to collaborate with Mensheviks . . . we are obliged therefore to cease publication of Comrade Ciliga's articles." It was the same with Serge, who until the time of his arrest in 1933 had been in contact with Trotsky's first wife Aleksandra. Serge too had returned from his sufferings convinced that only a non-sectarian approach to the struggle against Stalinism could bring success. He called for "freedom of opinion for all the different shadings of socialist approach", by which he meant including both anarchists and Mensheviks. As he explained in a letter to Trotsky, most of those in the gulag were "inclined to take the view that on the organisational question you were right [in 1904] against Lenin". Relations between Trotsky and Serge worsened dramatically.[33]

Trotsky's condemnation of his former comrades for calling for co-operation among socialists and communists coincided with the highpoint of the Left's revival in Europe, the formation of Popular Front governments in Spain and France. Yet even before it became clear whether these governments would prove Left-wing enough to have the sort of beneficial impact on the Soviet Union that Trotsky had hoped for in 1934, Stalin acted to reinforce his position and end the period of reconciliation associated with Kirov. Trotsky was on a fishing trip with Knudsen when in August 1936 news came that Zinoviev and Kamenev had been put on trial. Trotsky immediately started a press campaign to prove that, whatever confessions might have been made by the defendants, he had at no time conspired against the Soviet state. The Norwegian Government then came under intense diplomatic pressure to expel from the country someone whose involvement in terrorism had been "proved" by the death sentences passed on Zinoviev and Kamenev. In a questionable ruling the Norwegian Justice Minister decided that Trotsky's press campaign had broken the terms of his residence permit by interfering in domestic politics; although Trotsky had written exclusively about the Soviet Union, he had given an interview to a Norwegian Social Democrat newspaper. In September Trotsky was placed under house arrest until he was put on a boat sailing for Mexico on 19 December. Trotsky's memories of Norway were understandably bitter, but he did recall that "we carried away with us warm remembrances of the marvellous land of forests and fjords, of the snow beneath the January sun, of skis and sleighs, of children with china-blue eyes, corn-coloured hair, and of the slightly morose and slow-moving but serious and honest people."[34]

Trotsky arrived in Mexico on 9 January 1937 and immediately began a campaign to clear his name of the charges laid against him in the trial of Zinoviev and Kamenev and subsequently the second purge trial of Radek, Pyatakov and other of his supporters in January 1937. To establish his innocence he and his supporters organised "a counter-trial". The Dewey Commission took evidence in April 1937 and reported in September that the trials were frame-ups. While waiting for this verdict Trotsky made one last attempt to contact the Soviet leadership. On 17 June 1937 he sent a telegram to the Central Executive Committee of the Soviet: "Stalin's policies leading to complete collapse, internal as well as external; only salvation lies in radical about-face toward Soviet democracy, beginning with public review of last trials; on this matter offer total support."[35]

Frida Kahlo

One of those to meet Trotsky when he arrived at the oil port of Tampico on 9 January was the artist Frida Kahlo, the wife of the painter Diego Rivera, a former Mexican communist who had rallied to Trotsky's cause after witnessing in Moscow in 1927 the brutality with which Opposition demonstrators were attacked. Rivera put his house, Casa Azul, at Trotsky's disposal, and so it was inevitable that Trotsky and Frida came into close contact. Trotsky was always happy to flirt with a beautiful young woman and Frida, then 29, was both attracted to the charms of older men (her husband was already 50) and not averse to extra-marital liaisons. By the summer flirtation and the not-too-well-concealed exchange of *billets doux* had led to secret assignations in the flat of Frida's sister: the extent of Trotsky's subsequent remorse and the tone of letters passed years later by Frida to one of her friends show that a brief love affair developed between them. Natasha soon suspected something was going on, suspicions made worse by the fact that Trotsky and Frida always spoke in English, a language Natasha could not understand. By the start of July marital tension had reached such a point that Trotsky resolved to move away for a while. On 7 July Trotsky took up Rivera's suggestion that he take a few days' holiday at a ranch in the countryside. A day or so later Frida turned up at the ranch. This, however, was not the con-summation of the affair; Trotsky was out of his depth and had resolved to end it. In his last note to her he stated rather coldly and awkwardly: "Natasha and I wish you the best of health and real artistic success and I embrace you as our good and sincere friend."

While Trotsky was at the ranch, Natasha found out about Frida's visit and wrote demanding to know what was going on. Trotsky wrote of his "shame and self-hatred" and urged Natasha "to stop competing with a woman who means so little"; but he also reminded her, in correspond-ence that continued throughout the three weeks he was away, that when they had met in 1903 she had a lover, and in 1918 she had had her own flirtatious affair – something she denied, stressing that the young man concerned was infatuated with her but that she had not reciprocated such feelings.[36] Despite rumours to the contrary, all the evidence points to this being a unique episode in Trotsky's marriage. Less than two years earlier he confided in his diary entry for 27 March 1935: "Even now she still walks beautifully, without fatigue, and her gait is quite youthful, like her whole figure." He then recalled a night in Paris in 1903 when "we ran home from the Paris Opera to the rue Gassendi, 46, *au pas gymnastique*, holding hands . . . our combined age was 46." In a diary entry for 5 April

1935 he noted with tenderness, "Natasha and I have been together for almost 33 years, a third of a century!" A month later he recorded that Natasha was ill and how every time she was ill, "I feel anew the place she fills in my life". In February 1940 Trotsky drafted a will assigning the income from his royalties to Natasha. He wrote: "Fate gave me the happiness of being her husband; during the almost 40 years of our life together she remained an inexhaustible source of love, magnanimity and tenderness." Natasha was indeed magnanimous, for she effectively sacrificed her life to support an outcast prophet. On 6 June 1935, as preparations began for the move from France, a country she knew well, to Norway, a country she had never visited, Trotsky noted in his diary: "Never did Natasha 'reproach' me, never."[37]

And yet there was a lot she could have reproached him for. Natasha had to bear the brunt of much of Trotsky's strained relationship with his elder daughter. Even during their time in the Kremlin, Trotsky had infuriated Zina by his refusal to discuss politics with her. When Zina and her son Seva left the Soviet Union in mid January 1931 to be with her father in exile, it was to serve the revolutionary cause. Zina, however, was unwell, suffering from problems with her lungs, and not long after her arrival she was hospitalised. On returning to the family she began, rightly or wrongly, to be obsessed with thinking that she was an unwanted daughter, resenting in particular the role of her stepmother Natasha whom she had first met as a girl when visiting Vienna; this obsession gradually became a mental illness. In moments of tension Trotsky, understandably, always stood by Natasha, but he hardly helped matters by refusing to involve Zina in his correspondence with Russia on the grounds that she might divulge secret codes and addresses. By autumn 1931 it was clear that the operation on her lungs had not been a complete success, and so Trotsky insisted that she seek further medical advice in Berlin, in preparation for what he hoped would be her imminent return to Moscow. While she was in Berlin Trotsky never once wrote to her, despite a letter from his son Lev urging him at the very least to respond to a postcard she had sent him; she was desperate for him to write, he said, and had never meant to criticise Natasha.

While in Berlin Trotsky suggested she consult a psychiatrist, but her sense of isolation and desertion was then doubly reinforced by the decision of the Soviet Government to deprive all Trotsky's relatives abroad of their citizenship. She remained, unwanted by Trotsky, unable to return to her homeland, and separated from her son who had remained on Prinkipo and was now also stateless and unable to travel. By the end of December 1932 the last of these problems had been resolved, and Seva joined his mother in Berlin. But Zina was now in such a deep depression that she simply could not cope. The drift to the right in German politics was now palpable, and although Hitler was not yet in power, preparations to round up communists had already begun; on 5 January 1933, having been instructed by the police to leave Germany, Zina committed suicide. When the news reached her mother in Leningrad Aleksandra wrote to Trotsky: "You have reckoned only with her physical condition, but she was an adult and a fully developed being in need of intellectual discourse ... you, her father, could have saved her."[38]

Natasha stood by Trotsky through this terrible personal crisis; but two years later they would face a joint trauma when letters from their son Sergei suddenly ceased after a warning in his last letter that "my situation is very grave, graver than one could imagine". Sergei had indeed been arrested on 4 March 1935, but his parents never had any official confirmation of this. It was a far cry from the happy scenes of childhood in the Kremlin when Sergei and Lev, fighting in one of their rooms, crashed against a door and rolled into the room where the Politburo was meeting; at that time Stalin occupied the suite of rooms opposite and Natasha would chat to his "young wife, a charming creature both intelligent and spontaneous". Natasha certainly put up with a lot for Trotsky's sake, but remained devoted to him, writing of him in Mexico: "He still bore himself as of old; his head was held high, his gait sprightly and his gestures were animated; he seemed not to have aged, though his unruly locks had become grey."[39]

The Fourth International

In autumn 1937, with his personal crisis behind him, Trotsky turned to the degeneration of the Communist International as witnessed by events during the Spanish Civil War. By May 1937 the Popular Front Government in Republican Spain was in crisis, facing not only Franco's forces to the Right but internal dissent from the Left, from anarchists and anti-Stalin Marxists in the Unified Marxist Workers' Party (POUM). When both POUM and the anarchists took up arms against the Popular Front Government, the Soviet-backed security forces in Spain decided to bring in *cheka* advisers. Soon anarchists and POUMists were being kidnapped and assassinated by *cheka* agents operating within the Comintern. Trotsky saw this as the ultimate sign of degeneration. "The source of the contagion is the Communist International, or to put it more correctly, the *cheka*, for whom the apparatus of the Communist International serves only as a legal cover." It was, he decided, "high time to launch a world offensive against Stalinism", and this would be done by creating a Fourth International.[40]

Yet for Trotsky many of those groups expressing an interest in a campaign against Stalinism were not suitable for inclusion in the Fourth International. Serge was a case in point, for he had dared to draw a parallel between Stalin's brutality and Trotsky's suppression of the Kronstadt rebellion. In January 1938 Trotsky wrote *Hue and Cry over Kronstadt*, accusing Serge of attempting to discredit Trotskyism, "the only genuine revolutionary current which has never repudiated its banner and which alone represents the future". Trotsky repeated his view that, after victory in the Civil War, the most revolutionary elements of the Kronstadt garrison had been transferred to the front leaving "a great percentage of completely demoralised elements, wearing showy bell-bottom trousers and sporty haircuts". These were the sailors who had rebelled, and they had rebelled not for ideological reasons but to get improved rations. "SR-anarchist soviets" of the sort proposed by the rebels "could only have served as a bridge from the proletarian dictatorship to capitalist restoration", he stressed.[41] In the aftermath of this article Trotsky informed Serge that he was prepared to continue collaborating with him "but only on one condition, if you decide yourself that you belong to the camp of the Fourth International and not the camp of its adversaries". Serge kept his peace, but Ciliga then took up the issue of Kronstadt, forcing Trotsky in June 1938 to publish *More on the Suppression of Kronstadt* where he again stressed the role "of dandified and well-fed sailors, communists in name only" being the organisers of an insurrection which was justly repressed. By September 1938 relations between Trotsky and Serge had completely broken down and by the end of the year Trotsky was openly attacking Serge in the press.[42]

Trotsky not only faced criticism from former supporters, apparently loyal Trotskyists continued to threaten his authority. The Civil War in Spain saw Soviet military advisers supporting one side and Nazi and Fascist forces supporting the other; talk of a world war was commonplace, and so was the question of what Trotskyists should do in the event of the Soviet Union being involved in a war. Trotsky was clear: the Soviet Union was not a bourgeois state and its ruling bureaucracy was not a hostile class; the Soviet Union remained a workers' state, however degenerate, and had to be defended. He was equally convinced that the ruling bureaucracy would not find itself capable of organising the country's defence. Thus recognising the need to defend the USSR "does not at all signify a theoretical and political amnesty for the Soviet bureaucracy . . . the defence of the USSR means not only the supreme struggle against imperialism, but a preparation for the overthrow of the Bonapartist bureaucracy".

Yet many of his supporters could not accept this stance, and their repeated efforts to raise the issue within the various sympathetic parties prompted Trotsky to issue warnings in December 1937 worthy of Stalin.

Party democracy does not at all signify transforming the Party into an arena for the free exercise of sectarians, blunderers or aspiring individualists. Party democracy does not signify the right of the minority to upset the work of the majority. A revolutionary party is not a debating club, but a militant organisation. The problem of war, next to the problem of revolution, is the touchstone of a revolutionary party. Here no kind of equivocation is permissible.

Even Trotsky's attempt to soften these remarks had a Stalinist edge to it.

At the same time we can and must display the most attentive attitude to each sincere mistaken comrade; only in this manner can we guard the party from befuddledness and chaos and, in passing, reduce to a minimum the number of those ultra-Lefts who sooner or later will find themselves outside the party, sinking into political non-existence.

Not that such threats of discipline did any good. Towards the end of May 1938 Trotsky had to attack "certain ultra-Left phrasemongers" who would not accept that there could be no blanket response in the event of war: Trotskyists had to ask themselves which states were involved in a war and respond accordingly; sometimes "defeatism" would be appropriate, sometimes it would not. The proletariat in a capitalist country that found itself in an alliance with the USSR "must retain fully its irreconcilable hostility to the imperialist government of its own country", but the precise details of its actions would be very different to those of the proletariat in the state attacking the Soviet Union; for example, actions "such as burning of warehouses, setting off bombs, wrecking trains" would be quite inappropriate for those workers in countries allied to the Soviet Union.[43]

Having dealt with adversaries to both Left and Right, by summer 1938 preparations were under way for the formal establishment of Trotsky's long talked about Fourth International. These moves were delayed when the man designated as secretary of the new body, Rudolf Klement, was assassinated by the *cheka*. The Foundation Congress took place on 3 September in the home of Alfred Rosmer, with whom Trotsky had co-operated in 1916, but with whom his relations had been rather tense since his exile from the Soviet Union. Only the Polish delegation, guided by Trotsky's future biographer Isaac Deutscher, dared call a spade a spade and declare that the organisation was basically fictitious, uniting not the world proletariat but a few hundred sectarians. Six months after the founding of the Fourth International Trotsky could muse, as if wondering whether the effort of challenging Stalin's Comintern had all been in vain: "You cannot think of the Comintern as being merely an instrument of Stalin's foreign policy; in France in 1934 the French Communist Party had declined from 80,000 to 30,000, it was necessary to have a new policy."[44]

Assassination

The chain of events which were to culminate in Trotsky's assassination began in October 1938 when Frida Kahlo left to promote her work in France. In her absence, Rivera began to pursue a passing ambition to become the leading figure among Mexican Trotskyists; Trotsky was not convinced he was the right man for the job. Rivera was particularly pleased that, in autumn 1938, he had persuaded some local anarchists to recognise the Fourth International. Far from being delighted, Trotsky was furious, not so much for opening dealings with anarchists, but for the chaotic way Rivera carried out his mission. As he complained in a letter to Frida, what was the good of "a 'secretary' who never writes, never answers letters, never comes to meetings on time and always does the opposite of the common decision". The issue came to a head at the end of December when Rivera asked Trotsky's bodyguard to write a letter for him in French to one of the organisers of Frida's visit. In this letter he complained about some of Trotsky's methods of work, suggesting that Trotsky deliberately promoted himself and downplayed the contribution of others like Rivera. Unfortunately, the bodyguard left the letter on a desk where it was found by Natasha, who immediately took it to Trotsky. Challenged by Trotsky, Rivera first agreed to modify the letter, and then dug his heals in and refused, accusing Trotsky of deliberately intercepting the letter and acting like the *cheka*. By 12 January 1939 Rivera had announced he was leaving the Fourth International.[45]

Thus it was that on 5 May 1939 Trotsky moved into his own house on Avenida Viena, in the same suburb of Mexico City as the Casa Azul he had just left. The house was relatively isolated and surrounded by a shady garden. Two months after Trotsky and Natasha moved in, they were joined by Trotsky's grandson Seva. Since his mother's death he had lived with Trotsky's son Lev in Paris, where the *Bulletin of the Opposition* had been based since Hitler came to power in Germany. The group which produced the *Bulletin* had been penetrated by a high-level *cheka* agent, and on 16 February 1938 Lev died following complications after an operation for appendicitis; his partial recovery followed by a sudden relapse and agonising death fuelled stories of a *cheka* poisoning. With his uncle's death, the issue of Seva's future became an open question. Trotsky wanted him to come to Mexico, for he had lived quite happily with his grandparent for some of the time they were at Prinkipo. Lev's second wife Jeanne, however, recalled that at the time of Zina's suicide she had left a note asking her "to take good care" of Seva. After a bitter court battle, custody was given to Trotsky, and his old allies Alfred and Marguerite Rosmer brought Seva to Mexico City in July 1939. It would be through the Rosmers that Trotsky's future assassin, Ramon Mercader, who used the pseudonym "Frank Jacson", gained access to Trotsky's house.[46]

Stalin ordered Trotsky's assassination in March 1939 and detailed planning began in September. Arrangements were left to Naum Eitingnon, who had been deputy chief of the *cheka* in Spain during the Civil War, and he in turn chose Caridad Mercader, the mother of Ramon whom he had known in Spain, to help carry out the task. Ramon Mercader had taken the opportunity to get to know Sylvia Agelof, an American Trotskyist who had come to Paris to help organise the founding conference of the Fourth International. They were soon lovers. By the beginning of 1940 Sylvia was working in Trotsky's entourage, providing Mercader with the opportunity of gaining access to the house. Posing as a playboy businessman with a secondhand Buick and time on his hands, Sylvia got him to help entertain the Rosmers, taking them shopping, driving them on picnics with Seva, even taking Rosmer to the hospital; despite her years, Marguerite took a shine to Sylvia's dashing "husband". Towards the end of April he helped the Rosmers carry in some of their shopping bags, thus gaining access to Trotsky's garden for the first time.[47] On the basis of Mercader's information an armed attack was made on Trotsky's house at 4 a.m. on the morning of 24 May. It nearly succeeded. Over 60 bullets were fired into Trotsky and Natasha's bedroom, but they were not hit, although Seva was grazed on the foot. After this attack the house was converted into a virtual fortress, with double steel doors controlled by electric switches replacing the old wooden entrance, and the number of guards was tripled. A second assassination attempt could only succeed if it were made from inside, and so Mercader was given the task of carrying out the assassination himself.[48]

The key was still the Rosmers. They were due to leave Mexico on 28 May and Mercader offered to drive them to the ship. When he picked them up he was introduced to Trotsky for the first time. Gaining confidence, on 12 June he asked if he might leave his car in the safety of Trotsky's garden while he made a business trip to New York. After his return, on 29 July, Natasha asked him and Sylvia to have tea with her and there then followed several more visits: he took Sylvia and Natasha shopping on 1 August; on 8 August he turned up with flowers; and on 11 August he came into the house simply to pick up Sylvia, rather than his usual practice of waiting outside. Confident he could now gain access to the house, he had to gain access to Trotsky. This was not so easy, since he had always played the role of a non-political playboy. However, on his return from New York he claimed he had become absorbed in politics and wanted to side with Trotsky in a simmering dispute with some of his American followers. The outbreak of the Second World War had seen Soviet foreign policy at its most cynical. The signing of the Nazi-Soviet Pact, the dismemberment of Poland and the war with Finland had convinced many American Trotskyists that the Soviet Union was no longer a workers' state but an imperialist one and that the commitment of Trotskyists to defend it could no longer be supported. Trotsky stuck to his belief that the Soviet Union was a degenerate workers' state that had to be defended at all costs.

On 17 August Mercader arrived unannounced and asked if Trotsky would read through an article he had drafted on the subject. Somewhat reluctantly Trotsky agreed, reading it through and suggesting some changes. Mercader returned on the 20th at about 5 p.m. and asked if Trotsky could look through the redrafted article, typed this time, for he planned to return to New York the following day. Trotsky, who had been feeding his pet rabbits, agreed and the two men entered the study. Trotsky sat down, read the first page, and Mercader, standing over him, struck him with the ice-pick concealed under the raincoat he was wearing despite the fine weather.[49] The blow did not kill Trotsky outright, he died in hospital the following day at 7.25 p.m. As he lay awaiting the ambulance he managed to say in Russian, "Natasha, I love you" and in English to his bodyguards, "Take care of Natasha, she has been with me many, many years." Natasha recorded his final conscious moments thus:

The nurses began to cut his clothes. Suddenly he said to me distinctly but very sadly and gravely: "I do not want them to undress me . . . I want you to do it . . ." These were his last words to me. I undressed him, and pressed my lips to his. He returned the kiss, once, twice and again. Then he lost consciousness.[50]

Notes

1 A. Cummins (ed.), *Documents of Soviet History* (1998), p. 228.

2 G. R. Swain, "Stalin's Rise to Power", *Modern History Review*, No. 3, 2003, pp. 3–7.

3 P. Broué, *Trotsky* (Paris, 1988), pp. 547–50; D. Volkogonov, *Trotsky: the Eternal Revolutionary* (London, 1997), p. 309; J. van Heijenoort, *With Trotsky in Exile: From Prinkipo to Coyoacán* (Cambridge, Mass., 1978), p. 6.

4 *Minuvshee: istoricheskii almanakh*, Vol. VII (Moscow, 1992), pp. 278, 289; A. Vatlin, "On the Verge of the Break: Trotsky and the Comintern in 1928" in T. Brotherstone and P. Dukes (eds), *The Trotsky Reappraisal* (Edinburgh), pp. 59, 62.

5 N. Allen (ed.), *Leon Trotsky: the Challenge of the Left Opposition (1923–25)*, Vol. II, p. 121; V. Serge, *Memoirs of a Revolutionary* (Oxford, 1963), p. 258; V. Serge and N. Sedova Trotsky, *The Life and Death of Leon Trotsky* (New York, 1973), p. 175.

6 Broué, *Trotsky*, p. 577; Allen, *Challenge*, Vol. II, pp. 271–8.

7 *Minuvshee*, pp. 306, 310–13; Allen, *Challenge*, Vol. II, pp. 295, 304.

8 L. Trotsky, *Trotsky's Diary in Exile* (London, 1958), p. 39; Serge, *Memoirs*, pp. 253–4.

9 Volkogonov, *Trotsky*, pp. 314–16; L. Trotsky, *The Writings of Leon Trotsky 1929* (New York, 1975), pp. 26–7.

10 Volkogonov, *Trotsky*, p. 337.

11 Allen, *Challenge*, Vol. II, p. 369; Trotsky, *Writings 1929*, pp. 48–9, 83, 113.

12 Broué, *Trotsky*, pp. 629–35; Trotsky, *Writings 1929*, pp. 136, 162, 200.

13 "Rakovsky: Theses, 3 août 1929", *Cahiers Leon Trotsky*, No. 7–8, 1981, p. 81; Trotsky, *Writings 1929*, p. 358; I. Deutscher, *The Prophet Outcast, Trotsky: 1929–1940* (Oxford, 1970), p. 78.

14 Broué, *Trotsky*, p. 619; Volkogonov, *Trotsky*, p. 329; "L'affaire Bloumkin", *Cahier Leon Trotsky*, No. 7–8, 1981, p. 83.

15 Trotsky, *Writings 1929*, pp. 377, 403; *Writings 1930*, pp. 107–18.

16 Trotsky, *Writings 1930–31*, pp. 52–4, 57.

17 *Arkhiv Trotskogo*, Vol. IV, p. 264; Trotsky, *Writings 1930*, p. 85, *Writings 1930–31*, pp. 215, 222.

18 Trotsky, *Writings 1930–31*, p. 308; Serge and Sedova, *Life and Death*, p. 191.

19 Trotsky, *Writings 1932*, p. 19; Volkogonov, *Trotsky*, p. 330.

20 Trotsky, *Writings 1932*, pp. 64–9, 125.

21 J. A. Getty, *Origins of the Great Purges* (Cambridge, 1987), pp. 119–20; Broué, *Trotsky*, pp. 709–11; Deutscher, *Outcast*, p. 165.

22 *Report of Court Proceedings in the Case of the Anti-Soviet "Bloc of Rights and Trotskyites"* (Moscow, 1938), pp. 389, 391.

23 Trotsky, *Writings 1932*, pp. 247–54; 279–80; 328.

24 Trotsky, *Writings Supplement 1929–33*, pp. 169–70; *Writings 1932–33*, pp. 73–7.

25 Trotsky, *Writings 1932–33*, pp. 141–2, 235, 265, 319.

26 Trotsky, *Writings 1932–33*, p. 312; L. Trotskii, *Dnevniki i pis'ma* (Tenafly, 1986), pp. 56–8.

27 Trotsky, *Writings 1933–34*, p. 27.

28 Trotsky, *Writings 1933–34*, pp. 102–21.

29 For the call to form soviets, see Trotsky, *Writings 1933–34*, pp. 243–4.

30 Broué, *Trotsky*, p. 734; D. Cotterill (ed.), *The Serge-Trotsky Papers* (London, 1994), p. 48; Trotsky, *Writings 1934–35*, p. 70.

31 L. Trotsky, *Trotsky's Diary in Exile* (London, 1958), p. 35; Trotsky, *Writings 1934–35*, pp. 162–5, 183–4.

32 Trotsky, *Writings 1934–35*, p. 315, *Writings 1935–36*, pp. 220–2; Serge and Sedova, *Life and Death*, p. 206.

33 Trotsky, *Writings 1935–36*, p. 331; D. Cotteril (ed.), *The Serge-Trotsky Papers* (London, 1994), pp. 59–60.

34 Trotsky, *Writings 1936–37*, p. 41.

35 Deutscher, *Outcast*, pp. 371–82; Trotsky, *Writings 1936–37*, p. 350.

36 Volkogonov, *Trotsky*, p. 395; Deutscher, *Outcast*, pp. 384–5; Broué, *Trotsky*, p. 844; van Heijenoort, *With Trotsky*, pp. 111–18.

37 Trotsky, *Diary*, pp. 56, 72, 121, 139.

38 Trotsky, *My Life*, p. 231; Broué, *Trotsky*, pp. 691–7; Deutscher, *Outcast*, p. 196; Volkgonov, *Trotsky*, p. 350.

39 Deutscher, *Outcast*, p. 282; Volkogonov, *Trotsky*, p. 355; Serge and Sedova, *Life and Death*, pp. 82, 253.

40 Trotsky, *Writings 1937–38*, p. 28.

41 Trotsky, *Writings 1937–38*, pp. 134–45.

42 Cotterill, *Serge-Trotsky*, p. 109; Serge, *Memoirs*, p. 348; Trotsky, *Writings 1937–38*, pp. 376–8; Trotsky, *Writings 1938–39*, pp. 142, 194.

43 Trotsky, *Writings 1937–38*, pp. 71, 86, 333.

44 Deutscher, *Outcast*, pp. 419–22; Trotsky, *Writings 1938–39*, p. 265.

45 van Heijenoort, *With Trotsky*, pp. 132–8; Trotsky, *Writings 1938–39*, pp. 278, 292–3, 285–8.

46 Volkogonov, *Trotsky*, p. 359; van Heijenoort, *With Trotsky*, p. 37.

47 Volkogonov, *Trotsky*, pp. 445–7, 463; Broué, *Trotsky*, p. 934; van Heijenoort, *With Trotsky*, p. 146; Deutscher, *Outcast*, p. 484.

48 J. Hansen, "The Attempted Assassination of Leon Trotsky", in J. Hansen *et al.* (eds), *Leon Trotsky, the Man and his Work* (New York, 1969), p. 5.

49 Volkogonov, *Trotsky*, pp. 463–4; Broué, *Trotsky*, p. 934; Deutscher, *Outcast*, pp. 476–99; Serge and Sedova, *Life and Death*, pp. 264–6.

50 J. Hansen, "With Trotsky to the End" in Hansen (ed.), *Trotsky, the Man*, p. 17; Serge and Sedova, *Life and Death*, pp. 267–8.

Conclusion

In March 1935 Trotsky noted in his diary: "And I still think that the work in which I am engaged now, despite its extremely insufficient and fragmentary nature, is the most important work of my life – more important than 1917, more important than the period of the Civil War or any other."[1] It is impossible for the historian to accept such a judgement. In truth, it needs to be stood on its head. Any assessment of Trotsky's contribution to history must concentrate on his time working alongside Stalin, rather than his time opposing him. In 1917 it was Trotsky's experience of the 1905 Petrograd Soviet which showed the way towards a successful insurrection. If Lenin had had his way and the Bolshevik Party had staged a coup with the support of a few loyal military units there would have been no October Revolution. Trotsky strove to make the insurrection a non-party Soviet affair, and one which was defensive in nature rather than offensive. Similarly, if Trotsky had not been sent to Sviyazhsk in August 1918 and organised the recapture of Kazan, the Bolsheviks would not have marked the first anniversary of their insurrection. When Trotsky called on Lenin to report on his triumph at Kazan, Lenin commented "the game is won", and it was.[2] The Bolsheviks triumphed in the Civil War because of Trotsky's ability to work with military specialists, because of the style of work he introduced where widescale consultation was followed through by swift and determined action. This was the model he tried to introduce in Gosplan, freeing it from too much interference by the Party. The Soviet Union would have been a very different place if, in December 1923, Trotsky had decided to stick by the agreement he had signed with Stalin and Kamenev, allowing him to emerge in January 1924 as the head of Gosplan.

Any assessment of Trotsky during his years in power inevitably focuses on his ability as an organiser. Late in life he mused on the difference between his approach to organisation and that of Stalin.

There were two aspects to military work in the epoch of the Civil War. One was to select the necessary workers, to make proper disposition of them, to establish the necessary supervision over the commanding staff, to extirpate suspects, to exert pressure, to punish. All of these activities of the administrative machine suited Stalin's talents to perfection. But there was also another side, which had to do with the necessity of improvising an army out of human raw material, of appealing to the hearts of soldiers and commanders, arousing their better selves and inspiring them with confidence in the new leadership. Of this Stalin was utterly incapable. It is impossible, for example, to imagine Stalin appearing under the open sky before a regiment.[3]

Trotsky was the inspirational organiser.

At Kazan, like all Bolsheviks, he was brutal and ruthless, setting up "blocking battalions" to prevent desertion and taking as hostages the wives of unreliable officers. But at Kazan, as throughout the Civil War, he got things organised, he got supplies in place, he got telephones working, he got airplanes flying and it would be the same story throughout the Civil War. Even as a precocious apprentice, his organisational powers had been extraordinary. His comrade Ziv conceded that Trotsky ran the South Russia Workers' Union almost singlehanded. Ziv met Trotsky a few days before the St Petersburg Soviet was arrested in November 1905, and felt hurt that his old friend could only spare him a few minutes, but Trotsky had to dash from a meeting of the Soviet to an editorial meeting to get his paper on to the streets. After the Civil War, Trotsky was organising Labour Armies, combating typhus in Ekaterinburg, reconstructing the country's stock of railway locomotives; Captain McCullagh of the British Army, who met him at this time, said he could "switch from one important matter to another a dozen times in the course of a single day". As Lenin said of Trotsky in his Testament, he possessed "a disposition to be much attracted by the purely administrative side of affairs".[4]

Lenin had said something similar in March 1921. Then, at the height of the Trade Union Dispute, Lenin concluded that Trotsky was "in love with organisation". At the same time he noted that when it came to politics, Trotsky "has not got a clue".[5] Why did he find it so difficult to build up the sort of personal alliances which stand at the heart of successful politics? Trotsky was not used to working in a team. Unlike the other Bolshevik leaders who had been funded before the revolution from Bolshevik coffers as "professional revolutionaries", Trotsky had funded himself from his earnings as a journalist. The South Russia Workers' Union was his affair, Vienna *Pravda* was his affair, in 1917 the Military Revolutionary Committee was his affair, and for much of the Civil War he was away at the front running his own affair; and there were rows enough when he visited Moscow. Trotsky was simply not easy to work with. He made agreements and then wriggled out of them. He arrived early at Politburo meetings with military precision, and sat impatiently while the other members drifted in; but then, on the grounds that the Politburo was not competent to discuss economic issues of such complexity, he would take no part in debates and sit quietly with a French novel, throughout his life his favourite reading matter.[6] When challenged on such behaviour, he was petulant and imperious, bombarding his colleagues with long, repetitive and pedantic memoranda, self-righteously justifying his every decision and demanding apologies or explanations from his accusers.

However, there was another reason why he found building alliances difficult, his blind devotion to the cause. Trotsky's first wife Aleksandra told the American communist Max Eastman, when he was working on a biography of Trotsky's early life: "He can be very tender and sympathetic and he can be very assertive and arrogant; but in one thing he never changes – that is his devotion to the revolution; in all my revolutionary experience, I have never met any other person so completely consecrated." Natasha described him perhaps more accurately, as "hypnotised by the consummation of the task at hand". But, like other revolutionaries, he tended to identify himself with the revolution. Ziv felt that for Trotsky "the revolution and his active ego coincided; everything that was outside the revolution was outside his ego and therefore did not interest him and did not exist for him". Trotsky himself confirmed this in his own analysis of why he made so many enemies during the Civil War. He recalled:

In the great struggle that we were carrying on, the stakes were too big to permit me to consider side issues. As a result, I frequently trod on toes of personal prejudice, friendly favouritism or vanity. Stalin carefully picked up the men whose toes had been trodden on.[7]

Identifying himself with the revolution, not caring if potential comrades were offended, such traits had their positive side, but could easily become the sort of "too far-reaching self-confidence" that Lenin spoke of in his Testament. His old ally Lunacharskii noted the same failing: "His colossal arrogance and an inability or unwillingness to show any human kindness or to be attentive to people, the absence of that charm which always surrounded Lenin, condemned Trotsky to a certain loneliness." Natasha too was ready to recognise this failing: she stressed that "he was a fundamentally kind man", and it is true that during the Civil War he repeatedly intervened to help those of his former "bourgeois" friends arrested by the *cheka*[8]; but she accepted that his habit of judging people by what he called objective criteria could appear harsh. Both Lenin and

Lunacharskii warned that this self-identification with the revolution could not only lead to arrogance, but bad-tempered and ill-considered judgements. Lenin referred to him as temperamental while Lunacharskii made clear that "being a man of choleric temperament he is liable, although only temporarily, to be blinded by passion"; calling Stalin the gravedigger of the revolution was a case in point.[9]

It was after this incident that Pyatakov advised Trotsky to be "more sociable" because potential supporters saw him as haughty and arrogant. As part of a campaign to make him more accommodating, Trotsky was persuaded to attend a New Year's Eve party at the end of 1926 hosted by Kamenev. Natasha recalled that he returned almost at once, saying, "I cannot stand it, liqueurs, long dresses, and gossip; it was like a salon." Trotsky was not a man's man. He had given up smoking after the revolution and only drank on special occasions. He was also a bit of a prude: he abhorred smutty stories and was horrified when, at their first meeting after the seizure of power Stalin commented suggestively about Aleksandra Kollontai's new "toy boy", Pavel Dybenko. During the Civil War he sacked the commander of Armoured Train No. 26 "The Bolsheviks" because of the swearing and obscenities heard on board when it was standing in Konotop station in the presence of women and children. These purely personal attributes merely served to heighten his appearance of self-obsessed superiority.[10]

If Trotsky identified himself with the revolution so completely in this way, the only answer to the question why he failed to make the political alliances necessary for survival was that he was completely convinced that he was right, that political blindness referred to by Lenin. When he committed himself to the United Opposition in 1926 he compared himself to Karl Liebknecht, the German Spartacist leader killed by the *Freikorps* in 1919. When the train left Moscow for exile in Alma Ata, Trotsky told Natasha that he had not wanted to die in bed in the Kremlin. He wanted to continue the struggle, he believed in Thermidor, he believed he would have to take up arms against a peasant counter-revolution. He was the son of a Ukrainian kulak, his whole political awakening had revolved around understanding his father's true petit bourgeois money-grubbing essence. He had experienced kulak power and he believed that Voroshilov would stage a coup against Stalin and establish a military regime similar to that of Chiang Kai-shek in nationalist China; it would then be Trotsky's duty to lead the heroic and possibly unsuccessful resistance to that coup. Lunacharskii noted that Trotsky "treasures his historical role" and predicted that "he would probably be ready to make any personal sacrifice, not excluding the greatest sacrifice of all – that of his life – in order to go down in human memory surrounded by the aureole of a genuine revolutionary leader." He was prepared to sacrifice his life in the struggle against the chimera of Thermidor, that was why he was so unwilling to accept that such a struggle would never come.[11]

In one of their last confrontations, at the meeting of the Comintern Executive on 27 September 1927, Stalin ended his speech by accusing Trotsky to his face: "You are a Menshevik!"[12] Was Trotsky ever a Bolshevik? The question would have little importance if Trotsky had not used his years in exile to cultivate the myth that he was the "best Bolshevik", a consistent opponent of Stalin and Lenin's preferred successor. The case against Trotsky's Bolshevism is convincing. In the years before 1917, two things distinguished Bolsheviks from revolutionary socialists in general, of whom there were many among the Mensheviks. First there was the question of Party organisation, on which Lenin had split the party in 1903. Second there was the question of the peasantry, which emerged as crucial during 1906–7, the period of the First and Second Dumas, when the Bolsheviks looked to peasant parties as their allies rather than the liberals. On both these questions Trotsky disagreed with the Bolsheviks.

Trotsky never denied the intensity of his disagreements with Lenin on organisational matters; before 1917 denouncing Lenin's sectarianism was his *raison d'être*. In a letter to the Bolshevik historian M. S. Olminskii he explained after the revolution that it was only during 1917 when he saw how "Bolshevism managed to retain its revolutionary tight-knit organisation" and thus make "a rapid switch from a revolutionary democratic position to a revolutionary socialist one", that he saw the benefits of Lenin's theories on organisation.[13] Yet this conversion was skin deep. Once inside the Bolshevik Party, Trotsky found the Bolshevik concept of the Party almost unbearable: throughout the Civil War and the period of post-war reconstruction he chafed against Party interference and the sidelining of specialists, unwilling to accept that this was the Bolshevik way. Trotsky's ideas on Party organisation remained entirely consistent. In 1903 he had favoured Martov's definition of Party membership because it brought into the Party workers from the factories; they were needed not simply because they were workers, but because they could be learned from when it came to class struggle, they were the experts and during the 1905 Soviet Trotsky learned how to work with activists, rather than dictating to them. That was then his message between the revolutions: the expertise of legal labour activists was essential if the Party were to recover, organise strike action once again and overthrow the Tsar. After the Revolution other experts were needed, and Trotsky believed that really conscious workers would recognise that those once perceived as enemies – generals and factory managers – were now essential allies, who, as experts, should be consulted, not told what to do by a Party claiming a monopoly of knowledge.

During that clash at the Comintern Executive in September 1927 Stalin repeated his view that Trotsky was simply struggling against the Leninist regime in the Party; he was. According to Trotsky: "I had my own views, my own ways of working, and my own methods of carrying out a decision once it had been adopted; Lenin knew this well enough, and respected it."[14] The other Bolshevik leaders did not and could not handle Trotsky, although Stalin worked for three years to carry out Lenin's insistence that Trotsky be kept on board. By questioning the way the Party tried to administer the economy and calling for the experts to take major decisions Trotsky was acting as he had done throughout the Civil War, implying that the Party did not always know best. There was therefore a logic to Stalin returning to *Our Political Tasks* as he expelled Trotsky from the Party, for Trotsky's attitude was still essentially that the Party apparatus did not know best, just as he had once argued that underground committees were often staffed by radicalised students with no experience of the factory shop floor.

As to the peasantry, Trotsky always denied that he underestimated them, even though the very logic of the working class seizing power as early as 1905 implied that the peasantry could be ignored. Lenin summed up the difference between them in a speech to the Petrograd Party Conference in April 1917, before Trotsky returned to Russia. "Trotskyism says: no Tsar, but a workers' government. That is incorrect. The petit bourgeoisie exists and it cannot be left out of account. But it consists of two sections and the poorer section follows the working class."[15] Trotsky was not convinced. In *Results and Prospects* Trotsky asserted that "all historical experience shows that the peasantry are absolutely incapable of taking up an *independent* political role". The peasantry here is not divided into rich, poor and middle, but taken as a whole. At the Fifth Party Congress in 1907 he insisted that the Bolsheviks were wrong to talk of "the proletariat and the peasantry": this suggested independent activity by the peasants, so he demanded the wording "the proletariat supported by the peasantry".

When he argued in *Results and Prospects* that during the revolution's initial phase the peasants would rally to the proletariat's lead, he commented "it will not matter much even if the peasantry does this with a degree of consciousness not larger than that with which it usually rallies to a bourgeois regime". Peasant political consciousness was scarcely worth exploiting.[16] Although he wrote "from the very first moment after its taking power, the proletariat will have to find support in the antagonisms between the village poor and the village rich", he then noted that, "The heterogeneity of the peasantry creates difficulties and narrows the basis for a proletarian policy, the insufficient degree of class differentiation will create obstacles to the introduction among the peasantry of a developed class struggle upon which the urban proletariat could rely." The bulk of the peasantry would become passive, while the upper sections become active opponents of the regime and "cannot but have an influence on a section of intellectuals and the petit bourgeoisie of the towns".[17]

Trotsky's attitude to the peasantry was his Achilles' heel. Because he had doubts about how successfully the Bolsheviks could play the game of exploiting the level of differentiation among the peasantry, he lived in perpetual fear that his colleagues had misunderstood the difficulties involved and that, as he suggested in *Results and Prospects*, kulak leaders were organising and establishing contacts with the urban petit bourgeoisie. This was the origin of his obsession with the danger of the Thermidor counter-revolution. For Trotsky it had been an incipient problem from December 1923, but became acute when the Dnieper Dam Project was shunted into a siding; this was a decision of Stalin's bureaucracy, and the perfect illustration of how, unwittingly, that bureaucracy had become the tool of hostile forces. Because the problem was the Thermidorised bureaucracy, and not Stalin personally, Trotsky worked with Stalin in 1925 and early 1926, declining to join Zinoviev and Kamenev. For the self-same reason, he refused to follow Zinoviev and Kamenev back into the Party at the Fifteenth Party Congress in December 1927, preferring the path of exile. He was so attached to the concept of Thermidor that, against all the evidence, he insisted that Stalin's industrialisation campaign was not serious, to the extent that he could still see a Right-wing danger when in 1932 Stalin was at his weakest and even from exile he might have been able to help remove him. To paraphrase Lenin once again, Trotsky really had been blinded by passion.

As *Results and Prospects* made clear, the ultimate insurance against the Thermidor danger was a European Revolution. Yet Trotsky never understood the European labour movement. Before 1933 his interest in it stemmed entirely from the logic of the factional struggles in which he was involved. During autumn 1923 Trotsky differed from the other Bolshevik leaders on what to do in Germany only on points of detail. His criticisms all came after the event in the context of his bitter attack on Zinoviev and Kamenev. It was similar with the British General Strike, although on this occasion he had made some criticisms before the event of the work of the Anglo-Russian Joint Advisory Council. As to China, the vehemence with which he took up swords against Stalin on this issue, to the astonishment of all his colleagues, can only be understood if China is seen as a metaphor for a successful Thermidor, an example of how, if communists follow the wrong path a military dictator backed by the petit bourgeoisie can take over. It is hard to see how the outcome of the British General Strike would have been any different if, on its eve, the Anglo-Russian Joint Advisory Council had been dissolved. Similarly, if soviets had been established in Shanghai in March 1927 it is likely that Chiang Kai-shek would simply have acted a little earlier.

Trotsky's internationalism only became a serious issue in 1933 when he decided that the one way left to improve the situation within the Soviet Union was to establish a less antagonistic international climate abroad. With growing political crises maturing in France and Spain, the moment was opportune, and Trotsky's initial tactic of encouraging the radicalisation of the Left-wing of the socialist parties through a policy of "entryism" brought some prospect of success. It was that success which prompted Trotsky's optimistic diary entry for March 1935 that he was engaged in "the most important work of my life". By the end of that year he would cry out to Natasha: "I am tired of it all, all of it – you understand."[18]

Trotsky stated in his memoirs that he had not wanted or expected a government post after the Bolsheviks seized power; he had suggested to Lenin that he take over the direction of the press. Explaining his humility Trotsky stated: "From my youth on, or to be more precise, from my childhood on, I dreamed of being a writer; later I subordinated my literary work, as I did everything else, to the revolution."[19] Lenin, as Trotsky no doubt anticipated, took no notice of this unexpected request and insisted that Trotsky join the Bolshevik Government. Perhaps Trotsky should have stood his ground and remained a journalist, but if he had done so, the Bolsheviks would have been defeated at Sviyazhsk in August 1918 and have survived in power for less than a year.

Notes

1 L. Trotsky, *Trotsky's Diary in Exile* (Faber and Faber, 1958), p. 53.

2 Trotsky, *Diary*, p. 83.

3 L. Trotsky, *Stalin* (London, 1968), Vol. II, p. 49.

4 F. McCullagh, "Trotsky in Ekaterinburg", *Fortnightly Review*, pp. 547–8; J. M. Meijer (ed.), *The Trotsky Papers* (The Hague, 1964), Vol. II, p. 791.

5 R. Pipes, *The Unknown Lenin* (New Haven, 1998), p. 124.

6 B. Bazhanov, *Bazhanov and the Damnation of Stalin* (Ohio, 1990), pp. 44, 55.

7 M. Eastman, *Leon Trotsky: the Portrait of Youth* (Faber and Gwyer, 1926), p. 97; N. Sedova-Trotsky "How it Happened" in J. Hansen (ed.), *Leon Trotsky, the Man and his Work* (New York, 1969), p. 35; G. Ziv, *Trotskii: kharakteristika po lichnym vospominaniem* (New York, 1921), p. 12; L. Trotsky, *My Life* (New York, 1970), p. 442.

8 For an example, see the fate of Konstantin Rozenshtein in RGVA 33987.1.304, pp. 435–8.

9 A. Lunacharskii, *Revolutionary Silhouettes* (London, 1967), pp. 62, 68; V. Serge and N. Sedova Trotsky, *The Life and Death of Leon Trotsky* (New York, 1973), p. 253.

10 Serge and Sedova, *Life and Death*, p. 121; Trotsky, *Stalin*, Vol. II, p. 13; RGVA 4.3.202, p. 72.

11 Serge and Sedova, *Life and Death*, p. 157; Lunacharskii, *Revolutionary Silhouettes*, p. 68.

12 D. Volkogonov, *Trotsky: the Eternal Revolutionary* (London, 1997), p. 293.

13 Meijer (ed.), *Trotsky Papers*, Vol. II, pp. 643–5.

14 Trotsky, *My Life*, p. 477.

15 Cited by J. V. Stalin in *Collected Works* (Moscow, 1953), Vol. VIII, p. 189.

16 Trotsky, *Results and Prospects* (London, 1962), p. 204; L. Trotsky, *The Permanent Revolution* (London, 1962), pp. 73, 93.

17 Trotsky, *Results and Prospects*, pp. 208–9.

18 Serge and Sedova, *Life and Death*, p. 206.

19 Trotsky, *My Life*, p. 339.

Bibliographical Note

This is not a definitive bibliography, but lists the major sources used.

Of the numerous biographies of Trotsky, the following are the most useful:

P. Broué, *Trotsky* (Fayard: Paris, 1988)

I. Deutscher, *The Prophet Armed, Trotsky: 1879–1921* (OUP: Oxford, 1970)

I. Deutscher, *The Prophet Unarmed, Trotsky: 1921–1929* (OUP: Oxford, 1978)

I. Deutscher, *The Prophet Outcast, Trotsky: 1929–1940* (OUP: Oxford, 1970)

M. Eastman, *Leon Trotsky: the Portrait of Youth* (Faber and Gwyer: London, 1926)

I. Thatcher, *Trotsky* (Routledge: London, 2003)

D. Volkogonov, *Trotsky: the Eternal Revolutionary* (Harper Collins: London, 1997)

The following memories of Trotsky's contemporaries proved enlightening:

J. Hansen, "The Attempted Assassination of Leon Trotsky" in J. Hansen (ed.), *Leon Trotsky, the Man and his Work* (Merit: New York, 1969)

J. van Heijenoort, *With Trotsky in Exile: From Prinkipo to Coyoacán* (HUP: Cambridge, Mass., 1978)

A. Lunacharskii, *Revolutionary Silhouettes* (Penguin: London, 1967)

F. McCullagh, "Trotsky in Ekaterinburg", *Fortnightly Review*, Vol. 108, 1920.

L. Reissner, "Sviyazhsk" in J. Hansen (ed.), *Leon Trotsky, the Man and his Work* (Merit: New York, 1969)

V. Serge and N. Sedova Trotsky, *The Life and Death of Leon Trotsky* (Basic Books: New York, 1973)

G. Ziv, *Trotskii: kharakteristika po lichnym vospominaniem* (Narodnopravstvo: New York, 1921)

Of the more detailed studies, the following proved significant:

T. Brotherstone and P. Dukes (eds), *The Trotsky Reappraisal* (Edinburgh University Press: Edinburgh, 1992)

J. Channon, "Trotsky, the Peasants and Economic Policy: a Comment", *Economy and Society*, Vol. 14, 1985

R. B. Day, *Leon Trotsky and the Politics of Economic Isolation* (CUP: Cambridge, 1973)

B. Knei-Paz, *The Social and Political Thought of Leon Trotsky* (OUP: Oxford, 1978)

E. van Ree, "'Lenin's Last Struggle' Revisited," *Revolutionary Russia*, No. 2, 2001

I. Thatcher, *Leon Trotsky and World War One* (Palgrave-Macmillan: Basingstoke, 2000)

N. Valentinov, "Dopolnenie k 'Dnevniku' L Trotskogo", *Sotsialisticheskii vestnik*, No. 2–3, 1959

J. White, "Lenin, Trotsky and the Arts of Insurrection: the Congress of Soviets of the Northern Region 11–13 October 1917", *Slavonic and East European Review*, No. 1, 1999

I. Yurenev, "Mezhraionka, 1911–17", *Proletarskaya revolyutsiaya*, Nos. 1–2, 1924

Much of Trotsky's voluminous writing is available in English:

N. Allen (ed.), *Leon Trotsky: the Challenge of the Left Opposition* (Pathfinder Press: New York – three volumes, 1975 and 1981)

D. Cotterill (ed.), *The Serge-Trotsky Papers* (Pluto: London, 1994)

L. Evans and R. Block (eds), *Leon Trotsky on China* (Monad: New York, 1976)

J. M. Meijer (ed.), *The Trotsky Papers* (Mouton & Co.: The Hague, 1964 – two volumes)

P. Pomper (ed.), *Trotsky's Notebooks 1933–5* (Columbia University Press: New York, 1986)

L. Trotsky, *1905* (Penguin: Harmondsworth, 1971)

L. Trotsky, *The History of the Russian Revolution* (Sphere: London, 1965 – three volumes)

L. Trotsky, *How the Revolution Armed* (New Park: New York, 1979 – three volumes)

L. Trotsky, *My Life* (Pathfinder: New York, 1970)

L. Trotsky, *Our Political Tasks* (New Park: New York, 1979)

L. Trotsky, *Results and Prospects* (New Park: London, 1962)

L. Trotsky, *Stalin* (Panther: London, 1968 – two volumes)

L. Trotsky, *The Stalin School of Falsification* (Pathfinder: New York, 1971)

L. Trotsky, *Trotsky's Diary in Exile* (Faber and Faber: London, 1958)

L. Trotsky, *The Writings of Leon Trotsky* (Pathfinder: New York, from 1975 – this multi-volume collection contains Trotsky's published output from 1929–40)

V. Vilkova (ed.), *The Struggle for Power in Russia in 1923: From the Secret Archives of the Former Soviet Union* (Prometheus: New York, 1996)

A Russian edition of Trotsky's writings of the 1920s is invaluable:

Arkhiv Trotskogo (Terra: Moscow, 1990 – four volumes).

The other major Russian language source of Trotsky's writings used in this book was "The Military Papers of Leon Trotsky, 1918–24", a collection microfilmed in 1999 by Research Publications, an imprint of *Primary Source Media*, which contains material held in the Russian State Military Archive (RGVA).

Index